CAMBRIDGE STUDIES IN PHILOSOPHY

In defense of pure reason

This book is concerned with the alleged capacity of the human mind to arrive at beliefs and knowledge about the world on the basis of pure reason without any dependence on sensory experience. Most recent philosophers reject the view and argue that all substantive knowledge must be sensory in origin. Laurence BonJour provocatively reopens the debate by presenting the most comprehensive exposition and defense of the rationalist view that *a priori* insight is a genuine basis for knowledge.

As well as offering a systematic defense of *a priori* justification, BonJour provides a sustained critique of competing empiricist theories that either claim that *a priori* justification exists but is limited to mere tautologies or deny the existence of *a priori* justification altogether. The book concludes with a rationalist solution to the classical problem of induction.

This important and ground-breaking book will be at the center of debate about the theory of knowledge for many years to come.

CAMBRIDGE STUDIES IN PHILOSOPHY

General editor Ernest Sosa – Brown University

Advisory editors

Jonathan Dancy – (University of Reading)
John Haldane – (University of St. Andrews)
Gilbert Harman – (Princeton University)
Frank Jackson – (Australian National University)
William G. Lycan – (University of North Carolina at Chapel Hill)
Sydney Shoemaker – (Cornell University)
Judith J. Thomson – (Massachusetts Institute of Technology)

In defense of pure reason

A RATIONALIST ACCOUNT OF *A PRIORI*
JUSTIFICATION

Laurence BonJour

University of Washington

CAMBRIDGE
UNIVERSITY PRESS

PUBLISHED BY THE PRESS SYNDICATE OF THE UNIVERSITY OF CAMBRIDGE
The Pitt Building, Trumpington Street, Cambridge, CB2 1RP, United Kingdom

CAMBRIDGE UNIVERSITY PRESS
The Edinburgh Building, Cambridge CB2 2RU, United Kingdom
40 West 20th Street, New York, NY 10011-4211, USA
10 Stamford Road, Oakleigh, Melbourne 3166, Australia

First published 1998

Typeset in Bembo

Library of Congress Cataloging-in-Publication Data

BonJour, Laurence, 1943–

In defense of pure reason : a rationalist account of a priori
justification / Laurence BonJour.

p.   cm. – (Cambridge studies in philosophy)

Includes references and index.

ISBN 0–521–59236–4 (hb.) – ISBN 0–521–59745–5 (pb)

1. Rationalism.   2. Justification (Theory of knowledge)   3. A
priori.   I. Title.   II. Series.
BD181.B64   1997
121′.3–dc21   97–6563
                                                        CIP

*A catalog record for this book is available from
the British Library*

IBSN 0 521 59236 4 hardback
ISBN 0 521 59745 5 paperback

Transferred to digital printing 2002

Contents

Preface

My aim in this book is to explain and defend a *rationalist* conception of *a priori* justification and knowledge: a view according to which there is genuine *a priori* justification that is not limited in its scope to tautologies or matters of definition. Though taken largely for granted throughout most of the history of philosophy, such a view has fallen into increasing disrepute in the last two centuries and has been generally repudiated in recent times. Nonetheless, as explained further in Chapter 1, it is arguably difficult or impossible to make good sense of most if not all claims of empirical knowledge, and indeed of reasoning generally, while eschewing any *a priori* appeal. What this indicates, I think, is that the prevailing forms of empiricism are in fact untenable, and that a re-examination of rationalism is sorely needed.

Though this book is not primarily meta-philosophical in character, the need for an account of genuine and non-tautological *a priori* justification seems to me especially urgent for philosophy itself. While it is not my purpose to argue the matter in detail here, my conviction is that philosophy is *a priori* if it is anything (or at least if it is anything intellectually respectable); and that the practice of even those who most explicitly reject the idea of substantive *a priori* justification inevitably involves tacit appeal to insights and modes of reasoning that can only be understood as *a priori* in character, if they are justified at all. Thus the prevailing epistemological views in this area are at war with the very existence of philosophy as a rational discipline, and only a successful defense of rationalism can hope to resolve this problem.

While I am confident that such a defense is possible, the issues involved are both large and difficult, and I am far from sure that I have handled all of them in the optimum way. Thus I prefer to regard the explication and defense of rationalism as an ongoing project, toward which the present book is only an initial and perhaps relatively modest contribution. If I am right, this general project, despite its recent neglect, should be utterly central to the philosophical agenda. Thus my primary goal is not to resolve fully all of the issues discussed, but rather to bring them to the attention of others who may see further or deeper than I have managed to do so far.

The large-scale structure of the book is as follows. Chapter 1 is introductory, containing explanations of some of the key concepts, a *prima facie* defense of the indispensability of *a priori* justification, and a brief discussion of the often misunderstood views of Kant in this area. Chapters 2 and 3 offer detailed explication and criticism of the two leading empiricist alternatives to rationalism: the moderate empiricism of Hume, Kant (as argued in Chapter 1), and twentieth-century positivism; and the radical empiricism of Quine and his followers. Both of these views are argued to be entirely unsatisfactory. Moderate empiricism evaporates under scrutiny, turning out, if I am right, not to have been even a fully intelligible position, while radical empiricism collapses into a pervasive skepticism. With the usual qualifications that attach to arguments by elimination, these two chapters seem to me to constitute a very strong case for rationalism.

Chapter 4 then presents and develops a moderate, fallibilist version of rationalism, one that is more modest in its claims than many or most historical positions, but still quite strong enough to handle the epistemological desiderata in relation to which empiricism has been shown to be inadequate. Chapters 5 and 6 then explore and attempt to answer the leading objections, epistemological and metaphysical respectively, to this rationalist view. These three chapters are the heart of the book.

The final chapter, Chapter 7, is rather different in character. Having argued that a rationalist view of *a priori* justification is essential to philosophy, it seems valuable to show how an *a priori* approach could deal with a central philosophical issue, and the problem of induction was the obvious candidate. In this chapter I argue that the standard approaches to induction are thoroughly inadequate and that only a rationalist approach offers any hope of success. I then offer, somewhat more tentatively, a specific rationalist solution that seems to me highly promising, though all of the details are not filled in. (It is worth adding that in my view a rationalist approach is also the one hope for dealing satisfactorily with many other philosophical issues, from the venerable problem of the external world to the justification of moral and ethical claims. I once hoped to include here at least an outline discussion of some of these further issues, but they proved too large to fit reasonably into the present volume.)

This book has been in progress for a rather long time. Most of it was written in two intensive periods of work, the first during a sabbatical leave from the University of Washington in the academic year 1986–87, and the second during my tenure of a research fellowship from the National Endowment for the Humanities in the academic year 1990–91; I am extremely grateful to Washington and to N.E.H. for this support, without which it is unlikely that the book would have been completed. Many people have provided helpful comments, including especially Tony Anderson, Jay Atlas, Robert Audi, Al Casullo, Marc Cohen, Larry Colter, Pat Franken, Mark Hinchliff, Jennifer Lackey, C.D.C. Reeve, Bob Richman, Steve Rosenbaum, Ernie Sosa, Steve Sullivan, Bill Talbott, and Cass Weller. I am grateful to audiences at Western Washington University, the University of Nebraska, Illinois State University, Hope College, Pomona College, and Brown University, where portions of the book were presented; and to students over the years, mainly at the University of Washington, but also more briefly at Illinois Wesleyan University and Illinois State University, upon whose developing philosophical intelligences this material was honed and tested. I am also extremely grateful for the insightful comments of the referee for Cambridge University Press, which resulted in many improvements; though he is in fact no longer anonymous, he shall remain nameless here. Obviously none of these people is responsible for the problems and mistakes that undoubtedly remain.

My greatest debt is to my wife and partner, in life and in philosophy, Ann Baker: for unstinting philosophical criticism and stimulation, and for constant and unfailing support and sustenance in an abundance of other ways. Among many other things, she is the very embodiment of the sort of philosophical reader that I would like this book to have. I dedicate it to her with love and gratitude.

L.B.

Acknowledgments

Various portions of this book have appeared in earlier or condensed versions as journal articles, as detailed below:

A condensation of Chapters 1–3 appeared as "A Rationalist Manifesto," *Canadian Journal of Philosophy*, Supplementary Volume 18 (1992): 53–88.

Some parts of Chapter 3 were included in "Against Naturalized Epistemology," *Midwest Studies in Philosophy*, 19 (1995): 283–300.

A condensation of Chapters 4 and 5 appeared as "Toward a Moderate Rationalism," *Philosophical Topics*, 23 (1995): 47–78.

A preliminary version of much of Chapter 6 appeared as "Is Thought a Symbolic Process?" *Synthese*, 89 (1991): 331–52.

A very early version of Chapter 7 appeared as "A Reconsideration of the Problem of Induction," *Philosophical Topics*, 14 (1986): 93–124.

I am grateful to the various editors and publishers for permission to make use of material from those articles.

1

Introduction: the problem of a priori justification

§1.1. THE NEED FOR THE A PRIORI

Perhaps the most pervasive conviction within the Western epistemological tradition is that in order for a person's belief to constitute *knowledge* it is necessary (though not sufficient) that it be justified or warranted or rationally grounded, that the person have an adequate *reason* for accepting it. Moreover, this justifying reason must be of the right sort: though one might accept a belief for moral reasons or pragmatic reasons or religious reasons or reasons of some still further sort and be thereby in a sense justified, such reasons cannot satisfy the requirements for knowledge, no matter how powerful, in their own distinctive ways, they may happen to be. Knowledge requires instead that the belief in question be justified or rational in a way that is internally connected to the defining goal of the cognitive enterprise, that is, that there be a reason that enhances, to an appropriate degree, the chances that the belief is *true*. Justification of this distinctive, truth-conducive sort will be here referred to as *epistemic justification*.[1]

1 For more extensive discussion of the general conception of epistemic justification, see my book *The Structure of Empirical Knowledge* (BonJour 1985; hereafter cited as *SEK*), chapter 1. Certain recent philosophers have questioned, or seemed to question, this requirement for knowledge, arguing instead that knowledge requires only that the process leading to the acceptance of the belief in question be *reliable*, i.e., that it in fact produce or tend to produce true beliefs, even though the person in question may have no reason of any sort for thinking that this is so (where this variant requirement may be presented as either a competing account of justification or as an alternative to the justification requirement). See, e.g., Nozick (1981), chapter 3; and Goldman (1985). My conviction is that views of this kind are merely wrong-headed and ultimately uninteresting evasions of the central epistemological issues. But I have dealt extensively with them elsewhere (and no doubt will again in future work) and so will mostly neglect them in the present work, where my main aim is to consider one crucial element of a more traditional epistemological position. See *SEK*, chapter 3; "Nozick, Externalism, and Skepticism," in Luper-Foy (1987), pp. 297–313; and "Replies and Clarifications," in Bender (1989), pp. 276–92.

Historically, most epistemologists have distinguished two main sources from which the epistemic justification of a belief might arise. It has seemed obvious to all but a very few that many beliefs are justified by appeal to one's sensory (and introspective) *experience* of the world. But it has seemed equally obvious to most that there are other beliefs, including many of the most important ones that we have, that are justified in a way that does not depend at all on such an appeal to experience, justified, as it is usually put, by reason or pure thought alone. Beliefs justified entirely in the latter way are said to be justified *a priori,* while beliefs justified at least partially in the former way are said to be justified empirically or *a posteriori.* As this suggests, the justification of some (indeed probably most) beliefs may derive in part from each of these sources; as the terms are standardly used, the justification of such beliefs counts as *a posteriori,* but this terminological point should not be allowed to obscure the possibility that the *a priori* component may be both substantial and, in many cases, essential.

In spite of its historical prominence, however, the very idea of *a priori* epistemic justification has over the last half century or so been the target of severe and relentless skepticism. Thus it may be useful to begin our discussion by considering, briefly and provisionally, three reasons why this venerable idea should still be taken seriously.

First. The most familiar and obvious appeal is to putative examples of knowledge whose justification, it is alleged, can only be construed as *a priori.* Here the leading examples are propositions of logic and mathematics; but there are a multitude of others as well, ranging from seemingly commonsensical truths such as "nothing can be both red and green all over at the same time" or "if one event is later than a second and the second is later than a third, then the first is later than the third," on the one hand, to alleged truths of metaphysics such as "a physical object cannot be in two places at the same time" or "every event must have a cause," on the other. Although perhaps no one would wish to defend all of the particular examples that have been proposed in this connection, they are undeniably impressive when taken as a group, and it is no accident that the vast majority of historical philosophers, from Plato on down to Leibniz and Locke, would have regarded this general line of argument as both obvious and conclusive, so much so that the issue of whether there is *a priori* justification scarcely arises for them at all. As will emerge much later (mainly in §4.2), the perceived cogency of examples of these kinds, and perhaps others, is ultimately crucial for the defense of *a priori* justification. Nonetheless, the appeal to such examples can be resisted, at least initially, in ways that may seem to deprive it of much of its force. Some examples, such as the causal principle cited above, may be dismissed as not being epistemically justified at all; and others may be argued to be grounded ultimately, albeit tacitly, in experience. (I ignore for the moment the less extreme tactic of claiming that the propositions in question, though indeed justified *a priori*, rest on definitions or linguistic conventions in a way that deprives the concept of *a priori* justification of most of its epistemological force; this sort of response will be considered extensively in the next chapter.) Such rejoinders vary widely in their intuitive plausibility, both in general and in relation to the various specific examples, but they are at least dialectically tenable so long as the present argument stands alone.

Moreover, the perceived force of this sort of rejoinder has been greatly enhanced in modern times by the apparent collapse of the appeal to *a priori* justification in the case that would for a very long time have been cited as the most obvious example of all: that of Euclidean geometry. Since geometry had been taken for centuries to be the very paradigm of *a priori* knowledge, the advent of non-Euclidean geometries and the apparent discovery that Euclidean geometry, far from being unchallengeably justified and indeed certain on an *a priori* basis, was in fact false – indeed that this could seemingly be shown *empirically* – led quite naturally to a massive loss of confidence in alleged *a priori* justifications. While it is not in any way obviously legitimate to generalize in this way from what is arguably a rather special case, the collapse of this historically favorite example of *a priori* justification has deprived the general argument from examples of much of its persuasive power: who is to say, it is likely to be asked, that the result in the case of geometry will not eventually be found to extend to the other examples as well?[2] Thus it is important to see that there are other, more general considerations that can be used to buttress the appeal to examples.

Second. Contrary to the tendency in recent times for even those who accept the existence of *a priori* justification to downgrade its epistemological importance, it is arguable that the epistemic justification of at least the vast preponderance of what we think of as empirical knowledge must involve an indispensable *a priori* component – so that the only alternative to the existence of *a priori* justification is skepticism of a most radical kind.

The argument for this conclusion is extremely straightforward and obvious, so much so that it is very hard to understand the widespread failure to

---

2 A second example of failed *a priori* justification, which has been at least as influential in narrowly philosophical circles, is set theory, where propositions that seemed at one time to be justified *a priori* turned out to lead to contradiction.

acknowledge it. It derives from reflecting on the relation between knowledge and experience. For present purposes, I shall suppose that there are certain "foundational" beliefs that are fully justified by appeal to direct experience or sensory observation alone. We need not pause to worry about just which beliefs these are, for example, whether they concern ordinary physical objects or perhaps only private experiences; all that matters for present purposes is that, as will be true on any conception of direct experience that has any plausibility or indeed that has ever been held, such beliefs are particular rather than general in their content and are confined to situations observable at specific and fairly narrowly delineated places and times. The obvious and fundamental epistemological question then becomes whether it is possible to infer, in a way that brings with it epistemic justification, from these foundational beliefs to beliefs whose content goes beyond direct experience or observation: beliefs about the past, the future, and the unobserved aspects of the present; beliefs that are general in their content; or beliefs that have to do with kinds of things that are not directly observable.

If the answer to this question is "no," then the upshot is a quite deep form of skepticism (exactly how deep will depend on one's account of the foundational beliefs – perhaps even solipsism of the present moment). But if the answer is "yes," then such inferences must seemingly rely on either premises or principles of inference that are at least partially justified *a priori*. For if the conclusions of the inferences genuinely go beyond the content of direct experience, then it is impossible that those inferences could be entirely justified by appeal to that same experience. In this way, *a priori* justification may be seen to be essential if extremely severe forms of skepticism are to be avoided.

Third. The previous argument may be generalized in the following way. I have spoken so far as though the object of epistemic justification in general and *a priori* justification in particular is always a belief that some *proposition* or *thesis*, something capable of being either true or false, is true. But this way of putting things, though a harmless simplification when correctly understood, has the potential to be seriously misleading in one important respect, which must now be attended to. What it leaves out, or at least obscures, is perhaps the most cognitively indispensable application of the idea of the *a priori*: its application to arguments or inferences, to *reasoning*.

An *argument* is a set of beliefs or statements, or more precisely a set of propositions believed or stated, one of which (the conclusion) is claimed to follow from the others (the premises); the argumentative transition, in thought or discourse, from the premises to the conclusion is an *inference*. For any argument an issue that is closely analogous to the issue of epistemic justification for propositions can be raised: is there any reason for thinking that the conclusion of the argument either must be true or else is likely to be true *if* the premises are true? When such a reason exists, the argument in question may be said to be rationally cogent and the inference in question to be, in a somewhat modified sense, epistemically justified; where no such reason exists, the argument has no rational force and the inference is epistemically unjustified.[3] And the *a priori–a posteriori* distinction can also be extended to this variant kind of epistemic justification in an obvious way: if the reason for thinking that the conclusion will be true if the premise is true involves an appeal to experience of the world, in the sense explained above, then the inference is justified *a posteriori;* whereas if the reason is independent of any such appeal to experience, the inference is justified *a priori.* (As before, justification that is partially based on experience and partly independent of experience will be classified as *a posteriori,* but this of course does not alter the fact that such justification is partially *a priori* in character.)

Could an argument of any sort be entirely justified on empirical grounds? It seems clear on reflection that the answer to this question is "no." Any purely empirical ingredient can, after all, always be formulated as an additional empirical premise. When all such premises have been explicitly formulated, either the intended conclusion will be explicitly included among them or it will not. In the former case, no argument or inference is necessary, while in the latter case, the needed inference clearly goes beyond what can be derived entirely from experience.[4] Thus we see that the repudiation of all *a priori* justification is apparently tantamount to the repudiation of argument or reasoning generally, thus amounting in effect to intellectual suicide. This result will be examined further below, in Chapter 3, when I consider views, like those of Quine, that advocate such

3   For a particular person to be justified in accepting the conclusion of such an argument on the basis of a prior acceptance of its premises, the reason in question must, I assume, be in some way available to him.
4   This is not to deny that in practice we can and do employ empirical elements that function as principles of inference rather than as premises: e.g., the principle that a certain sort of frown indicates puzzlement on the part of the person exhibiting it or that a certain distinctive smell indicates that the food being cooked is starting to scorch. But the full justification of any inference that relies on such an empirical principle would presuppose an *a priori* justification for the transition (presumably inductive in character – see Chapter 7) from observations proper to the empirical principle in question and would also rely on *a priori* principles of logic to justify the transition from the empirical principle and specific observations to the conclusion. (I am indebted for this clarifying point to the referee.)

a repudiation, but it surely constitutes a strong *prima facie* reason for regarding the idea of *a priori* justification as philosophically and intellectually indispensable.

There is, of course, an intimate relation between the justification of inferences, as thus understood, and the justification of propositions or theses. For any argument, we may form the corresponding conditional, that is, the truth-functional conditional whose antecedent is the conjunction of the premises of the argument and whose consequent is its conclusion. The original inference will then be epistemically justified, in the sense just explained, if and only if this conditional proposition is epistemically justified in our original sense; and the classification of the justification as *a priori* or *a posteriori* will be the same for both inference and proposition. Because of this parallelism, it is sufficient for many purposes to confine our explicit attention to the *a priori* justification of propositions, and this is the course that will be largely followed here. Such an approach is apt to be misleading, however, insofar as it obscures the fact that the need for *a priori* justification is not confined merely to propositions accepted on a non-empirical basis, but extends also to reasoning itself.

These three arguments seem to me at the very least to constitute powerful *prima facie* reasons for resisting the prevailing skepticism concerning *a priori* justification. But while the need for *a priori* justification is in this way apparent, the precise character of the distinction between *a priori* and *a posteriori* justification remains more than a little obscure, and this obscurity is seriously compounded, as we shall see, by the still prevalent tendency to confuse or conflate it with other distinctions in the same dialectical vicinity. Thus it is necessary to begin by attempting to elucidate and clarify the main distinctions in the area: the *a priori*–*a posteriori* distinction itself, the necessary–contingent distinction, and, in a more provisional way, the analytic–synthetic distinction. This will be the main job of the next two sections. In the course of this discussion, we will also take a preliminary look at the main alternative positions on the nature and possibility of *a priori* justification, positions that will be considered in more detail in succeeding chapters.

§1.2. THE CONCEPT OF *A PRIORI* JUSTIFICATION

As the foregoing discussion suggests, the *a priori*–*a posteriori* distinction is an *epistemological* distinction, having to do with the ways in which the acceptance of a proposition may be epistemically justified, where that is understood to require having a reason for thinking that the proposition is true. In fact, as was already implicit in the foregoing discussion, there are two distinguishable aspects to the classical conception of *a priori* justification, one negative and the other positive: a proposition is justified *a priori* if it is justified (a) independently of any appeal to *experience* and (b) by appeal to reason or pure thought alone.[5] While these two sides of the concept have often been taken to go together, to pick out the same kind of justification, this should not be simply assumed. Thus it will be useful to speak for a while of the *negative* conception of *a priori* justification, reflected in aspect (a), distinguishing it from the *positive* conception of *a priori* justification, reflected in aspect (b).

One potential source of obscurity in the negative conception of *a priori* justification is the appeal to the idea of *experience*. While the general intent of this appeal seems clear enough at first glance, it turns out to be surprisingly difficult to delineate precisely. It is obvious at once that the broadest meaning of the term 'experience', that in which it refers to any sort of mental process that one consciously undergoes, is substantially too broad; in that sense, following a mathematical proof or even reflecting on a supposedly self-evident proposition would be an instance of experience, and *a priori* justification would be ruled out in a trivial and uninteresting way.[6] But it is just as obvious that the relevant concept of experience cannot be confined in its scope to the obvious paradigm of such experience, namely, the experience involved in ordinary sense-perception and deriving from the five standard senses. The justification of introspective knowledge pertaining to one's own states of mind should surely count as empirical, as should that of kinesthetic knowledge of the position and movements of one's body and that of knowledge of past events deriving, via memory, from previous episodes of perception. Moreover, if it should turn out (surprisingly) that there is genuine knowledge that results from

5 For such a proposition to be *known a priori* requires at least that it be true and that its *a priori* justification be sufficiently strong. I will not, however, make the common assumption that any proposition that has any degree of *a priori* justification automatically and necessarily meets these further conditions.

6 At least this will be so if it is assumed that epistemic justification requires that the person in question have a subjective grasp of the reason why his belief is likely to be true, for any such grasping of a reason would count as an experience in this broad sense. This result could perhaps be avoided by adopting a reliabilist view of *a priori* justification, analogous to the views mentioned in note 1 above, according to which the reason that justifies a person's belief need not be subjectively grasped; but such a view would be even more implausible here than it is in the case of empirical justification. (For arguments against reliabilism, see the works cited in note 1; though the views explicitly under discussion in those works are reliabilist theories of empirical justification and knowledge, the objections raised seem to me to apply equally well to the case of *a priori* justification.)

parapsychological or extrasensory capacities such as telepathy and clairvoyance, it seems apparent that its justification should also count as empirical, and not *a priori*, from the standpoint of the traditional distinction, whether or not it involves any distinctive sort of sensation or sensuous imagery.

My suggestion at this point is that the relevant notion of experience should be understood to include any sort of process that is perceptual in the broad sense of (a) being a causally conditioned response to particular, contingent features of the world and (b) yielding doxastic states that have as their content putative information concerning such particular, contingent features of the actual world as contrasted with other possible worlds. So understood, there would be no essential connotation that sensuous qualities or imagery are involved. And thus not only sense experience, but also introspection, memory, kinesthesia, and clairvoyance or telepathy (should these exist) would count as varieties of experience and the justification derived therefrom as *a posteriori*.[7] In contrast, "mathematical intuition," even though it undoubtedly counts as experience in the sense of a consciously undergone mental process, would not count as experience in this more specific sense so long as it is concerned with eternal, abstract, and necessarily existent objects and offers no information about the actual world as opposed to other possible worlds, that is, so long as its deliverances consist solely of (putatively) necessary truths.[8]

The foregoing discussion in effect appeals to the positive conception of *a priori* justification to clarify and sharpen the negative conception. What is wrong with regarding introspective or kinesthetic or clairvoyant knowledge as justified *a priori* is that things known in these ways – unlike, for example, pure mathematics (at least as traditionally conceived) – are not apparent to pure rational thought, but are rather the product of processes strongly analogous to sense perception. Of course nothing ultimately hangs on such issues of taxonomy. One could always insist on a version of the negative conception according to which any proposition whose justification did not appeal to ordinary sense experience or perhaps, more narrowly, to ordinary sensory and introspective experience would count as *a priori*. Such a conception would perhaps not be mistaken in any clear sense, but it would lump together kinds of justification that are very hetero-

---

7 An appeal to a dream or hallucination that seemed to be a cognitive process of one of these sorts would also count as an appeal to experience, albeit an unreliable one.

8 I am not concerned to argue right now that this is the correct view of mathematical intuition, only that it is a possible view, under which the justification resulting from such intuition would count as *a priori*.

geneous. More importantly, it would fail to highlight the epistemological issue that is, in my judgment, the most crucial: whether there is a mode of epistemic justification that depends only on pure reason or rational thought and not at all on any input of an experiential or quasi-experiential sort. Since it is this last issue that is the focus of the present book, I will construe the concept of *a priori* justification accordingly.

A second important source of unclarity in the negative conception of *a priori* justification has to do with the sense in which such justification is to be *independent* of experience. Here there are two distinct problems, the first of which concerns the issue of concept acquisition. A strict interpretation of the requirement of independence would seem to require that experience should be in no way a precondition for *a priori* justification, so that something justified *a priori* could have been so justified even if the person in question had never had any relevant experience at all. One reason that this is problematic is that many propositions commonly regarded as being justified or justifiable *a priori* involve concepts that are plausibly regarded as *empirical* concepts derived from experience.

Consider, for example, the claim that nothing can be red all over and green all over at the same time, one of the most widely invoked examples of alleged *a priori* justification. While I have no desire to defend such a view in detail here, it is very commonly assumed and is surely at least *prima facie* plausible that the concepts of redness and greenness are derived from experience in the sense that only someone who has had certain familiar kinds of visual experience can acquire such concepts. Indeed, such a thesis about concept acquisition has often been regarded as itself a necessary truth and indeed as justified *a priori*. But even if it is only contingently true, it would still follow that someone who has not had the requisite experiences would in fact be unable to understand the proposition in question and thus trivially could not be justified in believing it. It would follow, therefore, that having had the color experiences in question is a necessary condition for being justified in believing the proposition, so that the justification in question would apparently not count as *a priori* after all.

Here again, the issue of taxonomy is unimportant in itself. One could adopt a concept of *a priori* justification according to which no proposition containing concepts that must be derived from experience can count as being justified *a priori*; this would correspond to Kant's category of "pure *a priori* knowledge."[9] But this way of dividing up the ground would be inadvisable for at least two reasons. First, while the issue of concept acqui-

---

9 *Critique of Pure Reason*, 2nd edition (Kant 1787), Introduction, B3.

sition is important in its own right, it is not connected in any very close or essential way with the issue of justification; thus a conception of *a priori* justification that in effect conflates the two issues is less perspicuous than one that does not. Second, although the distinction between concepts that must be derived from experience and those that need not be is hard to draw with great confidence, it is at least debatable whether *any* concepts fall on the latter side of the divide and hence uncertain that any justification would count as *a priori* in the alternative sense indicated. For these reasons, I choose to follow Kant and the overall tradition by stipulating that a proposition will count as being justified *a priori* as long as no appeal to experience is needed for the proposition to be justified *once it is understood*, where it is allowed that experience may have been needed to achieve such an understanding.

There is, however, a further source of unclarity that needs to be considered at this point. It is at least possible that there are propositions for which the following situation obtains: experience is required in order to acquire the concepts needed to understand them, but any experience or set of experiences that suffices for such an understanding will also provide an adequate reason for thinking it that the proposition in question is true. Perhaps "I exist as a thinking thing" or even "I have experienced at some time a red visual sensation" express such propositions. But although such propositions will automatically be justified for anyone who understands them, they will not count as justified *a priori* according to the account being offered here. For someone who understands such a proposition will still have to appeal *again* to experience to find a reason for thinking it to be true; that the experiences appealed to may be the very same experiences via which the requisite concepts were acquired is simply irrelevant to the issue.[10]

The second problem pertaining to the idea of independence from experience concerns the question of whether *a priori* justification, in addition to being free of any positive appeal to experience, is independent of experience in the further sense of being incapable of being refuted by experience (or even, perhaps, incapable of having its justification weakened or undermined by experience). Traditional proponents of *a priori* justification have often made such claims on its behalf. But, as elaborated further in §1.4 and Chapter 4, such a claim is quite problematic and is in any case inessential to

---

10 For an account of *a priori* justification that differs on this point, see Kitcher (1973), pp. 21–9. Kitcher would classify such cases as being justified *a priori*. But this is at least in large part due to his refusal to explicitly invoke the concept of epistemic justification, thus leaving him no way to exclude them.

the main thrust of the idea of *a priori* justification: that of justification that derives from pure thought or reason alone with no positive dependence on experience. This being so, it would be a mistake to include this further dimension of independence in our primary conception of *a priori* justification. I will accordingly leave open the possibility that *a priori* justification, though not requiring positive experiential input, is nonetheless susceptible to refutation by experience. Whether this is in fact the case will be considered in §4.6.

In summation, I propose to count a proposition P as being justified *a priori* (for a particular person, at a particular time) if and only if that person has a reason for thinking P to be true that does not depend on any positive appeal to experience or other causally mediated, quasi-perceptual contact with contingent features of the world, but only on pure thought or reason, even if the person's ability to understand P in question derives, in whole or in part, from experience.

§1.3. THE *A PRIORI* AND THE NECESSARY

Understood in the way just indicated, the *a priori*–*a posteriori* distinction is obviously closely related to the distinction between necessary and contingent truths, and this no doubt accounts in substantial part for the tendency of many previous philosophers to treat the two distinctions as identical. As Kripke, among others, has pointed out,[11] however, this is a serious blunder, for the two distinctions, far from being identical, are not even distinctions of the same general kind: while the *a priori*–*a posteriori* distinction is, as we have seen, an *epistemological* distinction having to do with the way in which a claim or assertion is epistemically justified, the necessary–contingent distinction is a *metaphysical* distinction having to do with the status of a proposition in relation to the ways the world might have been (and having no immediate bearing on knowledge or justification).

A proposition is *necessary* (necessarily true) just in case it is true in all possible worlds, that is, true in any possible situation that obtains or might have obtained, such that, in the strongest possible sense, it had to be true and could not have been false; it is *contingent* if it is true in some possible worlds or situations and false in others, so that its truth value, whatever it in fact may actually be, might have been different (contingently true if the actual world is included in the former group of worlds, contingently false if it is included in the latter). A necessary falsehood, obviously enough, is

11 Kripke (1972), pp. 260–3, 275.

true in no possible world or situation. It is sometimes objected that this sort of characterization, relying as it does on the correlative notion of possibility, is essentially circular and thus of little help, but this seems to me mistaken. While it is obviously true that necessity and possibility are correlative, interdefinable concepts, it seems clear on reflection that it is the idea of possibility, of a world or situation that might have obtained, that is intuitively primary. A possible world is a way things might have been, a comprehensive situation that might have been real or actual, and this idea seems to be intuitively intelligible without any direct appeal to the notion of necessity.[12]

What is the relationship between these two distinctions? Though drawn on quite different bases, one epistemological and one metaphysical, it is of course still possible that they might turn out to fall in the same place within the class of propositions, that is, that necessity might in fact coincide with apriority and contingency with aposteriority. Such a coincidence thesis, as I will call it, has in fact often been held by those philosophers who do not simply conflate the two distinctions.

In fact, the conception of *a priori* justification adopted above already comes at least very close to incorporating part of the coincidence thesis: if *a priori* justification cannot appeal to any causally mediated process that yields information about this world as against other possible worlds, then whatever ground an *a priori* claim possesses, since it seemingly cannot pertain specifically to this world, will therefore extend just as well to any other possible world. It is tempting to conclude that propositions justified in this way must be justified in relation to any possible world if they are justified at all, and hence that apriority entails truth in all possible worlds, that is, necessity.

One challenge to this result has been offered by Kripke,[13] who argues that propositions like "the standard meter stick is one meter long" are both justified *a priori* and contingent. The idea is that although it is plain that no

---

12 For an opposing view, see Bealer (1982), pp. 205–9. Bealer rejects the possible worlds definition of necessity as circular and offers his own: a proposition is necessary if it corresponds to a necessary condition (possible state of affairs); and a condition x is necessary if it is identical to some specimen necessary condition (Bealer chooses the condition that x is self-identical), for unlike propositions, all necessarily equivalent conditions are identical. (Bealer has an elaborate and systematic argument for this view of conditions.) But I am unable to see why this does not finally amount to saying that a proposition is necessary if it is *necessarily* equivalent to some further proposition recognized as necessary – which seems both circular and unhelpful (since we are given no account of the necessity of the sample proposition .
13 Kripke (1972), p. 275.

special experience of the world is needed in order to be justified in believing that such a proposition is true, there obviously are other possible worlds in which it is false (worlds, e.g., in which the standard meter stick is subjected to substantial heat). But this example is not convincing. What seems to be justifiable *a priori* is not a claim about some particular object, a specific platinum–iridium bar in Paris, but rather a general thesis about the relation between a general concept or unit of measurement and any physical standard used to "fix the reference" of the corresponding term. This thesis, which I will not pause to formulate exactly, is indeed justified and known *a priori,* but it is also necessary; while its application to any particular object, being dependent on the empirical fact that the object in question was used (at the moment in question[14]) to "fix the reference," will be contingent but also *a posteriori.*

But although Kripke's objection thus fails, this does not mean that the first part of the coincidence thesis is correct. The obvious flaw in the earlier argument is the move from the claim that *a priori* justification would pertain equally to all possible worlds, so that the proposition in question would be *justified* in relation to any such world, to the conclusion that such a proposition must be *true* in all possible worlds as well and thus necessary. The implicit presupposition is that *a priori* justification guarantees the truth of the proposition justified, so that it would not be possible for a proposition to be justified *a priori* but be nonetheless false. But while such a view has indeed been part of the standard doctrine of *a priori* knowledge, it is by no means obviously correct and will have to be considered at length later in our discussion; thus the correctness of the first part of the coincidence thesis will remain for the moment an open question.

Kripke also argues against the other part of the coincidence thesis, namely, the claim that necessity entails apriority (or, equivalently, that aposteriority entails contingency), and here his argument is much more compelling. In the first place, it is clearly not the case that all necessary propositions that have been considered up to the present moment are in fact known or justified *a priori.* There are obviously many contradictory pairs of propositions in mathematics, logic, and other *a priori* sciences, neither of which is presently justified on an *a priori* basis, but such that it is intuitively clear that whichever of them is true will also be necessary. Kripke's example here is the famous mathematical proposition known as

---

14 Clearly the claim must be relativized to the precise moment at which the reference is "fixed," for even in this world there is no guarantee that the standard object will not be heated or otherwise deformed at the very next instant.

Goldbach's conjecture: that every even number greater than 2 is the sum of two prime numbers. From an intuitive standpoint, it is clear that either Goldbach's conjecture or the denial thereof is a necessary truth: if there is an even number greater than 2 that is not the sum of two primes, then it will have this status in every possible world; and if there is no such number, then this will also be the case in every possible world. But presumably no one presently is justified in believing *a priori* that the necessary claim in question, whichever it is, is true or necessary.[15] And it is also obvious that this situation might well remain unaltered throughout the entire future development of mathematics. Thus a necessary proposition need not ever be in fact known or justified *a priori.*

The natural suggestion at this point is to invoke the idea of an *a priori justifiable* proposition, one that *could* be justified *a priori* even if no one ever actually possesses such justification. And indeed, the phrase '*a priori* proposition' is perhaps most standardly used to refer to propositions that could be justified in such a way, whether or not they ever in fact are. But, as Kripke insists,[16] the meaning of this conception is quite vague. Must an *a priori* proposition be justifiable *a priori* for human minds, or at least for minds more or less like ours, or might it be *a priori* justifiable only for God or some other being whose powers in this regard are radically different in character from our own? Leibniz notoriously believed that God could directly perceive truths about infinite collections such as the infinity of possible worlds simply by examining all of them, and in this way could perhaps be justified in believing any and all necessary truths. But this sort of view, even if correct, seems simply irrelevant to the concepts of *a priori* justification and knowledge as they apply to human knowers. And if such supernatural possibilities are thus dismissed, there is no clear reason for believing that all necessary truths are justifiable *a priori,* even in principle. Even setting aside debatable examples such as the essentialist necessary truths argued for by Kripke,[17] there is no reason to think that, for example, Goldbach's conjecture or its denial (whichever is true) *must* be knowable or justifiable by human minds in any way that resembles ordinary cases of *a priori* justification. Why couldn't such a proposition be necessarily true even though there is no possible way to prove it nor any perspective from which its necessity can be intuitively grasped? Thus there is no clear argument for the second part of the coincidence thesis, and hence, no

15 Kripke (1972), p. 261–3.   16 Ibid., p. 260.
17 Ibid., passim.

matter how the issue with regard to the first part is finally resolved, no compelling reason to think that the two distinctions coincide.

One last suggestion that might be offered at this point is that even if necessary propositions need not be justified or even justifiable *a priori*, they must still be justified in that fashion if they are justified at all, or perhaps rather if they are justifiably thought to be necessary. But it is easy to see that both of these suggestions can easily be mistaken. There is no reason to deny that propositions of mathematics can be justified and known by appeal to the output of a computer, even if no *a priori* justification is thereby obtained; nor any reason to rule out the possibility that at least some necessary propositions might be justified via empirical survey or investigation. And there is also no reason to deny that if a proposition can be known at all in such ways, then it can also be known to be necessary, simply on the grounds that it is the sort of proposition that could be true at all only if it were necessary (where this last fact is presumably known *a priori*).

The immediate moral to be drawn is that the two distinctions in question, the *a priori–a posteriori* distinction and the necessary–contingent distinction, though related in important ways (including some that have yet to emerge), are quite distinct in both meaning and application, a very long philosophical tradition to the contrary notwithstanding.

§1.4. RATIONALISM AND EMPIRICISM

One main goal of this book is to arrive at an understanding of the nature, rationale, and limits of the *a priori* variety of epistemic justification. It is obvious that the initial conception of such justification offered above is predominantly negative in character: *a priori* justification is justification that does *not* depend on experience. But where then does such justification come from? How is the positive idea, briefly mentioned above, of justification by pure thought alone to be understood? Putting aside for the moment the ubiquitous possibility of skepticism, the answers to this question that are to be found in the epistemological literature are standardly classified under two main rubrics: rationalism and empiricism.

According to *rationalism*, *a priori* justification occurs when the mind directly or intuitively sees or grasps or apprehends (or perhaps merely seems to itself to see or grasp or apprehend)[18] a necessary fact about the

18 As we shall see in Chapter 4, the rationalist must concede, contrary to the main historical tradition, that what appears subjectively to be such a seeing or grasping or apprehending

nature or structure of reality. Such an apprehension may of course be discursively mediated by a series of steps of the same kind, as in a deductive argument. But in the simplest cases it is allegedly direct and unmediated, incapable of being reduced to or explained by any rational or cognitive process of a more basic sort – since any such explanation would tacitly presuppose apprehensions of this very same kind. According to the rationalist, the capacity for such direct intellectual insight into necessity is the fundamental requirement for reasoning and reflective intelligence generally. Perhaps in part because it is taken by them to be so pervasive and fundamental, rationalists have typically had little to say directly about this capacity, focusing instead on more specific problems and issues and taking the general capacity itself almost entirely for granted. This in turn has lent support to the charge that there is something mysterious, perhaps even somehow occult, about the capacity in question. From a rationalist perspective, however, as we will see further in Chapters 4 and 5, nothing could be further from the truth: the capacity for rational insight, though fundamental and irreducible, is in no way puzzling or especially in need of further explanation; indeed without such a capacity neither puzzles nor explanations would themselves be rationally intelligible.

As alluded to above, rationalists (along with at least most moderate empiricists) have standardly made two stronger claims about *a priori* justification: first that such justification not only involves no positive appeal to experience but also is incapable of being refuted or even undermined by experience to any degree; and, second, that knowledge justified in this way is certain or infallible, incapable of being mistaken. These two claims raise difficult and complicated issues that will be considered at length in Chapter 4. But neither of them is in any obvious way essential either to the central conception of *a priori* justification or to the main rationalist thesis that intellectual insight (or apparent insight) of the sort in question is an independent source of epistemic justification, one that is capable of providing at least a *prima facie* adequate reason for the acceptance of a claim as true in a case where positive support from experience is unavailable. Moreover, a moderate rationalism that does not endorse these stronger claims could still be quite sufficient to meet the demands posed by the three arguments for the existence of *a priori* justification discussed in §1.1. Thus it will be useful and will do no harm to limit ourselves for now to this more modest version

may fail to be one, most strikingly in the case where the proposition that seemed to be necessary turns out to be false. But he must insist nonetheless that in at least some such cases the apparent seeing or grasping or apprehending can still provide epistemic justification for accepting the claim in question. More on this below.

of rationalism (which will in fact ultimately prove to be the most defensible one).

Throughout most of the history of philosophy, rationalism was the dominant, indeed almost entirely unchallenged view of the nature of *a priori* justification. Plato was the first great proponent of rationalism; but though Aristotle accorded a more significant cognitive role to experience, he was just as much a rationalist in the sense specified, as were virtually all of his medieval successors. Descartes and Spinoza were rationalists, of course, as, on the whole, was Leibniz.[19] But so were Locke and pretty clearly also Berkeley (despite the absence of any very specific pronouncement by him on the issue).

It is thus not until Hume that we find a major philosopher who clearly repudiates the rationalist capacity for insight into necessary truths pertaining to reality, insisting that *a priori* justification concerns only "relations of our ideas" as opposed to "matters of fact." Superficial impressions to the contrary notwithstanding, Kant (as discussed further in the next section) is in fact much closer to a Humean version of empiricism than to rationalism, but, excepting only Mill, clear examples of empiricism are hard to find in the period after Kant until the advent of positivism in Comte and Mach. Since that time, however, empiricist skepticism about the *a priori* has become more and more prevalent and, mainly in a specific form deriving from Hume and Kant, has been the dominant view for most of the twentieth century, at least in the Anglo-American world.

The underlying motivation for empiricist doubts is a deep-seated skepticism about the supposed capacity for rational insight into necessity to which the rationalist appeals. To the self-proclaimed hard-headed empiricist, the idea of such a capacity, or at least of its existence in human animals, appears implausible on both metaphysical and scientific grounds, and becomes even more so as our knowledge of human beings and their place in the world develops. But until very recently most empiricists have also found the existence of *a priori* justification and knowledge, in logic and mathematics at least, quite undeniable. It is thus incumbent on such empiricists to offer an alternative account of this justification, one that from their standpoint is metaphysically and scientifically more palatable than rationalism.

---

19 By virtue of his insistence that all necessary truths rest at bottom on the law of identity, Leibniz is a somewhat more problematic case and may be seen as taking the first step toward the moderate empiricist idea that *a priori* justification pertains only to tautologies. What makes this construal one-sided at best is his attribution of *a priori* justification to metaphysical claims of the strongest sort imaginable.

Although hints can be found in various earlier authors, especially in Locke and Leibniz, the main idea on which such an alternative account relies does not emerge clearly until Hume and especially Kant. The view that results, which I will refer to here as *moderate empiricism,* attempts to concede the existence of *a priori* justification and *a priori* knowledge while minimizing its ultimate cognitive significance. The basic claim of the moderate empiricist is that *a priori* epistemic justification, though genuine enough in its own way, extends only to propositions that reflect relations among our concepts or meanings or linguistic conventions, rather than to those that make substantive claims about the character of the extra-conceptual world. *A priori* justified propositions are thus ultimately trivial or tautological in character, and hence the justification for believing them requires nothing as outlandish as the rationalist's alleged intuitive insight into necessity.

The moderate empiricist view is most standardly formulated as the claim that all *a priori* justifiable or knowable propositions are *analytic.* But, as is much more fully explained in the next chapter, the term 'analytic' is more than a little problematic, due to its having been defined in a wide variety of ways, by no means obviously equivalent to each other. This is a familiar enough situation in philosophy (and elsewhere), but the reason for it in this case is rather unusual and bears an important relation to the general problem at issue. In effect, the concept of analyticity has come to be specified more by the argumentative or dialectical role that it is supposed to fill than by any generally accepted definition. Specifically, the moderate empiricist hopes to establish two correlative theses: first, that genuine *a priori* justification pertains only to analytic propositions; and, second, that the *a priori* justification of analytic propositions can be adequately understood in a way that does not require or depend upon the alleged capacity for rational or intuitive insight into the nature of reality advocated by the rationalist. Specific definitions of 'analytic' put forth by various moderate empiricists are simply attempts to find some concept that can fill this role, and it is thus hardly surprising that they vary quite widely from one moderate empiricist to another. What is somewhat more surprising is that the conviction that there *must* be some specific concept that can do this job is often very strongly held even in the absence of any definite commitment as to which concept might in fact work. (Kant's original conception of analyticity will be examined in the next section, and a relatively complete canvass of the various conceptions of analyticity will be offered in Chapter 2.)

There are two questions that must be asked about positions of this general type. The first and more obvious one, to which the major share of attention has been devoted, is whether it is indeed true that all plausible cases of *a priori* justification involve propositions that are analytic in the sense specified by the position in question. As we shall see, this question is difficult enough for most of the specific versions of moderate empiricism to answer successfully. But the second and equally important question is whether the fact that a particular proposition is analytic in the chosen sense really yields a complete and adequate account of how acceptance of it is epistemically justified, an account that does not rely even tacitly on the rationalist appeal to substantive *a priori* insight which it is the main point of such positions to avoid. My main thesis concerning moderate empiricism, defended at length in Chapter 2, is that there is in fact no version of moderate empiricism, that is, no conception of analyticity, that can by itself account fully and adequately for even a *single* instance of *a priori* justification.

From a historical standpoint, moderate empiricism is clearly the main empiricist position on the subject of *a priori* justification; and although full-dress defenses of it have been infrequent of late, it continues, I believe, to be widely albeit somewhat less openly held. The most conspicuous recent position on the general topic of *a priori* justification, however, is a much more extreme version of empiricism. Associated mainly with Quine and his followers, this second and quite distinct version of empiricism, which I will here refer to as *radical empiricism,* rather than attempting to give an epistemologically innocuous account of *a priori* justification, denies outright its very existence. This might seem to indicate that for the radical empiricist, epistemic justification derives entirely from experience; but while, as we shall see, there is a sense in which this is so, such a characterization fails to give a very good picture of the radical empiricist view, because it fails to bring out the skeptical thrust of the position. Radical empiricism seems to me extremely problematic from an epistemological standpoint, but Chapter 3 will be devoted to an attempt to understand and evaluate it.

The central theses of this book are, first, that a rationalist view of at least the moderate sort indicated above is the only hope for a non-skeptical account of *a priori* justification and knowledge, and indeed for a non-skeptical account of knowledge generally (with the possible exception of those parts of empirical knowledge, if any, that can be fully justified by appeal to direct experience or observation alone); and, second, that such a view is defensible and fundamentally correct. Rationalism will be developed and defended in detail in Chapters 4, 5, and 6. As is usual in philosophical discussion, however, a substantial part of the argument in favor of rationalism will derive from the objections to competing views, in this case to the various versions of empiricism that will be considered in Chapters 2 and 3.

§1.5. KANT AND THE SYNTHETIC *A PRIORI*

Before turning to a detailed consideration of the two main varieties of empiricism, there is one more preliminary matter to be dealt with. Clearly the most seminal figure in the modern discussion of the nature and possibility of *a priori* justification and knowledge is Kant, who was the first to make relatively clear the main distinctions upon which the issue turns. In spite of this fact, however, Kant's own quite idiosyncratic views on the topic, and especially their relation to the more standard positions canvassed above, have not usually been well understood, a situation that has tended to cloud the overall discussion of these issues in important ways. My purpose in the present section is to outline Kant's position and clarify its essential nature. It will emerge that Kant, though often regarded as a rationalist, indeed by some as the arch rationalist, is in fact much closer to moderate empiricism in his basic epistemological commitments.

Kant was, as we have seen, the first to formulate explicitly the logical distinction between propositions or judgments that are analytic and those that are synthetic. In his version, a judgment of subject-predicate form is analytic when "the predicate B belongs to the subject A, as something which is (covertly) contained in this concept A." Such a judgment, "as adding nothing through the predicate to the concept of the subject, but merely breaking it up into those constituent concepts that have all along been thought in it, though confusedly," may also be called an "explicative" judgment. In contrast, a judgment is synthetic (or "ampliative") if the predicate concept lies outside the subject concept and thus adds something to it (A6–7=B10–11).[20] Thus, for example, the proposition "all brothers are male" is analytic in the Kantian sense, because the subject concept *brother* is equivalent to the concept *male sibling* and thus includes the predicate concept *male;* whereas the proposition "all brothers are lazy," whether or not it is true, is synthetic, because the concept *lazy* is not contained in the concept *brother.*

What is important is to understand clearly the crucial epistemological significance that this concept of analyticity is supposed by Kant to have:

20 All references to the *Critique of Pure Reason* will be to the translation by Norman Kemp Smith (Kant 1787) and will use the standard pagination.

once the proposition that all brothers are male is seen to be analytic, the epistemological problem of how I can be justified in believing that it is true without any appeal to experience is regarded by him as entirely solved. All that is required, says Kant, is to "extract" the predicate from the subject "in accordance with the principle of contradiction" (B12); that is, since the predicate concept merely repeats part of the subject concept, so that the denial of the proposition would result in an immediate contradiction, anyone can see at once that such a proposition must be true.

It is this alleged epistemological insight that Kant in effect bequeaths to the moderate empiricist. Whether the resulting account is as unproblematic as he thinks is a question to which we shall return in the next chapter, but it is clear that Kant never questions it for even a moment.[21] His main epistemological concern thus becomes the problem of the synthetic *a priori:* how can there be knowledge that is *a priori* in its justification and yet synthetic in its logical form? Since such knowledge would be justified neither by experience nor along the lines just sketched, how could it be justified at all? To this question, the moderate empiricist replies, of course, that it could not, concluding that there is no such knowledge.

But that there is synthetic *a priori* knowledge, Kant, on the surface at least, never questions. Of the variety of examples that he offers in support of this claim, it will suffice here to focus on the most prominent and familiar, the arithmetical proposition that 7 + 5 = 12. Clearly if we know anything at all *a priori,* the proposition that 7 + 5 = 12 will be an instance of such knowledge. Why does Kant think that this proposition is synthetic rather than analytic?

His basic argument is as follows:

if we look more closely, we find that the concept of the sum of 7 and 5 contains nothing save the union of the two numbers into one, and in this no thought is being taken as to what the single number may be which combines both. The concept of 12 is by no means already thought in merely thinking this union of 7 and 5; and I may analyze my concept of such a possible sum as long as I please, still I shall never find the 12 in it. (B15)

---

21 As has often been noted, providing thereby one main motive for variant conceptions of analyticity, it is a consequence of Kant's definition of 'analytic' that no judgment or proposition that is not of subject-predicate form can qualify as analytic, so that even seemingly obvious tautologies like "either it is raining or it is not raining" are excluded. Of course, if the concept of the synthetic is similarly restricted to subject-predicate judgments, as seems to be the case for Kant, such a judgment would also not count as synthetic, and thus not as synthetic *a priori.* But it would still be an apparently clear example of *a priori* knowledge that could not be accounted for by appeal to the idea of analyticity. Kant has little to say about such examples.

Kant has often been criticized for couching his argument here in psychological-sounding terms, and it has been suggested that he confuses the *logical* issue of whether "7 + 5 = 12" is analytic with the purely *psychological* question of whether one who is thinking of 7 plus 5 must think explicitly of 12.[22] Such criticisms are, however, at least largely misconceived. It is of course true that the issue is logical, in a broad sense, rather than psychological. But it is not, as it is usually taken by such critics to be, the issue of whether the idea of being equal to 12 follows *somehow* from the idea of being equal to the sum of 7 plus 5 nor even the issue of whether such a conclusion follows from the axioms of number theory. The issue that Kant wants to consider is the much narrower issue of whether this conclusion follows because the concept of 12 is actually, albeit covertly, *contained* in the very concept of the sum of 7 and 5, contained in the way that the concept of being male is contained in the concept of being a brother. For only such an explicit relation of containment would, he believes, allow us to account epistemologically for our knowledge that 7 + 5 = 12 in the way discussed above. And a natural way to put this question is to ask whether someone who adequately understands or grasps the meaning of '7 + 5' must thereby, *as a part of that very understanding* and not a further conclusion, grasp that the sum in question is equal to 12: a formulation that is obviously very close to Kant's own and is not in any objectionable sense psychological.

Once the question is formulated in this way, Kant's original answer is, I submit, quite obviously correct. One who fails at a particular point in time to realize that the sum of 7 and 5 is 12 is not thereby shown not to have understood the concept of the sum of 7 and 5 itself. (If simple reflection on the point does not suffice, it may be helpful to consider more complicated sorts of arithmetical problems.)[23] Thus it seems correct to say that the proposition that 7 + 5 = 12 is indeed synthetic *a priori* (assuming that it is *a priori* at all), given the original Kantian account of the analytic–synthetic distinction. And if this is so, there will obviously be many other propositions that will fall into this same category. (Whether there is some alterna-

22 See, e.g., Ayer (1946), pp. 77–8.
23 It would of course be possible to invent a sense of understanding in which one could not be said to have understood a concept until he had grasped all of its *a priori* implications, but it should be noticed at once that a concept of analyticity formulated by reference to this sense of understanding would fail to accomplish the moderate empiricist purpose of accounting for *a priori* justification purely by appeal to meaning and definition, with no need for any sort of rational insight: the main problem could simply be restated as that of explaining how we are able to make the transition from understanding a concept in the more ordinary, limited sense to the more grandiose sort of understanding thus stipulated.

tive concept of analyticity that both applies to such propositions and yields a perspicuous epistemological account of how they are justified is a question that will be deferred until the next chapter.)

It is, of course, Kant's avowed belief in the existence of synthetic *a priori* knowledge of this kind that makes him seem on the surface to be a rationalist. But this impression is nonetheless profoundly misleading. For despite the apparent cogency of the argument just discussed, Kant's acceptance of its conclusion turns out to be a very superficial acceptance, one that is decisively undermined, I will argue, by his own answer to the question of how such knowledge is possible. In the first place, according to that answer, such knowledge must be qualified in a way that makes it questionable whether his view really accounts for the original examples, such as the one just discussed, that he appeals to in order to motivate it. Secondly, and more importantly, Kant cannot ultimately maintain even the claim that this qualified knowledge is genuinely synthetic.

Synthetic *a priori* knowledge would *not* be possible, Kant argues, if the objects that such knowledge purports to describe were independent objects external to the knower, things-in-themselves that are part of independent, *an sich* reality. It is only if the objects of knowledge and the experience that presents them must somehow conform to the faculties of knowledge, rather than the other way around, that synthetic *a priori* knowledge becomes possible, a suggestion that constitutes Kant's famous "Copernican Revolution" in philosophy (Bxvii–xviii). The rough idea, of course, is that the mind so shapes or structures experience as to make the synthetic *a priori* propositions in question invariably come out true *within the experiential realm*. Thus, synthetic *a priori* knowledge, according to Kant, pertains only to the realm of appearances or phenomena, not to *an sich* reality.

The divergence from classical versions of rationalism is already obvious enough, but it might be thought that Kant is still a rationalist, albeit a substantially more modest one. To see why even this is mistaken, we need to explore more fully the idea that synthetic *a priori* knowledge is possible within the bounds of experience. Suppose that we are concerned with some specific proposition P that is apparently synthetic *a priori*. Kant's suggestion is then that we can know P *a priori* in spite of its synthetic character because the mind so operates in structuring or "synthesizing" experience as to make P invariably true within the experiential realm.

The first problem with this suggestion concerns the precise identity of the proposition that is supposed to be synthetic *a priori*. Our pre-theoretic intuition, for which Kant is supposedly trying to account, is that it is P

itself that has this status. But it is easy to see that Kant's position offers no reason at all for thinking that the original proposition P is even true, let alone justifiable or knowable *a priori*. What would have to be true if Kant's account were correct is, not the original proposition P, but rather the apparently quite different proposition: *within the bounds of experience, P;* call this proposition $P*$.[24] And thus, insofar as the original intuitive datum to be accounted for is the apparent *a priori* justification of P itself, Kant's explanation does not really even speak to the issue.

More importantly, this first problem leads at once to a second, which concerns the status of the further proposition $P*$ just formulated: is *this* proposition *a priori* or *a posteriori*, analytic or synthetic? Presumably $P*$ will have the same status as the Kantian thesis from which it immediately follows, namely, the thesis that the mind so operates as to make the original proposition P true within the realm of experience. Plainly Kant cannot hold that it is a merely empirical fact that the mind so operates without abandoning any attempt to account for the original intuition that P, or anything resembling P, is knowable *a priori*. But if the claim that the mind so operates is justifiable *a priori*, is it then analytic or synthetic? To say that it is synthetic, while yielding a specimen of synthetic *a priori* knowledge – even if not quite the one originally proposed – creates an unsolvable problem for Kant. For how would the synthetic *a priori* status of this new proposition be accounted for? To offer the same account that was originally offered for P would in effect require Kant to say that the mind so operates as to make it true that: the mind so operates as to make it true that $P*$. It is very doubtful that this new claim even makes sense, but even if it does, the same question can be raised about it, and so on *ad infinitum*, thus generating a regress that is clearly vicious. The upshot is that the *a priori* thesis about the operation of the mind that underlies $P*$, if it is not to be synthetic *a priori* in a way for which Kant's philosophy cannot account, must apparently be *analytic* if it is to be justified at all – which would thus imply that its consequence $P*$ is also analytic. Both of these claims are quite implausible, albeit the former more obviously so than the latter. But Kant is committed to them as long as he maintains his insistence that

24 A possible response here would be that P is meaningful only within the confines of experience, so that the specified limitation is in effect already built in and hence does not alter the identity of the proposition. The argument for such a view from within Kant's philosophical position is stronger for some propositions than for others, though it is not clear that he accepts it for any. I doubt, however, whether any such contention can be made compelling on general philosophical grounds. (And if it were, the result would still be, for reasons discussed below, that P, as long as its *a priori* status is capable of being accounted for by Kant's philosophy, cannot be synthetic after all.)

synthetic *a priori* knowledge that does not derive from imposition by the mind is impossible.[25]

Thus, in summary, Kant's apparent insistence on the existence of synthetic *a priori* knowledge entirely evaporates, and his position turns out not to be a rationalist position to any serious degree at all. The Kantian view of *a priori* justification, if consistently elaborated, provides no basis for even a restricted sort of synthetic *a priori* knowledge that would apply only within the realm of appearances: the original proposition *P* turns out not to be knowledge of any kind and very possibly not even true, while the implicit substitute *P** must turn out, assuming that the Kantian account of the supposed synthetic *a priori* is itself justified *a priori*, to be analytic *a priori*.

Of course this last claim is extremely implausible, raising the possibility that if Kant had ever faced clearly the problem of the epistemological status of his own philosophical claims, he might have retreated into a more traditional rationalism. As things stand, however, it is clear that Kant is not only not a rationalist, but, most strikingly, does not even regard rationalism as a significant option. Whereas Hume, the supposed paradigm of empiricism, at least feels some need to argue (though not in these terms) that pure reason cannot yield knowledge of *an sich* reality, Kant does not seem to entertain such a possibility even momentarily. On the contrary, it appears to be for him self-evident that we can have no *a priori* knowledge of independent reality except that which is analytic and hence ultimately trivial.[26]

For this reason, a Kantian view, in my judgment, does not constitute a significant further alternative with respect to the issue of *a priori* justification and accordingly need not be accorded any further consideration. In

25 A fuller discussion of this point would have to consider the details of Kant's arguments and in particular the famous, though notoriously obscure "Transcendental Deduction of the Categories," but such a consideration would not, I think, alter the foregoing conclusion. The initial premise of the Transcendental Deduction is apparently the claim that unity of consciousness exists, that my consciousness is unified. It is difficult to decide what epistemological status Kant ascribes to this claim itself. But in any case, the conditional thesis that if unity of consciousness exists, the mind must have imposed the order reflected in the categories on the manifold of sensible intuition must presumably be *a priori* (if in fact justified at all), as allegedly shown by Kant's argument, and cannot be synthetic *a priori* in the only way that Kant's views allow, for essentially the same reason discussed in the text. Hence Kant must apparently say that this thesis is analytic – and so also the specific principles such as the causal maxim (perhaps themselves made explicitly conditional on the existence of unity of consciousness) that allegedly follow from it.

26 This is expressed perhaps most clearly in the B preface, but is also lurking just under the surface of the argument in many other places. (This assertion on Kant's part constitutes, of course, a second instance of a seemingly synthetic *a priori* claim which his own account of the synthetic *a priori* cannot account for.)

particular, such a view has no apparent resources beyond those of moderate empiricism for dealing with the general problem, discussed in §1.1 above, of how observation-transcending inference and reasoning generally are to be justified. In the next two chapters, I will argue that the two more widely held empiricist views discussed above are, in their different ways, equally unsatisfactory.

A NOTE ON TERMINOLOGY

I have spoken so far and will for the most part continue to speak of the objects of (allegedly) *a priori* justification and knowledge (and indeed of knowledge and belief generally) as *propositions:* assertive contents of belief, judgment, or thought, possessing truth values, which may of course be linguistically expressed but which need not be and often are not thus expressed. This more or less traditional view seems to me pretty obviously correct, though I have no desire to argue very extensively for it at this point. (In the course of the discussion of moderate empiricism in Chapter 2, I will offer reasons for thinking that at least some instances of *a priori* justification need not in fact be linguistically expressible by the knowers in question.) Though various problems can be raised concerning the precise nature and ontological status of propositions understood in this way, some of which will be considered later on, in Chapter 6, these seem to me to be relevant only to the question of the correct philosophical account of such entities, and not to provide any serious reason for doubting their very existence.

There are many philosophers, however, primarily those in the general tradition of analytic philosophy, who prefer to speak in linguistic terms when discussing issues concerning justification, belief, and knowledge. Sometimes this variant terminology genuinely reflects a serious opposing view on the present issue. This is most obviously so in the case of Quine who regards belief as an attitude toward *sentences,* presumably understood as types of inscriptions and utterances, and explicitly disavows anything like propositions as standardly conceived. It is also true for some versions of moderate empiricism, roughly those that appeal to something like linguistic convention. In such cases, obviously, this issue will have to be explicitly attended to and the position in question dealt with in its own terms, lest important questions be begged.

Most typically, however, the use of such variant terminology seems to reflect no serious divergence concerning the objects of justification, belief, and knowledge. This is especially common with respect to the employment of the term 'statement', which often seems to refer merely to a content that could be overtly stated, but with no presumption being involved at all that any such overt statement has actually been made. In this usage, speaking of statements seems to amount to nothing more than a fashionable or ontologically squeamish way of referring obliquely to what others refer to as propositions. And some philosophers also shift more or less freely between 'proposition', 'statement', and sometimes, though less commonly, 'sentence'.[27] In dealing with views of these sorts, where the choice of terminology seems to reflect no substantive position on this issue, it would be both tedious and philosophically pointless to constantly take explicit notice of it. Thus in these cases, I will often adopt the practice of allowing the terminology to drift a bit in a way that would be objectionable if a more serious issue were involved. (Where it seems helpful in avoiding misunderstanding, I will occasionally highlight the situation by employing a disjunctive formulation.)

27 It is worth noting that the term 'proposition' is also sometimes used in a way that seems to include overt statements.

2

In search of moderate empiricism

§2.1. INTRODUCTION

As explained in the previous chapter, the moderate empiricist position on *a priori* knowledge holds that while such knowledge genuinely exists and has occasional importance in its own distinctive way, it is nonetheless merely *analytic* in character – that is, very roughly, merely a product of human concepts, meanings, definitions, or linguistic conventions. Such knowledge thus says nothing substantive about the world, and its justification can be accounted for without appealing to anything as problematic as the rationalist idea of rational insight into the character of *an sich* reality. Indeed, as we shall see later in this chapter, it is this alleged capacity to provide an unproblematic explanation of *a priori* justification that constitutes the main argument for moderate empiricism, even in the face of recalcitrant rationalist counterexamples.

For much of this century, this general sort of position had the status of virtually unquestioned orthodoxy for most philosophers in the Anglo-American tradition; and despite the recent prominence of the radical empiricist views that will be discussed in the next chapter, it seems likely that moderate empiricism continues to be the most widely held view of the nature and status of *a priori* justification. What is profoundly misleading about the foregoing picture, however, is the suggestion that there is anything like one reasonably specific position that can be identified as moderate empiricism. On the contrary, as we shall see more fully below, moderate empiricism turns out to encompass a stunning diversity of distinct and not obviously compatible views, reflected in widely divergent definitions of the key term 'analytic' – views seemingly unified by little more than the twin convictions, first, that *a priori* justification can be accounted for in *some* way that avoids rationalism and, second, that the explanation will have *something* to do with concepts or meaning or definitions or linguistic conventions. Even more strikingly, this diversity has seldom been explicitly recognized, and it continues to be widely assumed that the divergent definitions of 'analytic' are merely superficially different ways of getting at the same underlying idea. One consequence of this situation is that individual proponents of moderate empiricism sometimes slide promiscuously from one such conception to another in the course of their arguments, with no apparent recognition that they are doing so. (Indeed, it is hard to avoid suspecting that many of those who have regarded moderate empiricism as unquestionably correct have had no very specific version in mind.)

The obvious consequence of this situation is that there is no reasonably standard version of moderate empiricism upon which the attention of a critic can safely be focused. Any assessment of moderate empiricism that hopes to be even approximately definitive will have to deal with a wide variety of different positions whose connections with each other are unobvious at best. Such a discussion, which is the aim of the present chapter, will inevitably be somewhat messy, but there is simply no other way to deal adequately with the main issue.

As noted in Chapter 1, moderate empiricism can be understood as an attempt to defend two main theses. Formulated in terms of the concept of analyticity, these are: first, that genuine *a priori* justification is restricted to analytic propositions (or "statements"); and second, that the *a priori* justification of analytic propositions (or "statements") can be understood epistemologically in a way that does not require the sort of allegedly mysterious intuitive capacity advocated by rationalism and thus is epistemologically unproblematic from an empiricist point of view. The obvious problem for the moderate empiricist is to find a single, reasonably clear conception of analyticity in relation to which both of these theses can be established, and the various divergent conceptions of analyticity arise in this attempt.

In the recent history of this issue, most of the controversy between proponents of moderate empiricism and their badly outnumbered but persistent rationalist critics has concentrated on the first of these two theses, with rationalists proposing cases of allegedly synthetic *a priori* knowledge and empiricists attempting to show that the propositions in question are either analytic or else not genuine cases of *a priori* justification. This discussion has tended to focus on a relatively limited range of examples, of which the following are representative:

(1) Nothing can be red all over and green all over at the same time.
(2) All colored things are extended things.
(3) If person A is taller than person B and person B is taller than person C, then person A is taller than person C.
(4) There are no round squares.

(5) $2 + 3 = 5$.
(6) All cubes have 12 edges.

The discussion of such examples has, however, been generally inconclusive. This is not surprising since, as will be elaborated below, it is reasonably clear that most of the interesting ones are in fact analytic under some conceptions of analyticity and synthetic under others, so that no definite result is possible without distinguishing more carefully between the different conceptions of analyticity than has usually been done.

There is a deeper reason, however, why this sort of appeal to examples is unlikely by itself to impress a convinced moderate empiricist, a reason presented with admirable clarity in a recent discussion by Salmon.[1] Though he deals in passing with some of the standard examples, Salmon makes it clear that the issue does not, in his view, turn primarily on the ability of the moderate empiricist to deal with such specific cases, but rather on the fact that synthetic *a priori* knowledge, unlike analytic *a priori* knowledge, would constitute "a genuine epistemological mystery":

> After some exposure to formal logic one can see without much difficulty how linguistic stipulations can yield analytic statements that hold in any possible world. It is easy to see that "Snow is white or snow is not white" is true simply because of the meanings we attach to "or" and "not." Analytic a priori statements are no great mystery. . . . But how could we conceivably establish by pure thought that some logically consistent picture of the real world is false? How could we, without any aid of experience whatever, find out anything about our world in contradistinction to other possible worlds? Given a logically contingent formula – one that admits of true as well as false interpretations – how could we hope to decide on a completely a priori basis which of its interpretations are true and which are false? The empiricist says it is impossible to do so, and in this I think he is correct. Nevertheless, it is tempting to endow various principles with the status of synthetic a priori truths. It was to Kant's great credit that he saw the urgency of the question: *How is this possible?* (39)

As we shall see later in this chapter, Salmon's conception of what the rationalist is actually committed to is seriously askew, but this does not matter for present purposes. What is clear is that his reason for thinking that all *a priori* knowledge *must* be analytic, that synthetic *a priori* knowledge is impossible in principle, is far too fundamental to be dislodged by occasional rationalist counter-examples. As Salmon himself puts it at the very end of his discussion:

---

1 Salmon (1967), pp. 27–40. References in the text to Salmon are to the pages of this book. Though it occurs only incidentally in a work devoted to the problem of induction, Salmon's discussion of the synthetic *a priori* seems to me an excellent formulation of views that are very widely accepted in the philosophical community.

even if a recalcitrant example were given – one that seemed to defy all analysis as either analytic or a posteriori – it might still be reasonable to suppose that we had not exercised sufficient penetration in dealing with it. If we are left with a total epistemological mystery on the question of how synthetic a priori propositions are possible, it might be wise to suppose it more likely that our analytic acumen is deficient than that an epistemological miracle has occurred. (40)

Clearly the reasonableness of this sort of stance rests on two distinct but equally essential grounds: on the alleged mysteriousness of synthetic *a priori* knowledge, but just as much on the alleged *lack* of mystery pertaining to analytic *a priori* knowledge. More will be said about the former issue in Chapters 4, 5, and 6, below, where I will argue that the supposed mystery pertaining to rationalism and the synthetic *a priori* has been, at the very least, greatly exaggerated. It must be conceded in advance, however, that the rationalist account of *a priori* justification does not provide the sort of reduction to simpler and less problematic cognitive processes that the moderate empiricist account in terms of analyticity is often believed to do, indeed does not even attempt such a reduction; thus rationalism does require the ascription to human knowers of stronger and more complicated cognitive capacities, whether or not these are in some objectionable way mysterious or unintelligible. For this reason, there would still be some force to Salmon's dialectical stance, simply for reasons of parsimony, if the second of the two grounds, corresponding to the second of the two main moderate empiricist theses set out earlier, could be satisfactorily made out: the claim that the *a priori* justification of *analytic* propositions can be accounted for in a way that avoids the need for such stronger capacities and is entirely unproblematic from an epistemological standpoint.

This latter claim, rather than the recalcitrant examples, will accordingly be the main focus of the current chapter. I will argue that contrary to Salmon and to widely held opinion, there is in fact no conception of analyticity that is capable of providing an adequate and autonomous epistemological account of the generally acknowledged cases of *a priori* justification; indeed the ability of such conceptions to provide such an account of even a single piece of *a priori* knowledge will turn out to be very much in doubt.[2] (I suspect that the widespread impression to the contrary is due

2 A further point worth noting, though an extended discussion of it is impossible here, is that moderate empiricism cannot deal successfully with the problem of the justification of inference beyond direct observation (discussed in §1.1). If the moderate empiricist insists that all *a priori* justifiable claims or principles of inference must be analytic in something like the Kantian sense, then his only apparent hope for dealing with this problem is to insist in procrustean fashion that inferences that seem to go beyond direct observation to conclusions that are not already contained or implicit in the observational premises do not

partly to a failure to distinguish the various divergent conceptions of analyticity and partly to a failure to grasp clearly what the central epistemological issue really is; clear examples of these two mistakes are offered below, but I will not attempt here to document their pervasiveness.)

An adequate defense of the foregoing thesis will have to canvass the various divergent conceptions of analyticity already alluded to. I will begin this task in the next two sections, by considering two families of such conceptions that, albeit in quite different ways, utterly fail to even confront the main epistemological problem.

§2.2. REDUCTIVE CONCEPTIONS OF ANALYTICITY

One of the most widely accepted conceptions of analyticity, and also in some ways the clearest, is that proposed by Frege: a statement is analytic if and only if it is either (i) a substitution instance of a logically true statement or (ii) transformable into such a substitution instance by substituting synonyms for synonyms (or definitions for definable terms). Or, in nonlinguistic terms, a proposition is analytic if and only if it is either (i) an instance of a truth of logic as it stands or (ii) equivalent to such an instance by substitution of concepts for equivalent concepts (where by equivalence between concepts, I mean the relation that corresponds to synonymy between expressions, i.e., the relation in which the concepts *bachelor* and *unmarried man* stand to each other).[3] A proposition or statement is syn-

genuinely do so, but are really to be understood as reducible in content to collections or patterns of observations. This is, of course, the central motive behind highly dubious and by now obvious untenable reductive views such as the phenomenalist view of the status of physical objects and the behaviorist view of other minds. And there are many sorts of apparently trans-observational conclusions in relation to which reductive views of this sort have even less plausibility (e.g., historical statements) and some (e.g., laws of nature or statements about the future) for which no such view has ever seriously been proposed. The looser and more dubious conceptions of analyticity discussed in §§2.3–2.6 are also in part responses to this sort of problem, though no conception ever proposed is broad enough to even purport to handle all of the relevant kinds of cases.

3 On the most straightforward view, that relation is simply identity. If this is right, then the second clause of the non-linguistic version of the Fregean conception turns out to be unnecessary: e.g., the proposition that all brothers are male would turn out to satisfy the first clause by virtue of being the very same proposition as the proposition that all unmarried male siblings are male. The issue lurking here is, of course, the so-called paradox of analysis. If, as claimed by G. E. Moore and others, a conceptual analysis involves some non-linguistic and non-conventional relation between the analyzed concept (the concept of a brother) and the analyzing concept (the concept of a male sibling) other than mere identity, then something like the formulation in the text is required. But I will not pursue this issue here.

thetic if and only if it is not analytic.[4] I will assume, perhaps somewhat unrealistically, that just which propositions or statements count as truths of logic is clear enough for the moment. Ultimately I will argue that although it is far from obvious that there is any sharp line to be drawn between what is logic and what is not, this makes very little difference for epistemological purposes.[5]

It is easy to see how the Fregean conception of analyticity offers a genuine, albeit also limited, epistemological insight. If I am somehow justified *a priori* in believing that the proposition expressed by[6] "for any proposition P, not both P and not P" is a truth of logic, and I am able to recognize *a priori* that "it is not the case that the table is both brown and not brown" is an instance of this logical truth, then I am justified *a priori* on that basis in believing that the latter proposition is also true. But it is equally clear that this conception of analyticity is incapable of offering any epistemologically illuminating account of how the truths of logic themselves are epistemically justified or known. We can obviously say that true propositions of logic are themselves analytic, but this amounts to nothing more, on

4 As this suggests, 'analytic' and 'synthetic' are normally construed as mutually exclusive and jointly exhaustive terms, and it is only on such a construal that the issue between rationalists and empiricists can be correctly couched in terms of whether there is synthetic *a priori* knowledge. Some empiricists have clouded the issue by defining 'synthetic' independently. For example, Ayer (1946) offers the following definitions: "a proposition is analytic when its validity depends solely on the definitions of the symbols it contains and synthetic when its validity is determined by the facts of experience" (78).

Since the meaning of 'synthetic' seems on this definition to be simply identified with that of '*a posteriori*' ("validity" presumably means the proposition's being justified), there will obviously be no synthetic *a priori* knowledge. Equally obviously, however, this in no way rules out the possibility of non-analytic *a priori* knowledge, which would be quite enough to vindicate the rationalist claim.

5 One interesting proposal for demarcating the scope of logic has been offered by Dummett: "Sentences can be divided into atomic and complex ones: atomic sentences are formed out of basic constituents none of which are, or have been, formed from sentences, while complex sentences arise, through a step-by-step construction, from the application of certain sentence-forming devices to other sentences, or to 'incomplete' expressions such as predicates themselves formed from sentences . . . . The expressions which go to make up atomic sentences – proper names (individual constants), primitive predicates, and relational expressions – form one type: sentence-forming operators, such as sentential operators and quantifiers, which induce the reiterable transformations which lead from atomic to complex sentences form the other. . . . Logic properly so called may be thought of as concerned only with words and expressions of the second type" (Dummett 1981, pp. 21–2). But however useful it may be for other purposes, it is hard to see why Dummett's distinction should be accorded any *epistemological* significance.

6 Since both this explicit stipulation and the alternative of using "that" clauses would quickly become tiresome, I will adopt the convention that, in the absence of a clear stipulation to the contrary, sentences in double quotes are to be taken to refer to the proposition that the sentence standardly expresses, rather than to the sentence itself.

the present conception of analyticity, than the entirely trivial claim that logical truths are logical truths, which clearly offers no epistemological insight at all.[7]

The Fregean conception of analyticity is a paradigmatic example of what I call a *reductive* conception of analyticity: it explains the *a priori* epistemic justification of some propositions by appeal to that of other propositions, but is thus automatically incapable of saying anything epistemologically helpful about the *a priori* justification of the latter, reducing class of propositions (in this case the propositions of logic). Such a conception of analyticity is therefore incapable in principle of accounting for all instances of *a priori* justification in the way that the moderate empiricist program attempts to do, and it clearly offers only a partial epistemological account of the instances that it does apply to.

The original Kantian conception of analyticity, discussed in Chapter 1, is also a reductive conception, in fact just a restricted version of the Fregean conception. To say that, for example, the proposition "all bachelors are unmarried" is analytic on the Kantian conception again offers a modest degree of epistemological insight: if we are somehow justified on an *a priori* basis in accepting the proposition that the concept *bachelor* is equivalent to the concept *unmarried adult male,* and also that a proposition of the form that we may schematize as "all FGH's are F" is logically true for any concepts F, G, and H, then it will follow that we are justified *a priori* in accepting the proposition originally in question. But even if we set aside worries about how conceptual or definitional equivalences are known, it is clear that this sort of position is incapable of accounting for the *a priori* justification of the logical truth thus invoked. (As noted earlier, the Kantian account also fails to apply at all to *a priori* justifiable propositions that are not of subject-predicate form.)

A third example of a reductive conception of analyticity is that conception which defines an analytic proposition as one whose denial entails a contradiction, where what is intended is an *explicit* contradiction, which we may take to be a proposition of the form "P and not P." That a proposition is analytic on this conception may again help to explain how it is justified and hence knowable on an *a priori* basis. But such an account once again presupposes and hence cannot explain the *a priori* justification of other propositions: of the logical truth that a proposition that is ex-

7 For this reason, it would be clearer in some ways to follow Butchvarov and regard logical truths as themselves synthetic, reserving the label "analytic" for those propositions that are reducible and whose justification is thereby (partially) explained. (See Butchvarov 1970, pp. 106–8.)

plicitly contradictory in form is always false, of the logical truths underlying the inference that any proposition that entails a false proposition is itself false, and of the propositions of logic (together, perhaps, with definitions) that are needed to derive the contradiction.[8] In regard to the last of these classes of propositions, it is useful to observe that there is *no* proposition whose explicit denial is strictly identical to an explicit contradiction: even the denial of a proposition of the form "not both P and not P" requires an application of the hardly negligible principle of double negation in order to arrive at an explicit contradiction; and for most propositions that fall under this conception, substantially more logical machinery than that will be required.[9]

Reductive conceptions of analyticity, though perhaps useful for other purposes, are thus inherently incapable of providing by themselves an adequate basis for the moderate empiricist program: they are incapable in principle of accounting for all instances of *a priori* epistemic justification or indeed of accounting fully for any. It would be possible, of course, for a moderate empiricist to employ a reductive conception as one ingredient in his position, thereby reducing the general problem of accounting for *a priori* justification to the narrower problem of accounting for the *a priori* justification of the propositions in the reducing class, and then to offer some alternative account of the *a priori* justification of the latter class of propositions. For this reason, one main concern in our discussion of further conceptions of analyticity will be whether or not they are capable of accounting for the *a priori* justification of logical truths.[10]

8 I ignore here the fact that some of these logical ingredients would no doubt take the form of principles or rules of inference rather than theses or assertions. As noted in chapter 1, a principle of inference is, from an epistemological standpoint, just as much in need of epistemic justification as is an assertion, albeit in a somewhat modified sense: if one is to be epistemically justified in accepting conclusions on the basis of such a principle, one needs to have some reason for thinking that if a set of premises and a conclusion jointly satisfy the principle, then the conclusion will be true (or perhaps, for some kinds of principles, will be likely to be true) if the premises are true.

9 Obviously it will not help to enlarge the set of propositions that are counted as explicit contradictions, for while this may reduce the need for logical machinery, it at the same time expands the class of propositions whose necessary falsehood must be known *a priori* in some other way. And, as we will see in the next section, to remove the requirement that the contradiction be explicit deprives the resulting conception of analyticity of any clear epistemological force at all.

10 It would, of course, be needlessly confusing to formulate such a bipartite moderate empiricist position by using the term 'analytic' to cover both of the conceptions in question. It is also, of course, quite possible that the needed second conception of analyticity would, if adequate to account for logic, also suffice to account directly for the propositions dealt with by the reductive conception, thus rendering the latter superfluous.

The main focus of the present discussion is on the general shape of the moderate empiricist strategy, rather than on particular recalcitrant examples. It is worth noting in passing, however, that reductive conceptions of analyticity are almost certainly incapable of dealing adequately with all such example (such as those cited in the previous section) even apart from worries about the propositions in the reducing class. This is more immediately obvious for the Kantian and Fregean conceptions, but it is, I think, obvious enough for the third reductive conception as well, so long as the machinery used in deriving the explicit contradiction is restricted to plausible candidates for principles of logic and is not allowed to include substantive claims that are just as problematic as the proposition originally in question. (E.g., in attempting to show that the denial of "nothing can be red all over and green all over at the same time" leads to a contradiction, it is implicitly circular for a moderate empiricist to make use of the theses that red and green are colors, and that being one color excludes being another color.) Thus even if the justification of logic were somehow not a problem, a version of moderate empiricism that appeals to a reductive conception of analyticity would still be unable to defend the first of the two moderate empiricist theses, namely, the claim that all genuine examples of *a priori* justification pertain to analytic propositions.

§2.3. OBFUSCATING CONCEPTIONS OF ANALYTICITY

While reductive conceptions of analyticity offer genuine, albeit necessarily partial, epistemological illumination, other popular conceptions of analyticity in fact fail to offer any genuine insight at all into how the claim in question is epistemically justified, superficial appearances to the contrary notwithstanding. The basic problem with these conceptions is that they tacitly equate analyticity either with apriority itself or else with necessity (while offering in the latter case no further account, other than the rationalist's, of how claims of necessity are justified). Such conceptions of analyticity thus have the effect of obfuscating the essential epistemological issue instead of illuminating it: while seeming to promise an epistemological account that is different from and superior to that of the rationalist, they in fact depend on a tacit invocation of rational insight for whatever superficial plausibility they might seem to possess.

The most widely accepted of the obfuscating conceptions of analyticity (and probably, along with the Fregean conception, one of the two most widely accepted of all) is the definition of an analytic statement as one that is "true by virtue of meaning," that is, by virtue of the meanings or definitions of its component terms. This formula might, of course, be merely a vague way of indicating some other conception of analyticity, perhaps one of the reductive conceptions considered in the previous section or the appeal to linguistic convention discussed in §2.6. But if it is intended, as often seems to be the case, as an autonomous conception, the initial problem is to decide what it is supposed to mean: *how* is the truth of such a statement supposed to be a consequence of meaning? A natural interpretation, and one that often at least seems intended by those who employ this wording, is that an analytic statement, that is, an analytic proposition, is one that need only be understood to be recognized as true or, equivalently, that is such that a failure to accept it constitutes proof that its meaning or content has not been fully and accurately grasped.[11]

Now there can be very little doubt that many simple *a priori* justifiable claims, including in particular simple truths of logic, have such a status. To consider again one of the rationalist's favorite examples, it is hard to see how anyone who understands the claim that nothing can be red all over and green all over at the same time can fail to agree with it – and also hard to deny that such agreement is (somehow) justified. But exactly what light is this supposed to shed on the *way* in which such a claim is justified? How in particular is the appeal to one's grasp of the meaning or content of such a claim supposed to avoid the need for the rationalist's allegedly mysterious intuitive insight into necessity?

The proponents of this conception of analyticity offer no clear answers, indeed for the most part no answers at all, to such questions. And without such answers, it is hard to see that the present conception of analyticity differs in any essential way from the very conception that it was supposed to explain, namely the conception of *a priori* justification itself. As formulated by, for example, Chisholm, the traditional conception of an *a priori* justifiable proposition is precisely that of a proposition that is such that "once you understand it, you see that it is true."[12] And obviously if there *is* no difference between the two conceptions, then the moderate empiricist thesis that all *a priori* justifiable propositions are analytic becomes on this

11 Thus, e.g., Quinton, in a defense of moderate empiricism that will be examined more fully below, characterizes the position he is defending as the thesis that a non-derivative *a priori* truth is one whose "acceptance as true is a condition of understanding the terms it contains." (Presumably the way in which these terms are combined must also be understood.) See Anthony Quinton, "The *A Priori* and the Analytic," reprinted in Sleigh (1972), pp. 89–109; the passage quoted is on p. 90.
12 Chisholm (1977), p. 40. For an extended argument (albeit one that hardly seems needed) that this conception of analyticity is indistinguishable from the conception of the *a priori*, see Pap (1958), pp. 94–108.

conception true but entirely trivial, and the appeal to analyticity is stripped of any independent epistemological significance.

Is there any difference between the two conceptions? Plainly such a difference cannot lie merely in the appeal to the understanding of meaning or content (as though the rationalist idea of *a priori* justification was supposed to suggest, absurdly, that the truth or necessity of an *a priori* proposition can be grasped or apprehended whether or not its meaning or content is understood). Thus the difference, if any, must lie in the claim that an *a priori* proposition can somehow be justified or seen to be true *solely* by appeal to its meaning, without any need for the intuitive insight that the proposition thus understood is necessary, true in all possible worlds (though such an insight could presumably still be a derivative product of the proposition's analyticity). But such a claim could only be defended, I submit, by giving some articulated account of just *how* justification is supposed to result solely from meaning. And there is no apparent way to do this without in effect abandoning this conception of analyticity for one of the others.

We may gain some further insight into this issue by examining the employment of this conception of analyticity by one of the most distinguished proponents of moderate empiricism in this century, C. I. Lewis. As we shall see further in §2.4, Lewis's employment of the notion of analyticity, like that of a number of other moderate empiricists, involves several different conceptions that are by no means obviously equivalent to each other. But his official definition is a variant of the one with which we are presently concerned, and part of his defense of moderate empiricism, namely, his discussion of the justification of logic, involves a relatively direct appeal to that conception. Lewis defines an analytic statement as one "which can be certified by reference exclusively to defined or definable meanings."[13] He spends a substantial amount of space clarifying the precise kind of meaning that is relevant here. For our present purposes, it is enough to note that the meaning upon which analyticity depends is characterized as *intensional* meaning, initially explained as the concept or "criterion in mind" that determines the application of a term.

Lewis's view of logic differs significantly from Frege's. For Lewis, the principles of logic are merely a subset of the class of analytic truths, singled out because of their generality and consequent usefulness for the critique of inference. The classification of them as logic has no special epistemolog-

---

13 Lewis (1946), p. 35. Subsequent references to the pages of this book will be placed in the text.

ical significance, and they must thus be "certified" by reference to their intensional meanings like any other analytic truths.

The account of how this works is, however, disappointingly thin. Lewis discusses two main examples, beginning with the first figure AAA syllogism:

All *M* are *P.*
All *S* are *M.*
Therefore, all *S* are *P.*

For example:

All men are mortal.
All Greeks are men.
Therefore, all Greeks are mortal.

He points out, correctly, that the validity of the syllogism depends only on the transitivity of the relation expressed by 'All *X* is *Y*'. But as to how the fact of transitivity is itself to be known, we are offered only the following:

And how should one know the fact so stated? Obviously, by knowing what 'all' and 'is' mean, and understanding the syntax of expressions in the form, "All _____ is ------." One who understands meanings in English to that extent, will know that the relation so expressed is transitive. (118)

But merely listing the elements that would have to be grasped in order to understand the proposition provides no insight into *how* the proposition is known on the basis of those elements. Lewis seems to be saying merely that once those elements are understood, one can just see or grasp intuitively that the relation is transitive, a view that is, of course, entirely indiscernible from that of the rationalist.

Lewis also offers an account of how the principle of contradiction is justified or known on the basis of meaning, but this is, if anything, even thinner. He provides a summary account of the twelve elements that must be understood in order to understand a standard symbolized version of the principle. A complete listing of these would be needlessly tedious, but the following examples will adequately suggest the sort of items that are involved:

(1) The sign '⊢' is simply the sign of assertion; and the three dots after it (a larger number than occurs anywhere in what follows) indicate that the *whole* of what follows is asserted.
(5) The dot following '(x)' has the syntactic significance that "For all values of 'x'" qualifies all that follows.
(6) The tilde '~' is abbreviation for "It is false that."

Lewis then simply asserts that:

it is by reference to these constant meanings (as against the elements of purely variable signification . . .) and by reference to the syntax of the whole expression, that the analytic truth of this formal statement may be certified. (120–1)

But what we are *not* given, here as in the discussion of the syllogism, is any account of *how* the elements of meaning that are listed establish the truth of the statements in question without the need for rational insight into the necessary truth of the resulting proposition.

Indeed, Lewis's summation of this part of his discussion is entirely indistinguishable from the rationalist view that one who understands an *a priori* proposition can see or grasp that it is necessary:

whoever understands what the statement means may thereby know the truth of it without reference to any further consideration. . . . He is in position to observe that the truth of it is such as would impose no limitation on anything beyond limitation to what is consistently thinkable. (121–2)

While it does not seem to play any direct role in the account of logic just considered, it should be noted that in other places Lewis elaborates his notion of intensional meaning in a way that also obfuscates the main epistemological issue, albeit in a rather different way. Though, as already noted, the idea of intensional (or connotative) meaning is initially introduced in terms of a "criterion in mind" for the application of the term, it quickly becomes more demanding:

If application of the given term, 'A', to anything requires that another term, 'B', should also be applicable to that thing, then 'A' connotes 'B', and 'B' is contained in the intension of 'A'. (55)

And for the case of propositions (which are, for Lewis, just a special class of terms):

The *intension* of a proposition comprises whatever the proposition entails: and it includes nothing else. (55)
Alternatively, we might say that the intension of a proposition comprises whatever must be true of any possible world in order that this proposition should be true of or apply to it. (56)

Lewis thus identifies the intensional meaning of a term or proposition with everything that follows with necessity from its application to a thing or world, respectively.

The effect of this conception of intensional meaning is to make the vast majority of *a priori* justifiable propositions analytic in something very roughly analogous to the Kantian sense, but in a way that nonetheless, when properly understood, offers no significant epistemological insight.

Consider, for example, a slight variant of the familiar proposition concerning red and green:

A thing that is red all over is not green all over.

It is clear that the application of the phrase 'a thing which is red all over' does indeed entail or necessitate (though not formally) the application of the phrase 'not green all over', which is only to say that the original proposition is a necessary truth. But then, on the view of intensional meaning just described, 'not green all over' becomes part of the intensional meaning of 'a thing that is red all over', so that the proposition in question can indeed "be certified by reference to" its intensional meaning, as thus understood.[14]

The problem with all this, however, is that in order to be epistemically justified in accepting the proposition on this basis, one would need to have first grasped the full intensional meaning in question, that is, would have to know that not being green is thus included in being red. But since the obvious way in which one comes to know this is precisely by realizing that a relation of entailment obtains between red and not green, which is tantamount to knowing the original proposition, the account in question is completely circular from an epistemological standpoint. One cannot be epistemically justified in accepting a statement affirming a relation of entailment between two terms A and B (or, as in the present example, something tantamount to such a statement) by appeal to the intensional meaning of A, if the only way of establishing the relevant aspect of the intensional meaning of A is by coming to know that the entailment in question holds.

The underlying point here is that the initial "criterion in mind" in terms of which one understands a term or proposition plainly does not include in any straightforward way all that is in fact entailed or necessitated by it. Much of the epistemological problem of *a priori* knowledge is precisely the problem of how to justify the transition from our ordinary grasp of meaning or content to the further entailed consequences. And thus to simply include those consequences in the intensional meaning, as Lewis does, offers no real epistemological gain: the original problem simply recurs as the problem of how to justifiably make the transition from the narrower ordinary meaning to the full intensional meaning.

It is important to see that the issue at stake here is not merely a quarrel

14 I have formulated this in linguistic terms, since that is the way that Lewis actually formulates the applicable version of his account (quoted above). But it is clear that Lewis would be just as happy with a version couched in terms of one concept or intelligible content being included in another.

41

about different conceptions of meaning. We may grant that it is possible, albeit seemingly unlikely, that some cognitively superior being might somehow come to grasp as the meaning of 'red' the full Lewisian intensional meaning. For such a being, the statement that he would formulate as:

A thing which is red all over is not green all over

would be both justified *a priori* and analytic in something like the Kantian sense; such an appeal to analyticity would still be reductive in character, but it would nonetheless have some epistemological value relative to that specific statement. But an account along these lines has nothing at all to say about how it is that when the meaning of 'red' is understood in the more limited but still *prima facie* adequate way in which most ordinary mortals first learn it, one can still know *a priori* that being red entails, even though it does not explicitly include, not being green. And this, of course, is the epistemological problem raised by the original statement, when normally understood. The superior being's statement, though verbally identical, has a quite different meaning or content, and an epistemological account that is applicable to it sheds no light at all on the more ordinary case.[15]

I conclude that as Lewis employs it, the idea that *a priori* knowable propositions are analytic in the sense of being true by virtue of meaning yields no genuine epistemological insight into how such propositions are justified and thus fails to constitute a genuine alternative to rationalism. My claim is that this result generalizes to all moderate empiricist uses of this conception of analyticity, few if any of whose proponents have even as much to say as Lewis about how the resulting epistemological account is supposed to work.[16]

Traces of a still different, though equally obfuscating conception of analyticity are also to be found in Lewis. Sometimes he at least verges on equating analyticity, not with apriority, but rather with necessity:

---

15 It is also worth noting that even for the cognitively superior being, there will be examples of *a priori* justification that Lewis's account cannot handle. If we use 'red*' to symbolize the use of the word 'red' with the full Lewisian intensional meaning (and 'red' as usual to symbolize its use with the narrower, more standard meaning), then "all red things are red*" will be such an example.

16 This is not to deny, of course, that reflection on meanings or concepts can often be an important aid to *a priori* insight. Consider, for example, the proposition expressed by 'Nothing is north of the north pole'. Here it is highly plausible that reflection on the meanings of 'north of' and 'the north pole' (or on the concepts expressed by these phrases) can help one to grasp the necessity of this proposition. My claim is only that even in this very simple case an insight that is not somehow reducible to the reflections on meaning is still required. (I owe this example to the referee, who called my attention to the need for clarification on this point.)

An *analytic* proposition is one which would apply to or hold of every possible world . . . . An analytic proposition does not fail to have implications – though all entailments of it are likewise analytic or logically necessary propositions which would hold of any possible world. (57)

Lewis, like most moderate empiricists, is not at all careful about keeping the needed distinctions clear, and it is thus not quite clear whether these statements are intended as outright identifications of the concepts of analyticity and necessity or as mere theses about analytic propositions. In any case, an equation of analyticity with necessity would, of course, once again deprive the idea of analyticity of any independent epistemological significance: the issue would then be how we know that the proposition is necessary; and to say that we just see or intuitively grasp that it is necessary is obviously to return, illicitly for Lewis, to the rationalist view.

Whether or not Lewis is guilty of this particular mistake, it is clear that it has been committed by others. One version of it, which may or may not be couched in terms of analyticity, is made by those who attempt to give an epistemological account of logical truth in model-theoretic terms, that is, by appeal to truth tables or to the more general idea of truth in every model or domain. Thus, for example, Salmon, in the discussion cited earlier, offers the following account of the truths of logic:

A valid formula is one that comes out true on every interpretation in every nonempty domain. . . . A logical truth is any statement that results from any assignment of meanings to the symbols of a valid formula. . . . Notice, however, that the definition of "valid formula" makes no reference to possible domains; it refers only to domains – i.e., actual domains. The reason that the qualification "possible" is not needed is that there are no impossible domains – to say that a domain is impossible would mean that it could not exist – so "impossible domains" are not available to be chosen as domains of interpretation. (30)

Though he does not quite say so explicitly, Salmon seems to think that an account of this sort somehow sheds light on the epistemological question of how logical truths are known or how belief in them is justified. But the problem with such a view is that the domains in question must themselves conform to the laws of logic in order for the account to work: for example, no domain may count as possible in which a particular individual both has and fails to have a certain property. And hence, contrary to what Salmon's final sentence in the passage just quoted seems to suggest, an epistemological application of this account would require an *epistemically prior* knowledge of the truths of logic (or at least an adequate subset thereof, together with adequate and epistemically justified rules of inference) in order to know which domains to admit as possible, thus once again presupposing the very knowledge that it purports to account for.

It may help to consider a simple illustration of this point, involving the familiar truth table account of propositional logic. A propositional formula such as 'P → (Q → P)' is established as a logical truth by showing that it comes out true for all possible combinations of truth-values of the component formulas:

P	Q	Q → P	P → (Q → P)
T	T	T	T
T	F	T	T
F	T	F	T
F	F	T	T

But on reflection, it is obvious that the very way in which the table is constructed presupposes at least that each of the atomic propositions, P or Q, is either true or false and not both in each possible case (as represented by a line of the table); it thus presupposes knowledge of at least the principle of non-contradiction and the law of the excluded middle, whose justification cannot therefore be accounted for in this way.

A closely related view, which may be offered either as a definition of analyticity or as a correlative account of why the justification of logical or analytic *a priori* truths is epistemologically unproblematic or unmysterious, is the idea that such truths are "empty of factual content." Salmon is also one of the many proponents of this view:

factual content of a statement is a measure of the capacity of that statement to *rule out* possibilities . . . . [A logical truth] is an interpretation of a formula which cannot have a false interpretation – a formula that is true under any interpretation in any non-empty domain. Since it is true under any possible circumstances and is not incompatible with any description of a possible world, its content is zero. Any analytic statement will . . . share this characteristic. (32–3)

As a definition of one idea of factual content, this is unobjectionable. But the suggestion that Salmon and others seem to have in mind is that such an absence of factual content somehow explains the *a priori* justifiability of the proposition in question in an epistemologically unmysterious way. The idea is apparently that if a statement has no real content and hence could not be false, one does not need any further reason in order to be justified in accepting it as true. Unfortunately, however, to say that a proposition has zero factual content according to this account is to say no more than that it is necessary, true in all possible worlds, without offering the slightest insight into how this necessity is known or how a belief in it is to be justified. It is quite true, of course, that one who justifiably believed the statement to be necessary would be adequately justified in accepting it, but this is obviously entirely unhelpful from an epistemological standpoint.

It is also worth noting that both of these last two conceptions can be extended equally well to synthetic *a priori* propositions (so long as these are claimed to be necessary, along the lines of the traditional rationalist account mentioned above and further elaborated in Chapter 4). For if such a proposition is genuinely necessary, then no domain in which it fails to hold is genuinely possible; and hence such a proposition holds in all (possible) domains and has zero factual content. Thus if Salmon's account were epistemologically enlightening, the rationalist could avail himself of it as well. The issue between the rationalist and the moderate empiricist is not whether all *a priori* justifiable propositions have the features in question (holding in all possible domains and having zero factual content), but rather whether the knowledge or justified belief that a proposition has these features is somehow less mysterious, less dependent on rational insight, in the case of propositions that are logically true or analytic in some narrower and more interesting sense. On this question, Salmon's discussion sheds no light at all.

Salmon's confusion over this point is reflected in his characterization of the rationalist view in the passage quoted above (in §2.1). The rationalist does not hold that we can "find out anything about our world in contradistinction to other possible worlds" (39) on an *a priori* basis; his view, like Salmon's, is that *a priori* knowledge is confined to ruling out worlds that are impossible. But he also holds that once it is realized that knowledge of logic is on exactly the same epistemological footing as other putative *a priori* knowledge, there is no reason at all to think that only worlds that violate logic can be ruled out *a priori* in this way.

The last of the obfuscating conceptions of analyticity to be considered here defines an analytic proposition as one whose denial leads to a "contradiction," where this conception differs from the verbally similar reductive conception discussed above in not demanding that the contradiction be explicit. The most extreme version of this view simply construes a "contradiction" as any necessarily false proposition. But while it is undeniably true that it is self-contradictory, in this sense, to deny a genuine necessary truth (or to accept the conclusion while rejecting the premise of a valid inference), this fact once again sheds no significant light on the epistemological issue with which we are concerned: it is obviously no easier to justify the claim that the denial of a proposition is a "contradiction" in this sense than it is to justify the claim that the original proposition is necessary. Other superficially more plausible versions of this general approach move some distance in the direction of the reductive conception by counting as "contradictions" only some more restricted class of necessarily false propositions. These views partially inherit the defects of each of the two extreme conceptions, the proportions depending on how far the class of "contradictory" propositions has been expanded: a larger class of "contradictory" propositions will in general require less logical machinery to derive such a proposition from the denial of the original proposition in question, but will have to establish (or presuppose) the necessary falsehood of each of the propositions in this larger class.

To briefly sum up the discussion of the last two sections: I have argued that two large families of conceptions of analyticity fail, upon careful examination, to provide a suitable basis for a moderate empiricist position because they fail to adequately address the central epistemological issue. It does no good from an epistemological standpoint to account for the *a priori* justification of some propositions in terms of that of others if the *a priori* justification of the latter class of propositions cannot be adequately accounted for. And it is equally futile epistemologically to identify analyticity, explicitly or tacitly, with apriority or necessity: on the former identification, an appeal to analyticity merely reiterates that the claim in question has the epistemological status of which the moderate empiricist purports to be giving a further account, while the latter identification has no direct epistemological relevance at all. And in either case, the appearance of epistemological insight can derive only from a tacit and inadvertent appeal to the rationalist view that is supposedly being rejected. With these conceptions of analyticity thus dismissed as ultimately irrelevant from an epistemological standpoint, I turn in the next three sections to three somewhat more interesting conceptions – conceptions that, whatever their ultimate adequacy, do not misfire in these comparatively simple and straightforward ways.

§2.4. LEWIS'S APPEAL TO SENSE MEANING

The first of the conceptions to be considered also derives from Lewis and represents the closest he ever comes to giving a non-trivial account of how analytic truths are supposed to be "certified" by appeal to intensional meanings. The central ingredient of this conception is the idea of the *sense meaning* of an expression: "the criterion in terms of sense by which the application of expressions is determined" (131) (as opposed to criteria that could be formulated in terms of other expressions). Such a criterion must appeal, in Lewis's view, to imagery, but Lewis, following Kant, avoids the familiar pitfalls of Locke's conception of "abstract ideas"[17] by identifying the criterion with a "schema":

A sense meaning, when precise and explicit, is a schema; a rule or prescribed routine and an imagined result of it which will determine applicability of the expression in question. We cannot adequately imagine a chiliagon [a thousand-sided figure], but we easily imagine counting the sides of a polygon and getting 1000 as the result. We cannot imagine triangle in general, but we easily imagine following the periphery of a figure with the eye or a finger and discovering it to be a closed figure with three angles. (134)

He adds that this conception of sense meaning should not be construed so as to require that the applicability of an expression should be decisively verifiable in any particular instance (137).

Analytic propositions occur when one sense-meaning includes another:

We know that "All squares are rectangles" because in envisaging the test which a thing must satisfy if 'square' is to apply to it, we observe that the test it must satisfy if 'rectangle' is to apply is already included. (152)

Presumably the schema for the applicability of 'square' would involve four elements: (i) observing in sensory terms that the figure in question is closed and rectilinear; (ii) counting its sides and finding four; (iii) observing that its angles are all right angles (perhaps by seeing that two angles congruent with those of the figure can be combined into a straight line); and (iv) observing that all the sides are of equal length. And since the schema for the applicability of 'rectangle' would involve the first three of these elements (and nothing more), it will be satisfied whenever that for 'square' is.

This account is worthy of serious consideration because it is one of the very rare accounts that at least attempts the sort of job that a successful moderate empiricist account would have to accomplish: actually showing *how* appeal to the meanings in question yields *a priori* justification for the proposition at issue, rather than just asserting (as Lewis himself, as we have seen, does elsewhere) that it does. Nevertheless, there are limitations to its

---

17 In a much-discussed passage of his *Essay Concerning Human Understanding* (Book IV, chapter vii, section 9), Locke puzzles over the abstract or general idea of a triangle, which "must be neither Oblique, nor Rectangle, neither Equilateral, Equicural, nor Scalenon; but all of these and none at once. In effect, it is something imperfect, that cannot exist; an *Idea* wherein some parts of several different and inconsistent *Ideas* are put together" (Locke 1689), p. 596. It is clear that Locke is mistakenly thinking of such an idea as something like an image. But even if this mistake is corrected, it does not solve the problem of how to conceive of sensory criteria for the application of such a general term or concept without falling into the same difficulty.

applicability that are immediately obvious: First, it does not apply to *a priori* propositions involving terms that have no sensory criteria of application; in particular, it does not extend in any obvious way to logic or most of mathematics. (Lewis might want to claim that any meaningful term must possess such criteria, but this quasi-positivist thesis is very dubious.) Second, the account does not apply to propositions that are not of subject-predicate form. Just how serious a limitation this may be is not entirely clear, but it is certainly enough to make the account inadequate to deal with every plausible case of *a priori* justification.

Moreover, it is far from obvious that this account can deal adequately with all cases of *a priori* justification even in the limited area to which it applies. Consider, for example, the proposition that all cats are mammals. Are there really sensory schemata for 'cat' and for 'mammal' that are sufficiently definite to allow us to see via an "experiment in imagination" that the latter is included in the former?

More difficult still is an example that Lewis actually considers, the proposition that no squares are round (or, equivalently, that all squares are non-round):

> it is from that apprehension of what a thing must be in order to satisfy 'round square' that we know, in advance of any experience, that it will never apply. The experiment of trying to put together in imagination the sense meanings of 'round' and 'square' in the manner prescribed by the syntax of the phrase, is sufficient to assure this universal non-applicability *a priori*. (151–2)

Here, once again, it is crucially important not to lose sight of the main epistemological issue. There is little doubt that the sensory criteria for 'round' and 'square' are genuinely incompatible or mutually exclusive, nor that we can indeed know *a priori* that this is so. But does this incompatibility of criteria offer any real epistemological insight into the justification of the original proposition? One problem is that the claim that the criteria are incompatible seems, on the contrary, to amount merely to a partial restatement of the original claim whose justification is at issue, namely, that roundness is incompatible with squareness, that nothing can have both properties. But whether or not this is so, the main difficulty is that Lewis has nothing useful to say about how the claim that the criteria are incompatible is itself justified. Whereas in the case of "all squares are rectangles," the explicit inclusion of one set of criteria in the other might seem to offer at least some epistemological insight, in the present case Lewis seems to say simply that we see or apprehend that the criteria necessarily exclude each other, offering no real alternative to the rationalist account of how we do this, and thus providing no real basis for a successful moderate empiricism.

Nor is the difficulty confined to negative propositions. Consider, as a final example, the arithmetical proposition that $7 + 5 = 9 + 3$. Here again it is reasonably plausible to suppose that there are sensory criteria for the application of the terms on each side of the equation, criteria having to do with counting or removing or marking so many of the items in question and having so many more left over. And it is clear enough that we can know *a priori* that the satisfaction of one set of criteria necessitates or includes the satisfaction of the other. But once again, Lewis's position offers no real account of *how* this mutual necessitation or inclusion is known. Thus he can only echo the rationalist by saying that we simply see or apprehend that the relation in question must hold.

One last problem worth mentioning is that even in the cases where it seems to shed some epistemological light, such as the square-rectangle example, Lewis's appeal to sense meaning seems to rely essentially on something like the sensory equivalent of Kantian analyticity, thus seemingly presupposing the principle of logic that all FG are F. If this is so, it is at best a reductive account like those considered earlier.

My conclusion is that Lewis's most developed account, though perhaps moving very slightly in the right direction, fails once more to provide the basis for an adequate version of moderate empiricism. It fails to apply at all to many kinds of *a priori* propositions. For many of the ones to which it does apply, the resulting account is only superficially different from that of the rationalist. Finally, if it succeeds anywhere, it is with propositions that involve something like the Kantian conception of analyticity; and there it is arguably, like the Kantian view, a reductive account that again presupposes one or more principles of logic for which it cannot account.

§2.5. THE IDEA OF IMPLICIT DEFINITION

The penultimate conception of analyticity to be considered in this chapter involves the idea that certain *a priori* knowable statements, perhaps especially the principles of logic, constitute "implicit definitions" of the terms contained in them.[18] Unlike the conceptions considered so far, but like the more general appeal to linguistic convention to be considered in the next section, this conception depends essentially on a linguistic construal of the

18 Cf., e.g., Quinton, op. cit., pp. 101–6.

objects of *a priori* justification; indeed, though specifically invoked often enough to be worthy of separate consideration, it is basically a special case of the appeal to linguistic convention and is thus also subject for the most part to the objections to that view that will be developed there.[19] (Also like that more general conception, the appeal to implicit definition is sometimes not couched in terms of analyticity but simply developed on its own as a moderate empiricist account.)

The main problem here is to understand what the idea of an implicit definition really amounts to. In what sense are the statements in question really *definitions* – and how is this status supposed to yield an account of how they can be justified *a priori*? It is obvious that citing the truth of such statements may help a novice to understand the terms involved, but this fact, which also holds of course for many contingent, *a posteriori* statements, does not seem to warrant classifying them as definitions in any more interesting sense and thus appears to be epistemologically unhelpful. Thus, unless some more specific account is available, the idea of implicit definition seems to provide a merely verbal solution to the problem of *a priori* justification: why couldn't *any* statement that is justified *a priori* be labeled an implicit definition, with that label shedding no real light at all on how it is justified?

One account of the idea of implicit definition, perhaps the only clear one to be found in the literature, is offered by Butchvarov: offering a form of words as an "implicit definition" amounts to a stipulation that any previously unknown terms it contains are to be interpreted in such a way as to make the proposition expressed under that interpretation come out true (or, perhaps, necessarily true).[20] Thus, for example, one might stipulate that the sentence '40 @ 8 = 5' is to count as a (partial) implicit definition of the symbol '@'. This, along with other stipulations of the same kind, might be a useful way of conveying that '@' is to stand for the operation of long division (assuming that the other symbols in the sentence are already understood). But if this is the right account of implicit definition, then the justification of the proposition that 40 divided by 8 is equal to 5 (as opposed to that of the linguistic formula '40 @ 8 = 5') is not a result of the implicit definition, but is rather presupposed by it: if I were not justified in

19 It is perhaps not entirely clear that the idea of implicit definition must be construed linguistically, that one cannot give definitions, or something very much like definitions, of non-linguistic concepts. But, as will emerge, the only way that seems to be available for making clear what an *implicit* definition might amount to depends on a linguistic construal of the notion.

20 Butchvarov (1970), pp. 109–10.

advance, presumably *a priori*, in believing that forty divided by eight is equal to five, I would have no reason for interpreting '@' in the indicated way. Thus we must apparently be justified in some independent way in believing that the appropriate propositions are true if linguistic stipulations of this kind are to work, the implicit definition serving merely to convey a way in which the proposition that is already believed and justified may be expressed. The upshot is that on Butchvarov's account (as he himself recognizes and insists upon), the idea of implicit definition has no genuine epistemological significance.

Is there any alternate conception of implicit definition that can avoid this problem? I know of none and therefore can only conclude, pending some account not yet given, that this conception of analyticity also fails to provide a basis for a successful version of moderate empiricism.

§2.6. THE APPEAL TO LINGUISTIC CONVENTION

The final conception of analyticity to be considered here is that which defines an analytic statement as one that is true by virtue of the conventions or rules of language.[21] Unfortunately, however, if this definition is not intended, as it sometimes is, as a way of indicating either the idea of implicit definition or one of the other conceptions of analyticity discussed earlier, it is once again by no means clear just what it is supposed to amount to. It is obvious, of course, that language is highly dependent on *conventions:* socially established and accepted rules or practices that determine word meaning, grammatical structure, etc. But how such conventions are supposed to account for the truth or, especially, the epistemic justification of *a priori* justifiable propositions or even statements is anything but obvious. And unfortunately, those who appeal to this conception typically have relatively little to offer by way of explanation.

In the absence of any more detailed and explicit version of how the appeal to linguistic convention is supposed to work, the best way to proceed, I suggest, is to canvass the main objections that have been raised against this general conception. A consideration of these objections, most of them quite familiar, will be as good a way as any of determining what dialectical resources, if any, are available to such a view.

---

21 This conception is not always employed as a definition of analyticity; sometimes a reductive conception of analyticity, usually the Fregean conception, is adopted instead, and the appeal to linguistic convention is employed only to account for the propositions in the reducing class. But this difference does not affect the issues discussed in the text.

First. One serious problem for the proponent of the appeal to linguistic convention is to explain clearly the relation that is supposed to obtain, according to this view, between the actual conventions of language and the *a priori* statements that are claimed to be true and knowable by virtue of those conventions. This is a serious problem because the two most obvious possibilities for such an explanation seem to destroy the view before it ever gets off the ground. These are, first, that what we take to be *a priori* statements are really only formulations or expressions of the linguistic conventions in question and, second, that *a priori* statements are implicit claims or assertions that such-and-such conventions exist or have been adopted. The problems with these possibilities are obvious. On the latter view, the supposedly *a priori* statements turn out to be contingent and empirical in character, for it is surely a contingent fact, knowable only on some empirical basis, that certain conventions have in fact been adopted in a given linguistic community. On the former view, *a priori* statements turn out not to express propositions at all and to have no truth value, for the expression of a convention is presumably something like an imperative or perhaps a joint statement of intention, not something that can be true or false. Thus the upshot of the linguistic convention conception, on either of these interpretations, is that there is in fact no *a priori* justification at all; the resulting positions are thus in effect versions of radical empiricism rather than of moderate empiricism, and quite implausible versions at that.[22]

But if these alternatives are set aside, what then *is* the relation between the conventions and the *a priori* statements supposed to be? At this point, proponents of the linguistic convention conception have little to say except that *a priori* statements, though neither expressions nor descriptions of linguistic conventions, are nonetheless made true by such conventions.[23] This leaves the view quite obscure and thus sheds very little light on the epistemological issue of how such statements are *justified*. Even if it is granted that *a priori* statements are (somehow) made true by conventions, how does that justify me in accepting them if, as seems usually to be the case, I have no independent knowledge of those conventions? Perhaps some answer can be found that appeals to tacit or implicit knowledge of linguistic conventions, but it is at the very least quite uncertain how this would go – and until such an answer is at least roughly spelled out, the linguistic convention view does not even amount to a definite position.

Second. An even more serious problem is that *a priori* justifiable state-

---

22 For further discussion of such views, see Pap (1958), pp. 163–73, 182–5.
23 See, e.g., Quinton, op. cit., p. 99.

ments do not seem to possess the most obvious feature that typifies the products of more ordinary sorts of conventions. Ordinary conventions are *optional:* they represent choices, whether deliberate or not, from a wider range of possible conventions that would have led to significantly different results – a feature that is often, though it need not be, reflected in variation over time or place or community. An obvious and convenient example here is the convention in most countries of the world according to which automobiles are to be driven on the right side of the road: even if the contrary practice did not actually exist in Great Britain, Japan, and a few other places, it would be obvious that the convention of driving instead on the left represents a possible alternative, one that could easily have been adopted and indeed could be adopted now if there were some reason to do so; and there are no doubt further possibilities as well, albeit more complicated ones.

It is clear that the most obvious conventions of language, those governing the meanings of particular words, spelling, capitalization, the grammatical structure of sentences, etc., are similarly optional. It is easy to imagine the meanings of, for example, the words 'red' and 'green' being interchanged, or a new convention adopted according to which one capitalizes the final word in a sentence and uses a period at the beginning. But the conventions that generate *a priori* justification, if they exist at all, do not seem to be optional in this way, for the results of such conventions do not vary in any apparent way from language to language, and there is no reason to think that there are possible alternative conventions that would achieve different results. What possible alternative convention would make the principle of non-contradiction come out false? What convention might be adopted that would make it possible for something to be red all over and green all over at the same time? It is, of course, obvious that new conventions could change the meaning of the word 'not', or of the words 'red' and 'green', but there is no plausibility at all to the idea that such changes would result in the *falsity* of the principle of non-contradiction or of the proposition that nothing can be red all over and green all over at the same time, as opposed to merely altering the way in which those propositions are expressed. And the same seems to be true for virtually all other plausible examples of *a priori* justification.

None of this shows that there are not conventions of language corresponding to *a priori* claims, for example, a convention of English according to which one is not to assert the conjunction of a statement or proposition and its denial. But it does strongly suggest that the *a priori* justification in question does not result from such a convention. An alternative is that, as

Butchvarov suggests, such a convention (if it exists at all) merely reflects the prior and independent *a priori* insight that such a conjunctive assertion would inevitably be false:

> one could gladly admit that the sort of rules [thus suggested] are indeed present in language, explicitly or implicitly, and then one would point out that the obvious reason such rules are adopted is the necessary truth of the corresponding propositions. For example, one would admit that there is the rule "Don't say of anything that it is both red and green all over!" but would point out that the reason the rule is accepted is the necessary truth of the proposition "Nothing is both red and green all over"; one would admit that there is the rule "Don't contradict yourself!" but would point out that the rule is accepted only because of the necessary truth of the principle of noncontradiction.[24]

And if this is the situation, then the conventions in question obviously cannot provide the sort of deflationary explanation of *a priori* knowledge and justification that the moderate empiricist is seeking.

Third. Quinton argues as follows for the view that necessary truth (which for him is more or less the same notion as *a priori* knowable or justifiable truth) results from linguistic convention:

> A statement is a necessary truth because of the meanings of the words of which it is composed. The meanings that words have is assigned to them by convention. Therefore it is linguistic convention that makes a form of words express a necessary truth.[25]

But, as suggested by the discussion of the previous objection, this argument seems to depend for whatever plausibility it possesses on a failure to distinguish two quite distinct theses: (i) the thesis that it is a matter of linguistic convention that a certain sentence or form of words expresses whatever it does, in particular that it expresses a necessary or *a priori* justifiable proposition; and (ii) the quite different thesis that the truth or *a priori* justifiability of the proposition thus expressed is itself somehow a result of such a convention. The former thesis is no doubt true, but also trivial and quite irrelevant to our main epistemological concerns. It is obvious that the fact that the sentence 'either grass is green or grass is not green' expresses an *a priori* knowable proposition depends on the linguistic conventions that endow the various words in it with the meaning they have (along with other, syntactic conventions), in particular on the fact that the English word 'or' expresses disjunction rather than, for example, conjunction. These conventions are of the optional sort just discussed, and

24 Butchvarov (1970), pp. 126–7. Further references in this section to Butchvarov are to the pages of this book.
25 Quinton, op. cit., p. 97. Further references to Quinton are to the pages of this reprint.

if they were altered, the proposition in question would have to be expressed in some other way (or perhaps could not be expressed in English at all). But none of this has any tendency to show that the truth or *a priori* justifiability of the proposition itself depends on such conventions.

One way to see this point is to note that the sort of convention dependence in question is just as much a feature of empirical propositions: that 'grass is green' expresses a true proposition depends in part on the linguistic convention in virtue of which 'green' expresses the color it does and not, for example, that which is in fact expressed by 'red'. But this obviously has no tendency to show that the truth of the proposition in question is a result of linguistic convention, and there is no apparent reason why the result should be different for the *a priori* cases, which are quite parallel in the relevant respects.

It is interesting to note that C. I. Lewis himself, despite his sympathy for moderate empiricism, rejects the appeal to linguistic convention on precisely these grounds:

The manner in which any truth is to be told by means of language, depends on conventional linguistic usage. But the truth or falsity of what is expressed, is independent of any particular linguistic conventions affecting the expression of it. If the conventions were otherwise, the manner of telling would be different, but what is to be told, and the truth or falsity of it, would remain the same. That is something which no linguistic convention can touch.[26]

In the discussion quoted above, Quinton considers Lewis's objection and offers two replies. The first, to which he seems to attach less weight, is that the objection, if cogent, would show that no case of necessary truth was to be accounted for by linguistic convention, a result that Quinton thinks even opponents of the general appeal to linguistic convention would find implausible (99–100). I think that he is quite right that this conclusion follows, but wrong in supposing that there is anything implausible about it. On the contrary, the upshot of our discussion here is precisely that the idea of convention is unable to account for the truth or justification of *any* proposition.

The second reply is the assertion that the distinction relied on by the objection between "conventionally introduced relations between words" and "non-conventional relations between the meanings themselves" cannot be coherently drawn (100). But Quinton's argument for this assertion is confined to the case of verbal definitions (100–1): there he argues that if, for example, the meaning of 'bachelor' is really *identical* to that of 'unmar-

26 Lewis (1946), p. 148.

ried adult male', as the truth of the corresponding definition seems to require, then there is no room left for a non-conventional relation of meaning, as opposed to the conventional relation between the two expressions of standing for one and the same meaning. This argument raises interesting issues in the vicinity of the "paradox of analysis"[27] and may perhaps be correct for cases of this specific sort; but there is no apparent way to generalize it to other kinds of *a priori* claims.

Fourth. Perhaps the most decisive objection of all to the linguistic convention view is that it is possible to restate *a priori* claims in a hypothetical form that the appeal to convention cannot in principle account for. A version of this point is developed by Butchvarov:

> if it is true that nothing can be both *a* and *b* (e.g., nothing can be both red and green all over), it can be said that this is true because of the rules we have established for the use of "*a*" and "*b*." For, obviously, had we established certain other rules, it might not have been true that nothing can be both *a* and *b*. [I.e., the *sentence* 'nothing can be both *a* and *b*' might not have been true.] So far the linguistic theorist is right. However, when he draws the conclusion that the necessary truth of the proposition that nothing can be both *a* and *b* is due to the fact that by our rules "*a*" denotes this quality and "*b*" denotes that quality, he is faced with disaster. For in addition to asserting that it is necessarily true that nothing can be both *a* and *b*, we should be able to assert that it is necessarily true that *if* "*a*" denotes this quality and "*b*" denotes that quality, then nothing can be both *a* and *b*. But the necessary truth of this *hypothetical* proposition is no longer accounted for by the rules for the use of the terms "*a*" and "*b*." (136–7)

By putting a statement of the supposed linguistic conventions into the antecedent of the conditional, any capacity they may seem to have to account for the truth of the original statement is, as it were, canceled out.

Butchvarov generalizes the point in the following way: Suppose that "*p*" expresses a proposition that is necessarily true and justifiable *a priori*. To say that this is so because of what *p* means, as determined by linguistic conventions, is to say that it is so because of the necessary truth and *a priori* justifiability of some hypothetical proposition of the form: "If '*p*' is understood to mean *x*, then *p*."

> But this hypothetical proposition is necessarily true not because of the fact that it is "*p*" (rather than, say, "*q*") that is [conventionally] understood to mean *x*, but because of *x*, because of its characteristics, nature, content, etc. The hypothetical would be necessarily true regardless of what we put in place of "*p*." (138)

And thus, once again, the relevance of the supposed linguistic convention turns out to be spurious.

27 See note 2, above.

A somewhat related, though more general objection can be developed along the following lines. It is overwhelmingly implausible to suppose that there is a separate, independent linguistic convention determining the necessary truth and a priori justifiability of each of the infinitely or at least indefinitely many a priori justifiable statements. Thus there must be some limited set of conventions from which the truth of all these a priori statements follows. But now consider the status of the claim that if those conventions are adopted, then some particular a priori statement P is true. This claim must itself be necessarily true and justifiable a priori if the conventions are to account for the necessary truth and a priori justification of P, and yet its truth and justification apparently cannot be accounted for by appeal to those conventions. The point, in other words, is that once it is agreed, as it surely must be, that the set of conventions is finite and the set of a priori justifiable statements infinite, there must be logical relations between the conventions and the further statements that determine the a priori status of the latter and that must themselves be justified a priori if the account is to work. But the a priori status of these logical relations (whether regarded as statements or propositions, or as principles of inference) cannot itself be accounted for by those same conventions, on pain of obvious circularity.[28]

Fifth. A final objection is that there are some a priori knowable propositions that do not depend on language at all, and thus that the appeal to linguistic convention cannot hope to account for. Ewing, in the course of a lengthy critique of moderate empiricist views, offers some examples:

> it is surely plain that some a priori propositions, e.g., everything which has shape has size, a thing cannot be both red and green, if one thing is above another and the second is above a third the first is above the third, all three-sided rectilinear figures have three angles, could be seen to be true without the use of language. A person who was capable of forming visual images might quite well see the truth of any of these propositions without having to put them into words.[29]

I am inclined to regard examples of this kind as entirely convincing. But since some may want to claim, implausibly, that it is a mistake to think that such propositions could be even entertained by someone who could not formulate them linguistically, it may be useful to consider a simpler and perhaps clearer example: I am presently looking at two books on my desk. Both are darkish blue, but not quite the same shade of darkish blue, though

---

28 Versions of this point are offered by Pap (1958), p. 184; by Quine, in "Truth by Convention," reprinted in Quine (1966), pp. 70–99, at pp. 96–8; and by Harman (1967–68), p. 130.
29 A. C. Ewing (1939–40), p. 217.

my rather meager color vocabulary contains no names for these specific shades nor any other way of indicating them linguistically. On this basis, I come to believe and, so far as I can see, to know *a priori* a certain proposition that I can only indicate indirectly but cannot adequately express in language, the proposition that nothing could be both of these colors all over at the same time; and it seems clear that the *a priori* justification of this linguistically unformulated proposition cannot be accounted for by appeal to linguistic convention. (The proposition in question is, of course, not to be identified with the linguistically expressible proposition that no object can be two different colors all over at the same time, nor is it derivable from that proposition without the use of premises that are equally difficult to account for by appeal to linguistic convention.)[30]

Of the five objections considered, I submit that all but perhaps the first are clearly decisive against the idea that *a priori* justification can be adequately accounted for by the appeal to linguistic convention (and if the first fails to be decisive, this is only because the view in question is at that point shrouded in protective obscurity). All of these objections are quite obvious, and none of them (except possibly the fourth) is especially new, making it something of a mystery how the view in question has continued to be seriously advocated for so long. As I have already suggested, my view, though I have not tried to fully defend it here, is that this conception of analyticity and the version of moderate empiricism that employs it have, like the others discussed above, seemed plausible only because the various versions have not been clearly distinguished from one another. My hypothesis is that moderate empiricists have traded, whether knowingly or not, on the extreme ambiguity of the concept of analyticity, avoiding the objections to one conception by appeal to another and failing to appreciate that there is no conception, at least none developed so far, that is adequate for their needs once the ambiguity is resolved.

§2.7. A FINAL PROBLEM FOR THE MODERATE EMPIRICIST

We have seen that none of the standard conceptions of analyticity seems capable of providing the deflationary epistemological account of *a priori* justification that the moderate empiricist purports to offer. I will con-

---

30 It is also worth noting that examples of this kind seem to cast severe doubt on the pervasive assumption of analytic philosophers that thought is somehow essentially a linguistic process. See further below, in Chapter 6.

clude the discussion of moderate empiricism by considering briefly a different sort of issue, but one that is equally damaging to the prospects for such a view: the issue of the epistemological status of the moderate empiricist thesis itself. The moderate empiricist claims to know, and hence to be justified in believing, that all *a priori* knowable propositions are analytic. But it seems plain that this thesis cannot itself be plausibly regarded as a contingent, empirical claim. If regarded as a simple product of enumerative induction over examples of *a priori* justification, it is pretty clearly refuted by the apparent rationalist counter-examples; and there is no other very obvious account of how such a claim might be empirically justified. Moreover, the main thrust of the moderate empiricist position is clearly that there *could* not be synthetic *a priori* knowledge, that the very conception of such knowledge is untenable or absurd, not just that there in fact happen to be no instances. Thus the moderate empiricist thesis must apparently be justified *a priori,* if it is justified at all, and the obvious question to ask is whether it is itself analytic or synthetic. Since the latter possibility is obviously unacceptable if moderate empiricism is not to be in effect self-refuting, the thesis must apparently be analytic. But can it be held with any plausibility at all that the claim that all *a priori* knowledge is analytic is itself analytic in any of the senses of analyticity that have turned out to have at least mild epistemological value, that is, in either the Kantian or Fregean senses?

Quinton is one of the very few moderate empiricists who discusses the epistemological status of the moderate empiricist thesis, reasoning along the foregoing lines that since the moderate empiricist thesis cannot be construed as empirical, it must be analytic. Moreover, though Quinton is not very explicit on this point, the moderate empiricist must also hold, of course, that all analytic truths are justifiable *a priori;* and this converse claim must also be *a priori* justifiable and hence analytic. But if it is analytically true *both* that all *a priori* justifiable propositions are analytic and also that all analytic propositions are justifiable *a priori,* then it seemingly must be the case that the content of each concept is included in the other, so that the two concepts are simply *identical* and the two terms *synonymous.* At least this would have to be true on the Kantian or Fregean accounts of analyticity, and to avoid it by appeal to one of the obfuscating accounts would simply underline the epistemological circularity or irrelevance of those accounts. Now only a little reflection on the discussion of these two concepts in Chapter 1 and earlier in the present chapter will reveal that such a claim of synonymy is utterly preposterous on its face. But preposterous though it is, Quinton proceeds to bite the bullet.

As one might suspect, his attempt to defend a thesis that is patently indefensible proceeds for the most part by thoroughly confusing the three main distinctions. With one qualification that is irrelevant here, apriority is simply identified with necessity; and necessity is then explicated as a statement's being "true in itself," as opposed to being true in virtue of something outside itself. To the extent that it means anything at all, this is plainly wrong: necessary truths can depend on things outside themselves so long as the relevant facts concerning those further things are also necessary – a Platonistic account of mathematics is surely not ruled out by the very meaning of 'necessary'. Quinton then proceeds to argue that if the truth of a statement depends on nothing outside itself, then it must be due to the statement's meaning (since it is plainly not due to the "form of words," i.e., to the physical properties of the utterance or inscription); the statement must therefore be true by virtue of meaning. In this way, he arrives at the conclusion that apriority, that is, (for him) necessity, is the same concept as analyticity in the sense of truth by virtue of meaning.[31]

Quinton also argues for the identity of the correlative concept of a contingent statement and that of an empirical statement in a way that completely and illegitimately conflates metaphysical and epistemological issues:

The idea of the empirical is a development or elucidation of the idea of the contingent. It aims to explain how a statement can owe its truth to something else, what conditions the something else must satisfy if it is to confer truth on a statement. To require it to be experience is to say that unless it is something of whose existence we can in principle become aware then the form of words involved has not made out its claim to be a statement. (92)

But apart from the implicit verificationism, why should we think that anything "of whose existence we can become aware" must be identical with experience, and how do we get from "made true by experience" to "justified by appeal to experience"?

Quinton's argument illustrates clearly the contortions that a moderate empiricist must go through in attempting to make it possible for his claim to be both knowable and true. My conclusion is that there is no way that this feat can be accomplished and hence that moderate empiricism, in addition to having no adequate account available of its central concept of

31 Quinton attempts to argue from this conclusion to the further conclusion that *a priori* knowable propositions are also analytic in other senses. Two parts of that argument have already been in effect considered and rejected above in the discussions of implicit definition and linguistic convention; the third is utterly question-begging (cf. Quinton, op. cit., pp. 95–6).

analyticity, is in fact ultimately incoherent in the sense that any apparently adequate justification of its central thesis would be at the same time a putative counterexample to that thesis.

What is shocking, of course, is that a view as ill-defined, poorly defended, and in this way ultimately incoherent as moderate empiricism should have been held so long, so confidently, and often so complacently by so many philosophers. The diagnosis of this situation is nonetheless pretty obvious. It results from the joint acceptance of: (a) the view that *a priori* knowledge is cognitively pervasive and indispensable, especially but by no means only in philosophy; together with (b) the view that rationalism is fundamentally untenable. My thesis in the present book is in effect that while (a) is plainly correct, (b) is little more than an ill-considered prejudice. But before turning to an elaboration and defense of rationalism, we need to examine the second main form of empiricism, that advocated by Quine and his followers.[32]

32 While it seems to me implausible to credit Quine with anything approaching a full understanding of the failings of moderate empiricism, there is no doubt that serious if ill-defined doubts about the concept of analyticity were a large part of his motive for rejecting (a) by rejecting the idea of *a priori* justification altogether.

3

Quine and radical empiricism

§3.1. RADICAL EMPIRICISM AND SKEPTICISM

The conclusion of the preceding chapter was that the moderate empiricist approach to *a priori* justification does not succeed. Moderate empiricism turns out on examination to be in effect a mere schema for a position, one that is apparently incapable of being satisfactorily fleshed out into a realized view and that owes most of its initial appeal to this schematic character (and, I have suggested, to a pervasive failure to distinguish clearly between the various attempted realizations thereof).

What alternative then is left for the empiricist? The answer is both stark and obvious: if *a priori* justification cannot be accommodated within the empiricist framework in the way that the moderate empiricist attempts, then it must apparently be repudiated outright if empiricism is to be sustained. Such a course would have had very little appeal to most of the historical advocates of empiricism, with the single, somewhat problematic exception of Mill, but it has been seriously advocated in recent times, mainly by Quine and his followers. While this Quinean view seems to me very difficult to take seriously, the present chapter will be devoted to an attempt to understand and evaluate it.

Though it is not always so regarded, radical empiricism as thus understood is of course a form of skepticism, indeed seemingly one of the deepest and most threatening forms of skepticism. As explained in Chapter 1, skepticism about the very possibility of *a priori* justification appears to undermine the rational cogency of reasoning and argumentation generally, thus confining epistemic justification and knowledge to the relatively few beliefs (if any) that can be justified by direct experience or observation alone and leading to a nearly complete skepticism. To be sure, this result is neither acknowledged nor apparently intended by the leading radical empiricists: their view instead seems to be that most of science and much of common sense can be adequately justified on a purely empirical basis. We have already seen compelling reasons for doubting whether this is so, but the whole issue of whether radical empiricism leaves room for a non-skeptical positive epistemology will be reconsidered later on in §3.7. For the moment, however, my concern is not with the consequences of radical empiricism, but rather with the arguments for the main radical empiricist thesis itself.

One thing that is obvious at once is that radical empiricism is entirely impervious to any direct refutation. What, after all, is such an attempted refutation to appeal to? An appeal to *a priori* insight or argumentation would be obviously question-begging, while no appeal to direct experience seems to have any clear bearing on the possibility or impossibility of *a priori* justification. Thus the radical empiricist is in a relatively secure dialectical position, one from which he cannot be dislodged by any direct assault.

But this immunity to refutation does not of course constitute a positive reason for thinking that radical empiricism is correct. Moreover, it is purchased at a rather severe price, for it becomes equally difficult to see what positive argument there could be for radical empiricism: it is just as hard to see how the truth of such a view could be supported by direct experience as to see how it could be refuted by such experience; while to offer any sort of non-empirical argument would be obviously incompatible with the radical empiricist's central claim. This problem parallels one already noted at the end of Chapter 2 for moderate empiricism: as was the case there, no account of the justification of the main radical empiricist thesis that is not in direct conflict with its truth seems to be possible.

Perhaps the best way to proceed in this dialectically difficult situation is to begin with a close examination of the specific views and arguments of the philosopher whose work has done the most to make radical empiricism not only a respectable philosophical position but, in the eyes of many, intellectually mandatory, namely Quine himself. I will begin with a close scrutiny of Quine's classic paper "Two Dogmas of Empiricism,"[1] a work that is standardly cited as containing his main arguments against the *a priori*, and will then proceed to consider some further arguments growing out of Quine's later work.

---

1 Reprinted in Quine (1961), pp. 20–46. Page references to this reprint will use the abbreviation *TD*.

One who approaches "Two Dogmas of Empiricism" in search of Quine's supposedly compelling arguments against the idea of *a priori* justification is faced with an immediate and rather severe problem, one that in fact pertains to virtually all of Quine's own writings and to those of many of his supporters: on the surface at least, the main target of the article seems to be, not the concept of *a priori* justification at all, but instead the concept of analyticity (or the analytic–synthetic distinction), with the *a priori* receiving little if any explicit attention. This is more than a little odd, especially in light of Quine's unquestioned advocacy, here and elsewhere, of empiricism. For, as we have already seen, the concept of analyticity is fundamentally an empiricist tool for disarming the threat that *a priori* justification seems to pose to empiricism, so that a rejection of that concept would in itself play directly into the hands of the rationalist. This can hardly be Quine's intention, but it is hard to avoid the suspicion that on this point, as on a number of others, he has failed to fully appreciate the dialectical situation.[2]

In fact, it is easy to show that Quine's grasp of the main concepts and distinctions in the area, in "Two Dogmas" at least, is far from sure. Consider, for example, his initial formulation, at the very beginning of the article, of the first of the "dogmas" that he intends to reject:

a belief in some fundamental cleavage between truths which are *analytic,* or grounded in meanings independently of matters of fact, and truths which are *synthetic,* or grounded in fact. (*TD* 20)

The first part of the explication offered here for 'analytic' is standard enough, in effect a variant of the idea of truth by virtue of meaning (though this is also, as we have seen, one of the more obscure and problematic conceptions of analyticity). The problem is the explication suggested

---

2 Perhaps the closest Quine ever comes to an explicit consideration of the rationalist view is in the following passage from "Carnap and Logical Truth" (reprinted in Quine 1966, pp. 100–25): ". . . I do not suggest that the linguistic doctrine [of elementary logical truth] is false and some doctrine of ultimate and inexplicable insight into the obvious traits of reality is true, but only that there is no real difference between these pseudo-doctrines" (106).

The extreme implausibility of this last claim is by now too obvious to require further comment. Thus whatever Quine's intent may be, it does not change the fact that an argument directed solely against analyticity would tell at least as much in favor of the rationalist as in favor of radical empiricism.

for 'synthetic', with its appeal to the unexplained notion of "fact." The term 'synthetic' was of course originally introduced by Kant merely as the complement of 'analytic', and thus ought to mean nothing more than "not analytic"; in the original Kantian usage, a synthetic proposition is one whose predicate concept is *not* contained in its subject concept, and analogously for other definitions of 'analytic'. Given the proffered explication of 'analytic' as "grounded in meanings," 'synthetic' should thus mean simply "not grounded in meanings." But instead the explication actually given by Quine for 'synthetic', in addition to assuming without any very apparent warrant that there are no facts corresponding to analytic propositions, is obscure at best and threatens to collapse the analytic–synthetic distinction into the *a priori–a posteriori* distinction (if 'fact' is taken to mean "*empirical* fact") or else into the necessary–contingent distinction (if 'fact' is taken to mean "*contingent* fact"). Probably it means both, thus conflating all three distinctions.[3]

The impression of unsureness that this passage conveys is borne out on the whole by the balance of the article.[4] While it is reasonably clear from his subsequent writings that Quine intended in "Two Dogmas" to be rejecting the concepts of apriority and necessity along with the concept of analyticity – indeed that these other concepts were ultimately his primary targets – he makes almost no effort to distinguish them from each other, let alone from the concept of analyticity (or to distinguish the multiple conceptions of 'analytic' from each other). Such carelessness would be objectionable enough in any case, but it is all the more disconcerting here because Quine's major objection, at least to the concept of analyticity, is that it is *unintelligible,* an objection that is hard to take seriously when even minimal efforts at clarification have not been made.

My somewhat speculative diagnosis of this situation is that Quine's approach, here and elsewhere, is explained in part by his taking utterly for granted what is in effect a weaker, hypothetical version of the moderate empiricist thesis: *if there were* any propositions justified *a priori,* he assumes,

3 The definition of 'synthetic' could be made acceptable only by taking 'fact' to mean simply "fact independent of meaning," where this is understood to allow the possibility that there might be facts that are necessary or *a priori* knowable while still being independent of meaning. But there is no reason at all to think that Quine means to allow for such a possibility.

4 See, e.g., *TD* 57, where Quine, in the context of a discussion of the verification theory of meaning, says that "An analytic statement is that limiting case which is confirmed no matter what." This is, of course, a specification of the concept of an *a priori* justifiable statement, not of an analytic one.

they would be analytic. If such a thesis is accepted, then showing that there are no analytic propositions would also rule out the possibility of *a priori* justification. But while it is easy to see how someone with Quine's strongly empiricist intellectual ancestry might find such a thesis initially plausible, indeed perhaps so plausible as to be taken entirely for granted, it ceases to be plausible as soon as Quine's own claim, discussed in the next section, that the concept of analyticity is *unintelligible* is accepted or even taken as a serious possibility. The main appeal of the moderate empiricist view depends after all, as we have seen, on the idea that only analyticity could satisfactorily explain how *a priori* justification is possible (see especially the passages from Salmon quoted in §2.1). Since an unintelligible or even doubtfully intelligible concept could not provide the basis for such an explanation, the effect of Quine's own argument, if it has any serious force at all, is to destroy the main warrant for moderate empiricism, including that of the hypothetical version.

When we restore the distinctions that Quine (along with very many others, of course) has blurred, the situation seems to be as follows. Any attempt at an assessment of Quine's arguments will have to distinguish two quite distinct theses: (1) the thesis that the concept of analyticity (or the analytic–synthetic distinction) is so unclear as to be unintelligible, and (2) the thesis that there is no *a priori* justification or knowledge. "Two Dogmas" may be seen in this light to contain three distinguishable lines of argument. The first of these, in sections 1–4, is an argument for thesis (1); it has little direct bearing on thesis (2) unless something like the hypothetical version of moderate empiricism is assumed. The second argument, in section 5 of the paper, is aimed at reductionist views of meaning; its relevance to *a priori* justification or even to analyticity is far from obvious, but there is a connection that will be mentioned below. Only the third argument, appearing in sections 5 and 6 (mainly the latter), can be construed as having any direct bearing on thesis (2), and thus only this argument is directly relevant to the main concerns of the present book.

Before considering this last argument, however, it will be useful to have a brief look at the earlier argument against analyticity. Though I have already argued that the concept of analyticity is incapable in principle of accounting for all *a priori* justification, some of the reductive conceptions of analyticity, especially the Fregean conception, seem to me unobjectionable in themselves and will prove to be of some limited use later on in our discussion; while the epistemological importance of such conceptions has been greatly exaggerated, I do not think that they are, as Quine claims, simply unintelligible.

§3.3. "TWO DOGMAS OF EMPIRICISM": THE ARGUMENT AGAINST ANALYTICITY

Quine's main argument against the concept of analyticity, commonly referred to as "the circle of terms argument," consists essentially in a challenge to proponents of the concept to establish its legitimacy by providing a clear definition or explication. Quine's claim, elaborated in sections 1–4 of *TD*, is that all attempts to do this are forced to employ other terms, such as 'cognitive synonymy', 'definition', 'contradiction', 'semantic rule', etc., that are in Quine's view equally unintelligible. (These other terms could, he claims, just as well be defined in terms of 'analytic' – thus the "circle of terms.")

One thing to notice about this argument is that '*a priori*' is nowhere mentioned as one of the terms in the circle – nor could it properly be, since it can neither be used to define, nor is itself definable in terms of 'analytic'. 'Necessary' is included, but this is simply a mistake on Quine's part, revealing once again his tendency to conflate the relevant distinctions. He speaks of construing 'necessarily' "so narrowly . . . as to be truly applicable only to analytic statements," thus yielding the result that 'Necessarily all and only bachelors are unmarried men' will be true only if 'bachelor' and 'unmarried man' are cognitively synonymous (*TD* 29). But there is no such sense of 'necessarily' (unless one is arbitrarily invented): if the two terms in question are synonymous, the sentence in question will of course be true, but the reverse does not hold.[5]

Does the circle of terms argument have any genuine force against the concept of analyticity specifically? An answer to this question will depend on first achieving a clear idea of the sort of definition or explication that Quine is demanding. To this end it is useful to begin by considering a problem raised by Grice and Strawson.[6] At one point in his consideration of the concept of synonymy, Quine mentions the sort of synonymy that results from a stipulative definition of a newly introduced term or phrase, and remarks:

---

5 Perhaps this confusion again reflects an implicit assumption that any proposition that is justified *a priori* must be analytic. This, together with an equation of apriority with logical or metaphysical necessity, would yield the result that there is a sense of necessity limited to analytic statements; the point of the narrow construal would simply be to exclude species of necessity other than the logical or metaphysical one, such as nomological necessity.
6 H. P. Grice and P. F. Strawson, "In Defense of a Dogma," *Philosophical Review* LXV (1956), pp. 141–58; reprinted in Sleigh (1972), pp. 82–3. (Subsequent references to this article will be to the pages of this reprint.)

Here we have a really transparent case of synonymy created by definition; would that all species of synonymy were as intelligible. (*TD* 26)

The obvious question is why, once Quine admits that synonymy is intelligible in this case, the proponent of the notion cannot say simply that what he means by 'synonymy' in general is precisely the sort of relation between two linguistic expressions that is in this case created artificially. Given an intelligible concept of synonymy, one could then define analyticity in the Fregean way as reducibility to logical truth via the substitution of one synonymous expression for another. There might, of course, still be a further problem about how to determine whether these concepts apply to particular cases, but this would be no reason for regarding them as *unintelligible*. Why doesn't this sort of account satisfy Quine's demand for explication and establish that the concept of analyticity is after all intelligible?[7]

The answer to this question seems to be that what Quine wants is not just anything that might serve as an explanation of the concepts of analyticity, synonymity, etc., but specifically an account in terms of the distinctive *verbal behavior* (or dispositions to such behavior) that would be elicited by their being satisfied (*TD* 24).[8] Thus the problem for the envisaged account of synonymy would presumably be that the specific sort of behavior associated with the introduction of a new term via stipulative definition obviously is not present in relation to all alleged instances of synonymy, indeed not even present for future uses of the particular term that is stipulatively defined.[9]

When Quine's demand is understood in this way, it is at least reasonable to suppose that it cannot be satisfied. Whether or not this is so will depend in large part on how narrowly the notion of verbal behavior is construed, and there are complicated and difficult issues that might be raised in this connection. But it is certainly plausible to suppose that no strictly behavioral test would distinguish a supposedly analytic statement (e.g., 'all bach-

7 It is worth noting that Harman, in a reasonably authoritative exposition of Quine's views that will be considered further below, retracts the concession in question, by claiming in effect that all one can do in a case of explicit definition is "postulate" that the two terms or phrases are equivalent, i.e., co-extensive, without giving this claim any special status that would somehow guarantee its truth. This claim by Harman seems quite implausible, however, and I can see no reason at all to accept it. See Harman (1967–68), p. 140.

8 See in addition Quine (1960), p. 207. (This book will be hereafter cited as *WO*.) Quine also seems to suggest that he would be satisfied by an explication of the concept of analyticity that was given within the resources of an extensional language (*TD* 30–1). The issues that arise regarding the legitimacy of this alternate sort of demand are, I believe, parallel enough to those discussed in the text with respect to the demand for an explication in terms of verbal behavior not to require separate discussion.

9 For discussion of this point, see Quine, "Carnap and Logical Truth," *loc. cit.*, pp. 112–13.

elors are unmarried') from a synthetic and empirical statement that is simply extremely obvious (e.g., 'at some time in the history of the universe there has been at least one brown table') – at least so long as other locutions (such as 'necessary' and 'possible') whose intelligibility has been similarly challenged by Quine are not employed. The main question for present purposes, however, is why failure to meet this more specific challenge is supposed to have the significance that Quine attributes to it. How, that is, is it supposed to follow from the supposed fact that an explication in strictly behavioral terms cannot be given that the concepts in question are unintelligible in a way that makes them unacceptable for philosophical purposes?

I can find nothing approximating a satisfactory answer to this question in the writings of either Quine or his followers. There are admittedly many hints of something like the following line of reasoning: if the notion of analyticity is to be meaningful, it must be explainable in terms of empirical consequences; the truth of behaviorism in psychology means that the relevant sort of empirical consequences must be behavioral; hence, an acceptable explication of analyticity must be given in behavioral terms. But apart from the obvious doubts that can be raised about the second of these premises, the verificationist character of the first premise, whether or not it would (or should) have been acceptable to the positivistic moderate empiricists whom Quine has most directly in mind, makes it extremely dubious as a general philosophical thesis – and, more importantly, obviously question-begging when employed in the context of an argument concerned with the possibility of one species of *a priori* justification.

Underlying both behaviorism and verificationism is a more general view that seems to constitute the fundamental premise of Quine's whole philosophical outlook. This view, which he elsewhere refers to as *naturalism,* holds that there is no genuine knowledge outside of empirical science, and hence that philosophical issues can be dealt with only in a way that is continuous with science.[10] But since naturalism, thus understood, is more or less equivalent to and certainly includes the denial of the possibility of *a priori* justification of any sort, the appeal to naturalism is even more obviously question-begging if employed in an argument for such a claim.[11]

---

10 For some typically brief and sloganistic formulations of Quine's naturalism, see, e.g.: Quine (1969), pp. 26, 126–7; Quine (1981), pp. 21, 72; and Hahn and Schilpp (1986), pp. 156, 316, 430. A more extended development of naturalism in application to epistemology is to be found in Quine, "Epistemology Naturalized," in Quine (1969), pp. 69–90; this paper is discussed further below, in §3.6.

11 In a general discussion of Quine's philosophy, Roger Gibson remarks that "Quine's

If the behavioristic and naturalistic dimensions of Quine's position are set aside as question-begging, does any force remain in the circle of terms argument? On the one hand, it seems clear that not just any failure to meet a challenge of the general sort posed by Quine, that is, a challenge of the form "explain term or concept A without using related terms or concepts B, C, D, or E," means that the term or concept in question is unintelligible. As Grice and Strawson suggest, it is pretty clear that moral terms and semantic terms would also fail an analogous sort of test.[12] And more generally, it seems plausible that virtually any term that is not ostensively definable[13] would fail some test of this general form. On the other hand, it must also be conceded that there may well be sets of terms – for example, in areas like astrology – that really are unintelligible in spite of being interdefinable, and in relation to which a challenge of at least approximately this sort would be appropriate. Everything hinges on whether there is some acceptable way to get into the circle, though it seems highly doubtful, pace Quine, that there is any unproblematic and non-question-begging general characterization of the relevant standards of acceptability to be had.

When Quine's argument is approached from this perspective, the key move turns out to be one that occurs very early in the paper, with relatively little in the way of explicit discussion or argument:

> For the theory of meaning a conspicuous question is the nature of its objects: what sort of things are meanings? A felt need for meant entities may derive from an earlier failure to appreciate that meaning and reference are distinct. Once the theory of meaning is sharply separated from the theory of reference, it is a short step to recognizing as the primary business of the theory of meaning simply the syn-

behaviorism prescribes the content of almost all of his more important doctrines and theses by restricting, ahead of time, what are to count as acceptable answers to a multitude of philosophical questions" (Gibson 1982, p. xx).

It seems abundantly clear that the more general "naturalism" of which behaviorism is a consequence has the same status. But what the justification for such an antecedent restriction is supposed to be, indeed how in light of Quine's strictures against "a prior philosophy" it could be non-circularly justified, remains totally obscure. One thing at least is clear, however: "naturalism" in Quine's sense cannot itself be construed as an empirical thesis.

12 Op. cit., p. 79. Of course, Quine might well want to accept such a conclusion of unintelligibility for moral and semantic terms, but it nonetheless seems clearly unreasonable. At times Quine's philosophical methodology seems to consist largely of simply repudiating, "refusing to countenance," anything that would conflict with his conclusions. (In the tongue-in-cheek *Philosophical Lexicon*, the verb 'to quine' is defined as "to deny the existence of something real or important.")

13 It is questionable whether or not any terms are in fact ostensively definable as that notion has classically been understood, so this may not be a significant restriction.

onymy of linguistic forms and the analyticity of statements; meanings themselves, as obscure intermediary entities, may well be abandoned. (*TD* 22)

This is not much of an argument for "abandoning" meanings as a type of entity; and in any case it is not at all obvious that giving up the idea of meanings as entities requires giving up the whole idea that words have meaning, which is in effect what Quine proceeds to do. It is this rather casual dismissal of the idea of meaning that makes it seem plausible that synonymy must be explained by appeal to the idea of definition or that of interchangeability *salva veritate* or ultimately by appeal to analyticity itself, thus suggesting that there is no viable entry into the "circle of terms." But this is at least largely misdirection, for surely the most natural and obvious course of explanation is to explain synonymy as sameness of meaning and then explain analyticity in terms of synonymy in the Fregean way. Indeed, it is hard to imagine anyone who would seriously claim that the concepts of synonymy or of definition (in the relevant sense) are intelligible independently of the idea of sameness of meaning.

Is there any cogent reason for doubting the intelligibility of the idea of sameness of meaning? Grice and Strawson argue (76–8) that the concept of sameness of meaning is at bottom a perfectly ordinary one whose intelligibility cannot reasonably be doubted, even in the absence of behavioral criteria. Harman's response to this point is that the ordinary concept of sameness of meaning is different from the philosophical conception in that it is less demanding, so that, for example:

in 1966 the sentence "Lyndon Johnson has traveled to Vietnam" would be taken to mean the same (in the ordinary sense of "means the same") as the sentence "The President of the United States has traveled to Vietnam.[14]

Thus, he claims, philosophers "assume a type of distinction between dictionaries and encyclopedias which does not exist."[15] There is *something* to this point (as anyone who has ever tried to explain the philosophical notion of sameness of meaning to an introductory class will realize), but it is also badly overstated (as anyone who has succeeded in such an explanation will also realize). What is clearly true is that ordinary people do not sharply distinguish between meaning (roughly Fregean sense) and reference, and especially that they do not ordinarily concern themselves with differences of sense that do not, in a particular context, seem to have any possible effect on reference or truth value. But it still seems highly implausible to hold, as Harman and Quine must, that the philosophical concept of

14 Harman (1967–68), p. 142.
15 Ibid., p. 136.

sameness of meaning is so different from the ordinary one that the former cannot be made adequately intelligible as a refinement of the latter. It is in fact relatively easy to get ordinary people to recognize the difference in meaning between the two sentences that Harman cites by, for example, considering them to be uttered at a different time or in a counterfactual situation in which someone else is elected in 1964.

In any case, the appeal to the ordinary concept of sameness of meaning is inessential, for it is possible to give an independent explanation of sameness of meaning in a way that is suggested in passing by Grice and Strawson (77–8), one that appears to be entirely adequate: linguistic expressions have meaning, that is, they are not just sequences of marks or sounds but convey something further; moreover, what they convey is not in general determined or restricted by their purely physical characteristics; hence, *whatever* it is in virtue of which an expression is meaningful in the specific way that it is, it would apparently be possible for two expressions to have the *same* such further characteristic; and this would be a case of synonymy.

Harman offers the following reply on behalf of Quine:

such an argument assumes that there are such things as meanings, that a sentence may or may not "have" a meaning, [and] that the meaning one sentence has may be the same as [that of] another.[16]

But this is quite unconvincing, amounting to little more than a bare reiteration of Quine's position in the form of a listing of the claims that he rejects. Notice in particular that the sort of explanation at issue requires no prior view about what meaning is or how it results and certainly no view of meanings as "queer entities" whose existence might be metaphysically problematic.

If the concept of sameness of meaning can be thus made acceptable, it can then provide an unproblematic entry into the "circle of terms," allowing analyticity to be defined in the Fregean way as reducibility to logical truth via substitution of synonyms. One should still worry about the epistemological status of the presupposed notion of logical truth, and this worry, for reasons already discussed in Chapter 2, calls into question the epistemological value of the resulting conception. But this is not the problem that Quine is concerned with and would not in any case support a claim of unintelligibility.

I conclude that Quine, at least in "Two Dogmas of Empiricism," offers no compelling argument for the thesis that all conceptions of analyticity

16 Ibid., p. 134; compare Quine, *WO*, pp. 206–7.

are unintelligible; the Fregean conception in particular seems to survive unscathed.[17]

§3.4. "TWO DOGMAS OF EMPIRICISM": QUINE'S ARGUMENTS AGAINST *A PRIORI* JUSTIFICATION

The circle of terms argument makes no mention of the concept of *a priori* justification, and moreover there seems to be no plausible way to reorient it in this direction. Thus if "Two Dogmas of Empiricism" contains any telling argument for the main radical empiricist thesis that there is no *a priori* justification or knowledge, this argument must be found in the final two sections of the paper. The central claim of those sections is that "no statement is immune to revision" (TD 43) or, as Quineans like to say, that any statement can be "given up." As Quine has made clear elsewhere,[18] 'statement' here simply means sentence. The idea, apparently, is that something justified or known *a priori* (and thus claimed to be necessary) would have to be something that could never be revised or "given up," and hence that nothing has such a status.[19] (I assume for now that "giving up" a previously accepted statement means rejecting it as false.)

Contrary to what Quine seems to think, however, even the strong "give-up-ability" of a *sentence* has no direct bearing on the issue of *a priori* justification. For, as Grice and Strawson point out (86–7), a sentence once regarded as true may be given up in two very different ways: while still possessing the same meaning or after a change in its meaning. And it is perfectly clear that the latter sort of giving up has no bearing at all on the *a*

---

17 This is not to deny that some of Quine's arguments, in "Two Dogmas of Empiricism" and elsewhere, have substantial force against some conceptions of analyticity. What Harman calls "a full-blooded theory of analytic truth" involves the claims that analytic truths are true and are knowable "solely by virtue of meaning," and we have already seen that such a view is indeed quite dubious. Moreover, some of the reasons that it is dubious are those that Harman attributes to Quine (Harman 1967–68, pp. 128–31): (i) It is hard to see how the truth of a proposition can be independent of the way the world is and depend only on the meaning of a sentence; why aren't 'copper is a metal' and 'copper is copper' true because of the way the world is? (But it does not follow that they are true by virtue of contingent features of the world that can only be known empirically.) (ii) Setting out a group of postulates in some area does not guarantee truth; a scientific theory may be formulated in this way and still be false, and thus mere convention does not seem to account for either truth or knowability. Quine's mistake was in thinking that such arguments tell against all conceptions of analyticity and even somehow against the distinct concepts of apriority and necessity, a mistake due in large part to his utter failure to distinguish any of these concepts from the others.

18 See Quine (1970a), p. 2.

19 What is mainly at issue throughout is obviously *a priori* justification that is direct or intuitive, not that which relies on demonstration.

priori justifiability of the sentence prior to the change or of the proposition that it previously expressed. To take an extreme example, it would surely be possible for our linguistic conventions to be altered, perhaps by governmental decree, in such a way that the sentence 'two plus two equals four' would come to have the meaning that the sentence 'two plus two equals seven' presently has. In such a situation, the former sentence would no doubt be "given up," but this plainly has no bearing on the claim that this sentence with its *present* meaning expresses an *a priori* justifiable claim. Thus Quine must seemingly claim, not merely that any sentence may be given up, but that any sentence may be given up *without having changed in meaning*.

No doubt Quine himself, given his "repudiation" of the notion of meaning, would also repudiate this way of putting the matter. But such a repudiation does not help to avoid the underlying problem: it remains obvious that some cases of giving up sentences, those that it is at least initially natural to describe as cases involving meaning change, are trivial and uninteresting in relation to the issue of *a priori* justification. However such cases are properly to be characterized, Quine needs some way of excluding them if his claim of give-up-ability is to have even *prima facie* epistemological import, which means that *Quine himself* apparently needs something very much like the notion of meaning, or at least change of meaning, if he is to avoid an interpretation of his main premise that renders it trivial. Since Quine's repudiation of meaning seems to me, for reasons already discussed, inadequately supported in any case, I will continue to speak in terms of change of meaning; but I see no reason to think that the substitution of any alternative formulation that is adequate to avoid the trivialization of his thesis would alter anything of substance.[20]

Moreover, even if cases of meaning change are somehow set aside, the

---

20 It is interesting to note that Quine himself seems to recognize in one place the possibility of change of meaning, though he avoids using that phrase:

> . . . By a less extraordinary coincidence, . . . an eternal sentence that was true could become false because of some semantic change occurring in the continuing evolution of our own language. Here again we must view the discrepancy as a difference between two languages: English as of one date and English as of another. The string of sounds or characters in question is, and remains, an eternal sentence of earlier English, and a true one; it just happens to do duty as a falsehood in another language, later English. (Quine 1970a, p. 14)

> But then the shift to later English does not involve "giving up" the original sentence in any epistemologically interesting sense, and it is unclear why precisely the same thing cannot be said in the more specific case of an allegedly *a priori* claim. See also the discussion of deviant logics (ibid., chapter 6, especially p. 74).

bearing of Quine's claim of give-up-ability on the possibility of *a priori* justification remains uncertain. For it is also obvious, and something that no proponent of *a priori* justification need deny, that a sentence which expresses an *a priori* knowable proposition might be given up by a sufficiently irrational or perverse person, especially if giving up is interpreted in the crudely behavioral way that Quine's views would suggest. Thus Quine needs at least the claim that any sentence, without having changed its meaning, can be *rationally* or *justifiably* "given up." And even this substantially stronger claim may still not be strong enough. As will be discussed at length later, in Chapter 4, there is no clear reason, historical precedent to the contrary notwithstanding, why a proponent of *a priori* justification cannot admit or even insist that such justification is in fact both fallible and corrigible.

In any case, once the claim of give-up-ability is strengthened in these ways, it is no longer at all clear what the argument for it in these sections of Quine's paper is supposed to be. In section 5, Quine offers an extreme version of the familiar Duhemian view that our claims about the world cannot be experientially tested one at a time, in isolation from each other, but only when taken together; nothing less than "the whole of science," he claims, can be meaningfully confronted with experience. (This is where the rejection of reductionism comes in: if something like phenomenalism were true, then a particular physical object statement could be falsified or confirmed on its own.) And in section 6, we are presented with the familiar, closely related metaphor of the conceptual fabric or field of force that need only be kept in agreement with experience at the edges:

A conflict with experience at the periphery occasions readjustments in the interior of the field. . . . But the total field is so underdetermined by its boundary conditions, experience, that there is much latitude of choice as to what statements to reevaluate in the light of any single contrary experience. (*TD* 42–3)

It would be extremely generous to regard Quine's extremely loose and metaphorical discussion, here and elsewhere,[21] as a reasoned defense of these views. But the main problem is that their relevance to the issue at hand is obscure: how are the Duhemian view and the related metaphor of the fabric or web supposed to show that any sentence (with meaning unchanged) can rationally be given up?

In one of the better accounts of Quine's philosophy, Alex Orenstein offers the following summation of the point at issue:

21 Compare, e.g., *WO*, chapter 1.

We are forced to recognize that from the fact that sentences cannot be tested in isolation but only as parts of systems of sentences, it follows that every sentence at all logically relevant to a test risks the danger of experimental refutation. . . . No sentence can be singled out as being in principle incorrigible; for in the attempt to fit theory to observation, any one sentence may become a candidate for revision. Logic and mathematics, and all other purported a priori knowledge, are parts of our system of background assumptions and are in principle open to revision. If a priori knowledge is knowledge that is justifiable independently of experience, then Quine denies that there is any.[22]

Unfortunately, however, though I know of no better interpretation of the Quinean argument in question, the line of reasoning suggested by Orenstein is in fact utterly question-begging. What follows from the Duhemian view is only that the revisions prompted by recalcitrant experience need not be confined to the observational periphery, that is, that *the demands of experience* can equally well be satisfied by revisions in the non-observational interior, so that there can be no experiential test of a single sentence in isolation. But to conclude from this that any sentence can rationally be given up (without having changed in meaning), it must be assumed that *epistemic rationality is concerned solely with adjusting one's beliefs to experience:* for without such an assumption it remains possible that a particular revision, though adequate to satisfy the demands of experience, is ruled out for some other, non-experiential reason. And the claim of the proponent of *a priori* justification is of course precisely that there are propositions (or sentences with fixed meanings) that it is justifiable or rational to accept, and also unjustifiable or irrational to give up, for reasons that have nothing to do with adjusting one's beliefs to experience. Whether or not such a view is finally acceptable, the Duhemian view concerning the impossibility of experientially testing individual claims in isolation does not count against it in any way.[23]

22 Orenstein (1977), pp. 85–6.
23 The Duhemian thesis might have force against a moderate empiricist view that explained *a priori* justifiable propositions only negatively as those to which experience somehow just happens to be irrelevant; certain of the logical positivists at least suggest such a view, and it may be them that Quine has primarily in mind. The basic problem with such a purely negative conception of *a priori* justification is that the mere fact that experience is irrelevant to a claim provides no positive reason for thinking that it is true; thus justification of this sort would not genuinely constitute epistemic justification (as that concept was explained in §1.1). Since the positivists in question clearly did want to say that *a priori* claims were justified in this sense, it is doubtful that the remarks that suggest the purely negative view should be taken very seriously.
   Harman (1967–68, pp. 132–4) offers an interpretation of the present argument that avoids some of the problems we have noted, but at the cost of depriving the conclusion of the argument of any real significance as an argument against the *a priori*. His suggestion is

Thus Quine's main argument in "Two Dogmas of Empiricism" against the possibility of *a priori* justification and knowledge turns out to be totally lacking in force: it reaches the conclusion that there is no *a priori* justification only by adopting a conception of epistemic rationality that already tacitly assumes that this is so. This is not quite the end of the story, however, for there is a further, seemingly independent, Quinean doctrine, the doctrine of the indeterminacy of translation, that is often cited to buttress the argument against the *a priori*. This doctrine and its bearing on the issue of *a priori* justification will be considered in the next section.

§3.5. THE ARGUMENT FROM INDETERMINACY OF TRANSLATION

Though it has, as we shall shortly see, an enormously wider application, the thesis of the indeterminacy of translation is first developed by Quine in application to the situation of *radical translation*: the situation in which a linguist or anthropologist is attempting to translate into his own language statements made in a completely unknown language, one unrelated to his own, and is therefore forced to rely solely on the observed behavior of its speakers in relation to their environment (including, of course, other instances of linguistic behavior). Quine's claim, in brief, is that while such a radical translator can succeed, in principle at least, in translating observation sentences and truth-functional connectives in a determinate, non-arbitrary way, the possibility of such determinate, non-arbitrary translation does not extend to the rest of the unknown language. While the sentences that fall outside these quite narrow bounds can indeed be putatively translated in a way that will be consistent with all possible behavioral evidence, any such possible translation will, he claims, be only one of indefinitely many different alternatives, all of which are equally satisfactory from a behavioral standpoint and between which only an arbitrary choice is possible. For any system of "analytical hypotheses" equating locutions in the unknown language with words and phrases of, for example, English, there will always be other, alternative sets of analytical hypotheses, equally com-

that revising or "giving up" a sentence need not involve rejecting it as false, but may mean simply refusing to accept it or anything that can be translated into it. But on the most natural interpretation, this claim seems simply and trivially irrelevant: of course one can refuse to accept a sentence expressing any given proposition, but this has no bearing on whether or not such a proposition is justifiable *a priori* or necessary; it does not show that the proposition, as opposed to the sentence, in Harman's phrase, "fails to hold." Whereas if the claim is rather the more interesting one that such a refusal might be rational for any sentence at all, then no argument has been given for thinking that this is so.

patible with the behavior of the native speakers, but offering quite different translations between the two languages.[24]

A simple and by now familiar illustration will help to make clearer the basic thrust of the thesis. Quine imagines a (putative) word in the unknown language, 'gavagai', which is observed to be uttered in the presence of rabbits (or to which the native speakers respond affirmatively when rabbits are present). His claim is that although the translator can determine that 'gavagai' has *something* to do with rabbits, he will be unable to determine on a purely empirical, behavioral basis whether 'gavagai' should be translated into English as 'rabbit', or alternatively, for example, as 'temporal stage of a rabbit' or as 'undetached rabbit part' or as 'fusion of all rabbits' (in Goodman's sense) or perhaps even as 'rabbithood'. Which of these translations is chosen will of course have a bearing in turn on which native locutions can be equated with other English locutions, such as numerals, expressions for identity and diversity, etc. But Quine's claim is that it will always be possible to adjust the translations of these other locutions in such a way as to preserve any of the alternative translations of 'gavagai' (*WO* 51–4, 71–2).

Suppose that this thesis is granted for the sake of the argument. The natural conclusion, from an intuitive standpoint, might seem to be that the native speaker surely has one of these things (or perhaps some distinct further thing) explicitly in mind when he says 'gavagai', and that the translator is merely unable to tell which one. Quine's conclusion, however, is much more radical and intuitively paradoxical: insofar as such indeterminacy of translation exists, he claims, there is simply no right answer, no fact of the matter as to what the native speaker really means (*WO* 26–7, 73). And this indeterminacy allegedly extends not only to the native speaker's meaning, but even to the state of mind of the native speaker that might be thought to embody that meaning.[25]

This is surely paradoxical enough. But the most crucial point is that while Quine develops his argument mainly in relation to the case of radical translation, he makes it quite clear that its significance is not intended to be confined to that rather unusual situation. Consider once more the 'gavagai'

---

24 The indeterminacy thesis was first developed in *WO*, chapter 2. It has since been elaborated and refined in many other places. Though a full account of the thesis would involve many further details and ramifications, such an account is inessential for present purposes.

25 Quine would not, of course, use the term 'meaning'; but for reasons already considered above, I can see no real basis for such a stance and hence no reason to deprive ourselves of this useful formulation.

example, but now imagine that *we* are the native speakers, and that someone else is trying to decide between analogous choices in his language for
the translation of our locution 'rabbit'. Quine argues that just as we cannot
determine on an empirical basis whether 'gavagai' means rabbit, rabbit-
stage, undetached rabbit-part, rabbit fusion, or rabbithood, so also the
radical translator of our language will be unable to decide in a non-
arbitrary way between an analogous set of alternatives. But then, Quine
claims, there is, just as in the original case, no fact of the matter as to which
of the alternatives captures what we really mean when we say 'there is a
rabbit', so that the indeterminacy again extends just as much to the content
of the belief that is expressed. The result is, as Harman puts it,[26] that
psychological attitudes like belief turn out to be attitudes only to *sentences,*
not to determinate propositions or meanings.

How is the thesis of the indeterminacy of translation, which we now see
would be better described, but for Quinean scruples, as the thesis of the
indeterminacy of meaning and belief, supposed to be relevant to the issue
of *a priori* knowledge and justification? Though I have been unable to find a
place where Quine himself speaks very explicitly to this point, the main
relevance seems to be the way in which the indeterminacy thesis buttresses
the quasi-Duhemian argument in section 6 of "Two Dogmas" and thus
makes possible a reply to the objection offered above to that argument. If
sentences have no isolable meanings, if their cognitive significance is
merely a function of their *de facto* connections with other sentences in the
"web of belief" and with experiences or stimuli, then there can apparently
be no reason why any sentence whose abandonment or revision would
eliminate a conflict with "recalcitrant experience" isn't just as open to
rational revision as any other. In particular, there would be nothing on the
basis of which any particular sentence could be recognized as necessarily
true or as justified independently of experience in a way that would rule
out such a revision. The effect of the indeterminacy would thus be to
deprive individual sentences of any autonomous significance that could
provide a basis for singling them out as being justified *a priori*.

But could the broad version of the indeterminacy thesis that extends
even to thought content possibly be correct? Despite Quine's claims, it is
very tempting to take his argument as instead an unintended *reductio ad
absurdum* of whatever considerations (which I have not yet attempted to
specify) are supposed to generate it. For surely, the intuitive argument
would go, I do have something definite in mind when I use the word

26 Harman (1967–68), pp. 147–8.

'rabbit', whether or not someone else can determine from the outside what that is, and hence any argument that leads to the denial of this obvious fact must be unsound.

How Quine would reply to this sort of objection is reasonably clear: he would say that my "having something definite in mind" reflects only my adoption of what he calls the "homophonic" translation of my own idiolect, that is, translating 'rabbit' as 'rabbit':

Staying aboard in our own language and not rocking the boat, we are borne smoothly along on it and all is well; 'rabbit' denotes rabbits, and there is no sense in asking 'Rabbits in what sense of "rabbit"?'[27]

But this response very obviously fails to address the basic problem. For to believe the *sentence* '"Rabbit" denotes rabbits' is, from a Quinean standpoint, quite compatible with having nothing at all in mind that would qualify, from an intuitive standpoint, as a determinate conception of a rabbit. As Quine himself says in another place, " 'Caesar' designates Caesar and 'rabbit' denotes rabbits, whatever *they* are."[28] Moreover, the "homophonic" translation of my own idiolect is in no way mandatory: "Reference goes inscrutable if, rocking the boat, we contemplate a permutational mapping of our language on itself,"[29] and such a "permutational mapping" is always a theoretically available possibility. Thus it is apparently only by ignoring alternatives that I know to be in fact available that I can seem to myself to know what I mean even in Quine's naturalistically purified sense.

What then are Quine's reasons or arguments for these intuitively incredible results? The argument for the thesis of the indeterminacy of translation proper, that is, for that part of the claim that bears narrowly on language and translation, is both complicated and fairly obscure. One key issue is just what information is available to the radical translator.[30] A second is whether the indeterminacy of translation is merely a special case of Quine's thesis that theories are always underdetermined by observational evidence or whether it involves, as Quine claims, a further and somehow more radical sort of indeterminacy.[31]

Fortunately, however, it is unnecessary to enter into these difficult issues, for what is relevant here is not the narrow claim of indeterminacy of

27 Quine (1981), p. 20.
28 Quine, "Reply to Robert Nozick," in Hahn and Schilpp (1986), p. 367.
29 Quine (1981), p. 20.
30 On this, see especially Michael Dummett, "The Significance of Quine's Indeterminacy Thesis," reprinted in Dummett (1978), pp. 375–419.
31 See Quine (1970b); and also Dummett, ibid.

translation, but rather the broader thesis of indeterminacy of meaning and of belief. And although Quine says little about it, it is clear enough how the transition from the narrower to the broader thesis is supposed to be made. The basic appeal once again is to behaviorism and verificationism, and ultimately to the "naturalism" that lurks behind them. But then the overall argument becomes once again question-begging, albeit in a more complicated way, when employed as an argument against the possibility of *a priori* justification: the argument against the isolable meanings that *a priori* justification requires depends on assuming that knowledge is confined to empirical science, so construed as to exclude both *a priori* justification and the sort of quasi-introspective justification that would be relevant to my grasp of my own meanings. Or, putting the matter the other way round, if *a priori* justification and knowledge genuinely exist, then naturalism is false and cannot support the corollaries needed to move from the narrow thesis of indeterminacy of translation to the broader thesis of indeterminacy of meaning and belief.

The indicated conclusion is that even if the narrow thesis of indeterminacy of translation is conceded for the sake of the argument, it yields no further argument against the possibility of *a priori* justification and knowledge that is not entirely question-begging. Nor, to the best of my knowledge, is there any further Quinean argument that does any better in this regard.

Moreover, as already noted briefly in §3.1, there is a powerful general argument that seems to show that there could in principle be no adequate justification for Quine's claim that there is no *a priori* justification. After all, the justification of such a claim would have to itself be either *a priori* or *a posteriori* in character. For a Quinean, it obviously cannot be *a priori*, but there seems to be no plausible way to construe it as *a posteriori*. Quine himself, surprisingly enough, does not seem to even see this problem. Harman tries to meet it by claiming that Quine rejects the notions of analyticity, meaning, etc., as elements of bad *empirical* theories and that the underlying argument is that they have no *explanatory* power, where this presumably means empirical explanatory power.[32] But the problem with this is that the rationalist and moderate empiricist views in question are obviously not intended as empirical theories at all, and the only reason for so construing them seems to be simply a refusal, once again essentially question-begging, to admit that they might be anything else. Moreover, the sorts of arguments that Quine offers against these views do not look at

32 See Harman (1967–68), pp. 125–7.

81

all like empirical arguments. If they can be construed at all as the sorts of arguments that would have a bearing on empirical theories, then they seem to be appeals to what are usually regarded as *a priori* standards for acceptable theories, for example, that they must possess explanatory power. And as we will see below (§3.7), Quine has no adequate alternative account of the justification of such standards. Thus, as suggested above, there seems to be no account available within the Quinean position of how that position can itself be justified.

One dialectical possibility remains open to Quine, however. While conceding, as he apparently must, that he has no non-question-begging argument against the idea of *a priori* justification, he might still want to argue that there are nonetheless two reasons why this idea should not be taken seriously: first, because the idea of *a priori* justification, even if not strictly refutable, remains obscure and highly problematic; and, second, because there is no reputable cognitive endeavor that requires any sort of *a priori* appeal. A consideration of the first of these reasons will be deferred to Chapters 4, 5, and 6, where a moderate version of the traditional rationalist conception of *a priori* justification will be elaborated, clarified, and defended. But even before that is done, it is clear that this suggested Quinean move will have little appeal unless the second reason can be defended, that is, unless Quine can establish that at least the bulk of scientific and common-sense knowledge can be adequately justified on a purely empirical basis. We have already seen, in Chapter 1, persuasive reasons at a general level for doubting whether this is so. The last main task of the present chapter is to pursue this issue further by examining in detail what sort of positive epistemological position is possible within the constraints laid down by Quine's views. Before doing this, however, it is necessary to digress somewhat to examine Quine's attempt to reorient or redefine epistemology itself.

§3.6. QUINE'S "NATURALIZED EPISTEMOLOGY"

Though elaborated somewhat in later works, Quine's main epistemological position seems to be essentially that suggested by the final section of "Two Dogmas of Empiricism." What we believe is a huge, interconnected "web" or "fabric" of sentences, a web that impinges on experience only at the edges (*TD* 42). We revise this web or fabric more or less continuously in an effort to keep the edge "squared with experience."

Many questions can be raised about this by now familiar but still undeniably fuzzy picture. But the central issue is what bearing it has or is supposed to have on the *epistemic justification* of our beliefs, that is, with whether we have any *reason* to think that they are *true*. Quine's predominant view seems to be that the web picture is simply a *psychological* description: we simply do treat some sentences as more relevant or "germane" to a particular experience than others and some as generally less open to revision than others, and we do revise or modify our system of sentences accordingly. But the problem at this point is obvious: merely from the psychological fact that we do operate in this way, it does not follow in any obvious way that the beliefs that result are epistemically *justified* or *rational,* so that, if true, they would constitute knowledge.[33] Why, it may well be asked, should Quine be taken to have even offered an *epistemology?*

Part of the answer to this question is that a major element of Quine's philosophical program is a radical and extremely problematic reinterpretation of what epistemology itself is all about. In his paper "Epistemology Naturalized," he argues that epistemology ("or something like it") should be reconstrued as "a chapter of psychology," an empirical study of the relation between "a certain experimentally controlled input – certain patterns of irradiation in assorted frequencies, for instance" and an output consisting of "a description of the three-dimensional external world and its history."[34] Quine's claim, in first approximation, is that while such a "naturalized epistemology" admittedly falls short of achieving the goals of traditional epistemology, it goes as far in that direction as turns out to be possible, and far enough to be a reasonable, albeit less ambitious substitute.

The rationale offered for such a reconstrual is basically that the epistemological project, as traditionally conceived, has failed more or less irredeemably and hence must be replaced by a more viable substitute. This view depends in part on a fairly narrow conception of traditional epistemology, roughly that put forward by positivistic empiricism, according to which epistemology (or at least the part of epistemology that is concerned with "natural knowledge," that is, knowledge of the physical world) involves two correlative goals: (i) to explain the relevant concepts, for example, the concept of a physical body, in sensory terms ("the conceptual side of epistemology"); and (ii) on the basis of this explanation, to justify claims about the physical world on the basis of sense experience ("the doctrinal side of epistemology") (EN 71). It is obviously these goals that motivate phenomenalism, as advocated by Hume, Ayer, Lewis, and

---

33 I ignore here the (irrelevant) complications required to deal with the Gettier problem.
34 Quine, "Epistemology Naturalized," in Quine (1969), pp. 69–90; the quoted passage at pp. 82–3. Further references in this section to this paper will use the abbreviation '*EN*'.

many others. But, argues Quine, it is clear by now that neither of these goals, at least as traditionally conceived, can be achieved. The attempt to reduce physicalistic concepts to phenomenal ones fails to yield genuine translations; and, since sensory generalizations at least would be required, the attempt to *prove* physical statements on the basis of sensory evidence would be defeated in any case by the problem of induction. What is left, once these goals are (regretfully?) abandoned, is the attempt "simply to understand the link between observation and science," and there is no reason not to appeal to psychology in achieving this end. In particular, the worry that an epistemological appeal to the results of natural science would be circular no longer applies when we abandon the goal of justification (EN 75–6).

There are many problems with this line of argument. A relatively minor one is that Quine's picture of "the conceptual side" and "the doctrinal side" of traditional epistemology as more or less equally important vastly exaggerates the importance of the former. Construed in the reductive way in which Quine construes it, "the conceptual side" of epistemology is a feature only of the narrowest and most implausible versions of empiricism and even there is primarily motivated by the attempt to satisfy "the doctrinal side." Thus the failure to achieve the aim of "the conceptual side," to which Quine devotes a much larger proportion of his attention in *EN,* does very little to show that traditional epistemology has failed and hence needs to be replaced by the suggested Quinean surrogate.

More importantly, Quine's discussion seriously muddies the waters by failing to distinguish a stronger and a weaker conception of "the doctrinal side" of traditional epistemology. According to the stronger conception, deriving from Descartes, the goal is to achieve certainty in our beliefs about the world, to establish that they are infallibly and indubitably true. For the weaker conception, on the other hand, the goal is the more modest one of showing that there are good reasons, even if perhaps not conclusive ones, for thinking that our beliefs are true; complete certainty, while it would of course still be desirable, is not essential. Though his discussion of "the doctrinal side" is too sketchy to allow much confidence on this point, Quine seems to slide illegitimately from the relatively uncontroversial claim that the stronger, Cartesian goal cannot be attained for "natural knowledge" to the much less obvious claim that the more modest goal is not achievable either. Thus we are told that statements about bodies cannot be "proved" from observation sentences, that "the Cartesian quest for certainty" is a "lost cause," that claims about the external world cannot be "strictly derived" "from sensory evidence" (*EN* 74–5); but on this basis it is apparently concluded that the entire "doctrinal side" of traditional epistemology, which Quine characterizes in one place as concerned with "the justification of our knowledge of truths about nature" (*EN* 71), must be abandoned. And this, of course, simply does not follow.[35]

What might cast doubt on this reading of Quine's argument is his employment of the term 'evidence' to characterize even the project of naturalistic epistemology. Thus he claims that despite the failure of traditional epistemology, it remains unassailable "that whatever evidence there is for science is sensory evidence" (*EN* 75). And further on we are told that the goal of naturalistic epistemology is "to see how evidence relates to theory, and in what ways one's theory of nature transcends any available evidence" (*EN* 83); and also that "observation sentences are the repository of evidence for scientific hypotheses" (*EN* 88). I do not see any way, however, to take these remarks at face value, for surely the standard normative concept of evidence, that is, the concept of a *reason,* perhaps of a certain restricted sort, for thinking that some claim is true, is not a concept of empirical psychology. Psychology can describe the causal relations between sensory stimulations and beliefs of various sorts, but it cannot offer any assessment of the rational cogency of any such transition. Perhaps there is some other, naturalistically acceptable conception of evidence that Quine has in mind, but if so this would not count against the conclusion that Quine has entirely abandoned "the doctrinal side" of traditional epistemology.[36]

It thus seems clear that naturalized epistemology has nothing whatsoever to say about whether we have any reason to think that our beliefs about the world are true. And hence, if Quine is right that naturalized

35 Though this is by no means apparent from the actual texts, it is possible that Quine would want to argue that the goal of even the more modest construal of "the doctrinal side" is still rendered unachievable by the complete intractability of the problem of induction. I do not think that such a pessimistic view of induction is warranted, but a discussion of that issue must be deferred to chapter 7.

36 For further criticism in a similar vein of the idea of naturalized epistemology, see Kim (1988), a paper that unaccountably did not come to my attention until after the present chapter was written. Kim argues that epistemology is essentially a normative inquiry that cannot be fitted into a descriptive science such as psychology. He adds the interesting argument, deriving from Davidson's theory of radical interpretation, that a purely descriptive psychology cannot even ascribe *beliefs* to people, since belief ascription relies essentially on normative standards of rationality and coherence. If this is so, then the Quinean project of giving a purely psychological description of the causal relations between sensory input and resulting beliefs, in addition to failing to speak at all to the main epistemological issues, would be impossible in principle. (I should add, however, that Davidson's view seems to me essentially verificationist in character and so quite implausible.)

epistemology is the best we can do, the result is a thoroughgoing version of skepticism: we have a set of beliefs, that is, we accept a set of sentences, that describe the external world[37]; part of that very set of beliefs describes how the beliefs are *caused* by observation, that is, by sensory stimulation; but we have no cogent reason of any sort for thinking that *any* of these beliefs are true. And if knowledge necessarily involves the possession of such reasons, as most philosophers would still insist, then we also have no knowledge.[38] This may indeed, as Quine suggests at one place, be "the human predicament" (*EN* 72). But it is surely extremely unsatisfactory and implausible from both a theoretical and a practical standpoint.[39]

To see how Quine would respond to this sort of objection, we need to look at his conception of skepticism:

Scepticism is an offshoot of science. The basis for scepticism is the awareness of illusion, the discovery that we must not always believe our eyes. Scepticism battens on mirages, on seemingly bent sticks in water, on rainbows, after-images, double images, dreams. But in what sense are these illusions? In the sense that they seem to be material objects which they in fact are not. Illusions are illusions only relative to a prior acceptance of genuine bodies with which to contrast them. . . . The positing of bodies is already rudimentary physical science; and it is only after that stage that the sceptic's invidious distinctions can make sense.[40]

Thus skepticism, in Quine's view, arises only from *within* science; "sceptical doubts are scientific doubts," and hence can best be answered by science itself:

Retaining our present beliefs about nature, we can still ask how we can have arrived at them. Science tells us that our only source of information about the external world is through the impact of light rays and molecules upon our sensory surfaces. Stimulated in these ways, we somehow evolve an elaborate and useful science. How do we do this, and why does the resulting science work so well? These are . . .

---

37 Or rather we believe that (accept a sentence saying that?) we have such beliefs or accept such sentences.

38 It is important, however, to see that the main issue here does not turn on the term 'knowledge'. Even if, as some believe, the ordinary meaning of 'knowledge' does not require epistemic justification in the sense advocated here, but only something like reliable or truth-conducive causation of belief (see the brief discussion of externalist theories at the end of this chapter), it would remain true even for beliefs that constitute knowledge in this sense that we have no reason at all for thinking them to be true, and that result is enough in itself to constitute a very deep and intuitively paradoxical version of skepticism.

39 Notice also that the belief that this is the best that we can do, that naturalized epistemology is all that is possible, is obviously not itself a psychological claim and thus cannot be part of the content of such an epistemology.

40 Quine, "The Nature of Natural Knowledge," in Guttenplan (1975), pp. 67–81; the quoted passage is from p. 67. (This paper will be cited in this section as '*NN*'.)

scientific questions about a species of primates, and they are open to investigation in natural science, the very science whose acquisition is being investigated. (*NN* 68)

Thus, Quine claims, naturalized epistemology is in principle quite adequate to deal with skepticism.

But this view of the skeptical challenge is seriously inadequate in two distinct ways. In the first place, while it is of course true that skeptics have often appealed to various sorts of illusions to motivate their doubts, such an appeal is in no way essential to the basic thrust of skepticism. The fundamental skeptical move is to challenge the adequacy of our reasons for accepting our beliefs, and such a challenge can be mounted without any appeal to illusion. A prominent example of such a challenge is Hume's skepticism about induction, mentioned in passing by Quine himself (*EN* 71–2), but there are many, many others. Such a challenge can in principle be raised against any alleged piece of knowledge: is the justification that is available for the belief in question genuinely adequate to show that it is (at least) likely to be true? To the difficult issues raised by these other versions of skepticism, Quine's naturalized epistemology has apparently nothing at all to say. This is a very serious deficiency if one takes traditional epistemology at all seriously, and the point is that Quine has offered no reason at all for not taking it seriously.

Moreover, even if we restrict our attention to the more limited versions of skepticism that essentially involve an appeal to illusions, the sort of response that is offered by naturalized epistemology totally misses the main issue – which is, of course, justification. What the skeptic questions is whether, once the possibility of illusion is appreciated, our sensory experiences any longer constitute good *reasons* for accepting our various beliefs about the world. Such a skeptic need not doubt that our beliefs are caused in some way, nor still less that an account of how they are caused can be given within our body of beliefs about how the world operates. What he doubts is whether we have any reason for thinking that any of our beliefs about the world, including those that are involved in such an account, are true, and to this issue of justification, naturalized epistemology once again has nothing to say.

Another, quite different way to appreciate the irrelevance of naturalized epistemology to traditional epistemological issues is to consider its application to bodies of belief where a substantial degree of skepticism seems warranted, for example, to religious belief and belief in various sorts of alleged occult phenomena. For just as naturalized epistemology can say nothing positive about the justification of science and common sense, and

87

is thus impotent in the face of skepticism, so also it can say nothing distinctively negative about the justification of these less reputable sorts of belief. There is, after all, no reason to doubt that occult beliefs are caused in some way by the total sensory experience of the individual, and thus no reason to doubt that psychology can offer an empirical account of how they are produced.[41] Such an account would no doubt differ in major ways from that which would apply to more properly scientific beliefs, but the differences would not, within psychology, have any *justificatory* significance. Thus the only epistemology that is possible on Quine's view apparently cannot distinguish between science and occult belief in any way that would constitute a reason for preferring the former to the latter.

Though it seems to me for these reasons to offer nothing that qualifies as a genuine epistemological account, it is important to realize that the idea of naturalized epistemology is in no way a mere aberration on Quine's part. On the contrary, once the very possibility of *a priori* justification is dismissed, it is hard to see what epistemology itself could be other than the genetic psychology of the cognitive process, and thus Quine has no choice but to do the best he can with such a view.[42]

One final issue remains. While the joint unavoidability and failure of naturalized epistemology is already enough to show that Quine cannot argue, as suggested at the end of the previous section, that all reputable cognitive endeavors can be accounted for on a purely empirical basis, it is perhaps still worth asking whether a Quinelike account of the justification of empirical knowledge might succeed if a naturalistically acceptable construal of the epistemological claims themselves is not insisted on, for it is this sort of claim that has typically been advanced by others in the broadly Quinean tradition, few of whom have in fact fully followed Quine in his advocacy of naturalized epistemology.[43]

---

41 Of course, some occult beliefs may conflict with the sort of psychology that Quine has in mind. It is, however, not clear why such a conflict poses any problem once issues of justification are set aside; and in any case, there will be or could be other, occult versions of psychology that Quine can offer no reason for not taking just as seriously as the scientific brand.

42 Of course even this desperate expedient is not really available if, as already argued above, psychology itself, like any discipline that involves claims that go beyond observation, requires the support of *a priori* principles if its own claims are to be epistemically justified. I am indebted to the referee for reminding me of this point.

43 Though many of these others continue to employ the phrase, it seems clear in most cases that the epistemological claims put forth are not, and are not claimed to be, simply claims of psychology. "Naturalized epistemology" has in fact become a fairly pervasive philosophical catchphrase, one that has no clear and univocal meaning.

§3.7. CAN RADICAL EMPIRICISM AVOID SKEPTICISM?

The question, then, is whether a Quinelike view that eschews any appeal to the *a priori* can give an adequate account of the justification of empirical knowledge – even if the issue of the epistemic status of the requisite epistemological claims themselves is set aside.

One problem that arises immediately in assessing Quine's positive epistemology is that it is far from clear just what status the claims that are justified by its lights are alleged by him to have. The obvious question is whether a Quinean approach can yield any reason for thinking that empirical claims, especially those that are not strictly observational in character, are likely to be true, that is, are epistemically justified in the sense discussed in §1.1, above. If the answer to this question is "no," as argued below, then Quine is in a clear sense a skeptic about such claims. At the same time, however, it must be acknowledged that Quine may not intend to claim that his position avoids this sort of skepticism. Thus a full investigation of Quinean epistemology must also consider whether there is some other sense in which some non-observational empirical claims can be rationally preferred to others without any appeal to the *a priori*. As will emerge, the answer to this second question is also negative.

What, then, is Quine's account of the justification of empirical knowledge, especially of that part which is not directly observational in character? Return to the metaphor of the conceptual fabric or web: We have already taken preliminary note of the distinction Quine draws between observational and non-observational beliefs or sentences, that is, between those that are at the "edge" of the "web of belief" and those that are in the "interior," a distinction of which he offers the following less metaphorical, though still rather vague account:

Certain statements, though *about* physical objects and not sense experience, seem peculiarly germane to sense experience – and in a selective way: some statements to some experiences, others to others. Such statements, especially germane to particular experiences, I picture as near the periphery. But in this relation of "germaneness" I envisage nothing more than a loose association reflecting the relative likelihood, in practice, of our choosing one statement rather than another for revision in the event of recalcitrant experience. (*TD* 43)

In the face of such recalcitrant experience, we revise or modify the system accordingly. The sentences that constitute principles of logic and reasoning are those that are toward the center of the web, that is, that are "in practice" less likely to be revised in this way. But their status is not essentially different from other elements in the system, and no sentence is entirely immune to revision. This account is elaborated and developed in many of Quine's later writings, except that talk of experience is replaced by behavioristically and "naturalistically" more respectable talk of "sensory stimulations."

Neither Quine nor his close followers have offered any clear account of precisely how the justification of observational beliefs, those at the edge of the web, is supposed to work (assuming that it is different in principle from that of non-observational beliefs).[44] The observational beliefs are said to be directly, or at least more directly, connected with experience (or sensory stimulations), but the precise epistemic significance of this more direct connection remains obscure. In particular, while it is clear that the justification of an observational belief can be overturned by the further sorts of considerations, discussed below, that apply to non-observational beliefs, it is not clear whether the justification of observational beliefs must always appeal to such further considerations or whether it is merely defeasible by reference to them. Here, however, I will focus primarily on non-observational or theoretical beliefs, those that are in the "interior" of the web, assuming for the sake of the argument that the justification of observational claims can be accounted for in some acceptable way.

How then are the "interior," theoretical beliefs justified? Or, to begin with a simpler question, in virtue of what is one such belief *more* justified, more reasonable to accept, than another? When faced with conflicting or recalcitrant experience, we are supposedly forced to revise our web of belief, our system of accepted sentences, but the experience itself does not fully determine which revision to make. What then does determine, or at least constrain, such revisions? Though the details are obscure, the broad outlines of Quine's answer are clear enough: he appeals to familiar standards like simplicity, scope, fecundity, and explanatory adequacy, adding to them a fairly strong principle of conservatism: roughly that we make the least change in our overall view that is otherwise satisfactory.[45] Thus a system of beliefs that meets these standards to some specified degree will be more justified, by Quinean lights, than one that meets them to a lesser degree, and this difference in justification will extend, *mutatis mutandis,* to the component beliefs of such systems.[46]

---

44 Though a possibility in the vicinity will be examined toward the end of the present section.

45 See, e.g., Quine, *WO,* pp. 19–23; and Harman (1967–68b), pp. 349–50.

46 I ignore here the problems posed by the apparent fact that one particular belief can belong in principle to many, indeed indefinitely many, different systems of belief. On the basis of

There are two immediate problems with this sort of response (beyond the undeniable fuzziness of the various specific standards, as explained both by Quine and by others), together with a third, even more serious one that will eventually emerge. First, it is unclear what the connection is supposed to be between the satisfaction of such standards and *epistemic* justification, where the latter concept is understood in the way offered in Chapter 1, that is, in terms of having a reason for thinking that a belief is likely to be *true*. What reason can be offered for thinking that a system of beliefs which is simpler, more conservative, explanatorily more adequate, etc., is thereby more likely to be true, that following such standards is at least somewhat conducive to finding the truth? Someone who had not rejected the possibility of *a priori* justification might attempt to offer an *a priori* argument for the truth-conduciveness of at least some of these standards,[47] though it is doubtful whether such an attempt could have much plausibility in the case of conservatism or the general notion of simplicity. (Why, after all, should it be thought that the beliefs I happen to hold are *ipso facto* more likely to be true, or that the world is somehow more likely to be simple than complex?) But Quine has in any case ruled out such an appeal. Moreover, it is clear at once that any attempt at an empirical argument for this sort of conclusion would inevitably be question-begging, since it would have to appeal to at least some of these very standards. Thus Quine's own strictures rule out the possibility of his having any reason for regarding his standards of non-observational justification as truth-conducive and hence of his having any reason for construing the justification that they yield as epistemic justification.[48] And this means that the Quinean epistemological view amounts to complete skepticism regarding at least non-observational empirical knowledge. It thus fails utterly to sustain the earlier suggested claim that purely empirical justification is sufficient for all reputable epistemic purposes.

his holism, Quine would presumably deny, most implausibly in my view, that this is really possible.

47 For my own earlier attempt to sketch such an argument for a notion of coherence that includes the idea of explanatory adequacy as a major component, see *SEK*, chapter 8.

48 It is important to be clear that the issue here is not merely a verbal issue concerning the proper understanding of the term 'justification' as it occurs in epistemic contexts. What has been shown is that a Quinean epistemological view can offer no (non-question-begging) reason for thinking that the beliefs it sanctions are thereby any more likely to be true. And that is enough to make such a position a very strong version of skepticism, one that is unable to vindicate the ordinary claims of science and common sense, no matter what use is made of the term 'justification'.

Second, and even more damagingly, it is unclear why these standards impose any real constraint at all on possible revisions. After all, any such standard, since it cannot on Quinean grounds be justified or shown to be epistemically relevant independently of considerations of adjustment to experience, is itself merely one more strand (or node?) in the web, and thus equally open to revision.[49] Thus in any situation in which one possible revision of one's system of beliefs might seem to be more justified than another by appeal to such epistemic standards, one need apparently only revise or abandon the standards themselves to make the alternative revision at least as acceptable.

The Quinean response would presumably be that such wholesale revision of one's epistemic standards, though possible, is itself less likely to be justified or epistemically reasonable – that in terms of the web metaphor, such standards are, as is also claimed for the principles of logic, closer to the center of the web and hence more insulated from the impact of experience. But it is impossible to find any adequate rationale for such a view within the resources of the Quinean position. Construed as a mere psychological claim about what we are in fact disposed to revise, such a picture of the status of epistemic standards might well be correct; but there is no apparent basis on this construal for ascribing to it any epistemic significance, no reason to think that frequent and wholesale revision of one's epistemic standards is less likely to lead to the truth or is in any other clear way epistemically or rationally unacceptable. To appeal to the very standards themselves, for example, to the principle of conservatism in order to defend the reluctance to revise the principle of conservatism, is obviously circular; while any further standard, even a meta-standard having to do with the revision of first-level standards, will itself be equally open to revision.[50]

---

49 It is less than clear just how such epistemic standards are to be represented in a Quinean framework. It is more natural to take them as principles or rules rather than as beliefs, i.e., in linguistic terms, roughly as imperative sentences rather than declarative ones. Quine has little to say about this issue, however, and I shall not worry about it here. It is clear in any case that such standards, however they may best be represented, cannot for a Quinean be construed as immune to the possibility of revision.

50 As Harman points out, "Quine's theory of evidence may also be thought of as a coherence theory of evidence: a person attempts to make his total conceptual scheme as coherent as possible . . . ," where the various standards mentioned above constitute the components of the idea of coherence (Harman 1967–68, p. 351). In these terms, the point being made in the text is the familiar one that the epistemic authority of coherence cannot itself be established by appeal to coherence. For more discussion, see *SEK*, pp. 108–10.

Moreover, it is important to see that this problem arises not only for relatively abstruse standards like conservatism and simplicity, but also for simpler and seemingly less problematic logical standards including even the principle of consistency or non-contradiction itself. If there are any constraints at all according to which some revisions of the system of beliefs in the face of recalcitrant experience are in an interesting sense more justified than others, it seems clear that they must include at a minimum the idea that a system that is free of contradiction is preferable, at least where other things are equal, to one that contains contradictions. But Quine's view can apparently offer no reason at all why the principle of non-contradiction, once its apparent *a priori* credentials are set aside, should not be as freely revised or abandoned as any other part of the system, making it no less epistemically reasonable to accept the contradictory system.

Thus, even apart from worries about their relevance to epistemic justification, the Quinean constraints on justified revision of one's system of beliefs come to very little. At best, they make some total systems (including epistemic principles and principles of logic) less justified than others. But for any less global issue, any question of common sense fact or scientific theory that does not include the specification of such principles, it will seemingly always be possible to find a revision of one's system of beliefs containing any answer one likes (together with appropriately adjusted epistemic and logical principles) that is as justified on Quinean grounds as any alternative revision. The inescapable conclusion is that all such specific answers are equally justified from a Quinean standpoint, which can only mean that none are in fact justified at all. The result is an almost total skepticism, limited at most by our ability to say that some answers (presumably relatively global ones) are preferable to others *if* certain epistemic and logical principles rather than others are (for no good reason) adopted.

But even this bleak picture is more optimistic than the Quinean view really warrants. I have been conceding for the sake of the argument that at least some revision is required in certain cases: that "recalcitrant experience" could demand the revision of at least some non-observational beliefs or other components of the system (perhaps via the mediation of observational beliefs), and also that adopting certain revisions would demand the accompanying revision of epistemic or logical principles. But in fact the Quinean position can ultimately offer no reason at all why *any* revisions are *ever* required; this is the third problem mentioned above and the most serious of all. Remember that for Quine the elements of the system are merely *sentences*, having no meanings beyond their roles in the system, and also that there is of course no *a priori* background logic that connects and relates such sentences. (The set of sentences of course includes sentences of logic, but these are again only further elements of the system.) Thus the basis for any supposed incompatibility within any set of sentences (such as that which supposedly creates a need for revision in the face of experience) can apparently only be some further sentence in the system that says explicitly that the acceptance of such a set is objectionable and hence that the system of beliefs must be revised. But if we now consider the enlarged set of sentences that includes that one, the same situation repeats itself: that set of sentences can only be incompatible and hence in need of revision by virtue of some still further sentence, and so on, thus generating an infinite demand for further sentences if the incompatibility is to be genuine. And since the total set of sentences is presumably finite, this regressive demand will eventually fail to be satisfied, meaning that the alleged incompatibility or need for revision does not really exist after all. The upshot is that even the revision of one's epistemic or logical principles discussed earlier turns out not to be necessary, since at some level there will inevitably fail to be a further sentence saying that the total set of sentences that includes those principles and that seems intuitively to be inconsistent really is inconsistent. This means that *any* non-observational sentence or set of such sentences can always be retained.[51]

This point is sufficiently tricky to make a schematic illustration desirable. Suppose then that I find myself in the following situation: I accept some sentence *P* and also, perhaps as a result of observation, its intuitive denial *not-P,* and in addition I accept a third sentence *PNC* that is intuitively a formulation of the principle of non-contradiction. From a rationalist standpoint, I can know *a priori* that *PNC* is true, so that *P* and *not-P* cannot both be true, and hence that the chance that my set of beliefs is true will be greatly enhanced if one of them is rejected; if my concern is finding the truth, I revise accordingly. But Quine rejects such a view and instead apparently must hold the view that one of *P* and *not-P* must be given up solely because I accept the further sentence *PNC,* where this sentence, though not unrevisable, is claimed to have a status that makes it less reasonable to revise it in at least most cases than to give up one of the other sentences. The point made earlier was that a Quinean has and can have no epistemic reason for assigning such a status to *PNC,* and hence that the

51 Here is a particularly good example of something that is quite common in philosophy and perhaps especially in discussions in the vicinity of the *a priori:* a philosopher tacitly and unwittingly relying on something that he has explicitly eschewed or "quined" (see above, note 12).

option of rejecting *PNC* while retaining both *P* and *not-P* is for him epistemically just as reasonable as giving up one of the latter. But the present point is that once meaning and *a priori* logic are excluded, there is nothing about the *sentences P, not-P,* and *PNC*, taken by themselves, that makes them incompatible or demanding of revision. Thus a genuine incompatibility requires at least that the system contain a further sentence, *MPNC* (a meta-principle of non-contradiction), that says explicitly that the other three sentences are incompatible. And now the problem repeats itself: for *P, not-P, PNC,* and *MPNC* to be incompatible will require a further sentence *MMPNC*, etc., and eventually the further sentence will simply not be present.[52]

In fact, the picture just presented is oversimplified in one obvious but ultimately unimportant respect. What actually happens, of course, is that at one of these stages, perhaps the one including *PNC* but more likely the one including only *P* and *not-P,* our actual cognitive *practice* is such as to treat the sentences in question as incompatible: when we realize that we have accepted such a set of sentences, we in fact revise. But of course practices are, for Quine, no more sacrosanct or unrevisable and no more justifiable *a priori* than are sentences; and he can hardly claim that the presence of such a practice is essential to the *meaning* of *PNC*. Thus the question of whether such a practice is epistemically reasonable, of why it should not be freely revised or abandoned, cannot be avoided, and once again Quine has no resources available to answer it. For this reason, the presence of such a practice, though undeniable as a matter of psychology, is epistemically irrelevant and cannot be used to show that revision is epistemically required.

One interesting upshot of this last point is that the familiar Quinean metaphor of the cognitive web or fabric is in fact deeply inappropriate. What we have on a Quinean view is just a set or bundle of sentences, sentences that are not connected by any background of *a priori* logic and that turn out to be incapable of somehow connecting themselves.

Thus the skepticism that seemed almost total from our earlier perspective turns out to be utterly complete: from a Quinean perspective, there is

---

52 Ironically enough, the point here is similar to an argument that Quine, and Harman following him, offers against the moderate empiricist appeal to convention (see note 15 of chapter 2 and the associated text): just as the logical force of the conventionalist's conventions cannot derive from the conventions themselves, so also the logical force of the sentences of the web cannot be given merely by other sentences in the web. Hence, if those sentences are all there is, they lose all logical force and the need for revision collapses (except, possibly, for sentences that are strictly observational, if there are any of these).

not only no reason for thinking that any non-observational belief is true, but also no reason why we cannot accept or retain any set of non-observational sentences at all, no matter how seemingly contradictory or incoherent it may be and no matter what sentences seemingly expressing epistemic or logical standards it may contain. Any such set is as justified by Quinean standards as any other, which means of course that none is justified at all. And the immediate point, to repeat once more, is not that such an extreme skepticism might not, for all we have seen so far, be correct, but only that it surely precludes Quineans from arguing that the possibility of *a priori* justification, even if not otherwise ruled out, need not be taken seriously because no clearly reputable epistemic goal or project requires it. In this way, both Quinean epistemology and the Quinean case against the *a priori* come to nothing.

In concluding this chapter, I will mention briefly one further possible move that Quine or Quineans might want to make, though I know of no place where Quine himself says anything very explicit in this direction. It might be possible to avoid the extreme skeptical outcome while retaining something approaching a Quinean view by adopting an *externalist* theory of epistemic justification, according to which epistemic justification or warrant need not involve the possession by the believer of anything like a *reason* for thinking that his belief is true. In the most common version of such a view, a belief is justified if it is produced or caused in a reliable way, whether or not the believer has any reason to think that this is so.[53] One problem with this suggestion is that proponents of externalism have typically concerned themselves with the justification of observational beliefs, leaving it unclear whether and how an externalist view can be extended to cover all reasonable cognitive endeavors. But the basic difficulty is that externalism, like naturalized epistemology, seems to simply change the subject without really speaking to the issues that an adequate epistemology must address. I have discussed this issue in great detail elsewhere and cannot go very far into it here.[54] But the essential point is that whatever account externalists may offer for concepts like knowledge or justification, there is still a plain and undeniable sense in which if externalism is the final story, we have no reason to think that any of our beliefs are true; and this result obviously amounts by itself to a very strong and intuitively implausible version of skepticism. This in turn is enough to show that an externalist view does no better than Quine's own in showing that the idea of *a priori*

53 See note 1 of chapter 1, and the references offered there.
54 See the references in note 1 of chapter 1.

96

justification can safely be dismissed.[55] Whether anything philosophically defensible can be made of that idea will be the concern of the next three chapters.

55 As the referee quite correctly points out, an externalist need not reject the *a priori*, though most actual externalists have done so. But I am mainly interested here in the possibility of using externalism to shore up Quine's position concerning the *a priori*, not in what an independent externalist view might say about this subject.

4

A moderate rationalism

§4.1. INTRODUCTION

The argument of the previous chapters leads to the striking or perhaps even startling conclusion that empiricist positions on *a priori* justification and knowledge, despite their apparent dominance throughout most of the twentieth century, are epistemological dead ends: the moderate empiricist attempt to reconcile *a priori* justification with empiricism by invoking the concept of analyticity does not succeed, indeed does not really get off the ground; and the radical empiricist attempt to dispense entirely with such justification ends in a nearly total skepticism. The indicated conclusion is that a viable non-skeptical epistemology, rather than downgrading or rejecting *a priori* insight, must accept it more or less at face value as a genuine and autonomous source of epistemic justification and knowledge. This is the main thesis of epistemological rationalism and also the central thesis of the present book.

Obviously, however, such a result can be no more than tentative until the rationalist view has been explored more fully and shown to be defensible. For even if the objections to the two positive empiricist views are indeed decisive, as claimed here, the possibility remains that the negative empiricist claim is correct: that *a priori* justification as understood by the rationalist simply does not exist. If this were correct, then skepticism would be the correct conclusion with respect to *a priori* justification, even if, as argued above, such a skepticism would inevitably encompass most (or perhaps even all) putative empirical knowledge as well. A thoroughgoing skepticism of this sort is obviously massively implausible from a commonsense or intuitive standpoint, but this cannot, in my judgment, be taken as a conclusive philosophical objection to it, so long as no clear epistemological alternative has been successfully explicated and defended.[1]

---

1 For more on the difficult issue of the proper dialectical stance to take vis-à-vis skepticism, see *SEK*, §1.3.

It is important to be clear at the outset, however, about what can reasonably be demanded of a defense of rationalism. It is obvious at once that there can be no general *a priori* argument in favor of the rationalist view and against skepticism concerning the *a priori* that is not intrinsically question-begging. Nor does any straightforwardly empirical consideration appear to be relevant here: the truth or falsity of rationalism is obviously not a matter of direct observation; and any sort of inductive or explanatory inference from observational data would, as we have already seen, have to be justified *a priori* if it is to be justified at all, thereby rendering the argument again circular.[2]

Thus, in a way that parallels many other philosophical issues, the case in favor of rationalism must ultimately depend on intuitive and dialectical considerations rather than on direct argument. Such a case will, I suggest, involve three main components: first, the arguments against competing views offered in earlier chapters (including, of course, the general argument that the repudiation of *a priori* justification restricts knowledge to the results of direct observation and amounts to intellectual suicide); second, an exhibition of the basic intuitive or phenomenological plausibility of the view in relation to particular examples, which will lead to a fuller statement of the rationalist position; and, third, responses to the leading and allegedly decisive objections.

The first of these components has already been presented in the preceding chapters (though some further elaboration, in the slightly more specific context of the classical Humean problem of induction, will be offered later, in Chapter 7). I begin the account of the second component in the next section by considering a modest selection of the wide variety of examples that illustrate and indeed at an intuitive level virtually demand a rationalist construal. My claim is that the *prima facie* case for rationalism that is provided by examples of these kinds is extremely obvious and compelling, sufficiently so when taken together with the failure of the alternative positive views to put the burden of proof heavily upon the opponents of rationalism. The balance of the present chapter will then be devoted to stating, refining, and clarifying the basic rationalist position. What emerges is what may be reasonably described as a moderate version of rationalism, one that rejects the traditional claim that *a priori* insight is infallible, while

---

2 As we shall see later on, there is a sense in which the truth of the general rationalist thesis (assuming that it is true) can only be an empirical matter, though not in a way that provides any direct response to skepticism about the *a priori*.

nevertheless preserving its status as a fundamental source of epistemic justification.

As already noted, rationalism has been generally repudiated in recent times, and indeed has often not been regarded as even a significant epistemological option.[3] My own suspicion is that much of the explanation for this repudiation is relatively superficial in character, that it is due more to arbitrary winds of philosophical fashion and a certain philosophical failure of nerve than to serious argument. Indeed, I think it is very plausible to think that many of those who claim to reject rationalism are in fact, though perhaps unbeknownst to themselves, committed to rationalism by their own philosophical practice. But be that as it may, it is clear that there are also objections to rationalism that need to be examined and assessed – objections which, though widely regarded as more or less conclusive, are seldom very fully articulated. Some of these objections are straightforwardly epistemological in character; these will be considered in Chapter 5. Other objections are aimed at the perceived metaphysical commitments of rationalism; these more metaphysically oriented objections will be examined in Chapter 6.

§4.2. *A PRIORI* JUSTIFICATION: SOME INTUITIVE EXAMPLES[4]

In this section, we will consider several examples that illustrate the nature of *a priori* justification as viewed by the rationalist, beginning with what is perhaps the most familiar example of all.

Consider then, once again, the proposition that nothing can be red all over and green all over at the same time. Suppose that this proposition is presented for my consideration (or, more or less equivalently, that I am somehow called upon to consider the cogency of the inference from the premise that a certain object is red all over at a particular time to the conclusion that it is not green all over at that same time). After extremely

---

3 For example: in Chapter 7, I will argue that only an *a priori* justification can even hope to solve the problem of induction; but it is a striking fact that discussions of induction often fail to even list such a justification as one of the dialectical alternatives. See, e.g., Skyrms (1966), chapter 2.

4 All of the examples in this section are putative examples of immediate or intuitive *a priori* justification. There is also, of course, justification that depends on a series of *a priori* inferential steps, each step being itself a matter of immediate intuition. The nature of such *demonstrative* justification, and in particular the issue of whether it relies on memory in such a way as to render it no longer *a priori* in character, will be considered below, in §4.6.

brief consideration, I accept the proposition (or inference) and moreover am strongly inclined at the intuitive level to think that such an acceptance is more than adequately justified from an epistemic standpoint, that is, that I have a good, indeed an excellent reason for thinking that the claim in question is true (or that the inference is truth-preserving). But what is the basis, if any, for this (apparent) justification?

The overwhelmingly natural and obvious response to this question would go roughly as follows. First, I *understand* the proposition in question. This means that I comprehend or grasp the property indicated by the word 'red' and also that indicated by the word 'green', that I have adequate conceptions of redness and greenness (which is not, of course, to say that I know everything about even their intrinsic natures, let alone their relational properties). Similarly, I understand the relation of incompatibility or exclusion that is conveyed by the rest of the words in the verbal formulation of the proposition, together with the way in which this relation is predicated of the two properties by the syntax of the sentence. Second, given this understanding of the ingredients of the proposition, I am able to see or grasp or apprehend in a seemingly direct and unmediated way that the claim in question cannot fail to be true – that the natures of redness and greenness are such as to preclude their being jointly realized.[5] It is this direct insight into the necessity of the claim in question that seems, at least *prima facie*, to justify my accepting it as true.

It may be helpful to recur briefly at this point to the issue of analyticity. It is natural enough in a case of this kind to characterize the sentence that formulates the proposition in question as being "true by virtue of meaning," where this means simply that it must be true by virtue of the con-

---

5 Many attempts have been made to argue that this sort of example is either not genuinely *a priori* or even not genuinely true – usually by moderate empiricists attempting to avoid what would otherwise be a clear example of synthetic *a priori* justification. The most recent such attempt, by C. L. Hardin in his book *Color for Philosophers*, construes the claim in question as empirical, but in doing so is forced to treat many analogous claims, e.g., the claim that nothing can be red and blue all over at the same time, as false. According to Hardin, this latter claim is falsified by the existence of purple objects. But while there may be a sense in which a purple object is red and blue all over at the same time, and in which it is then an empirical fact that nothing can be red and green all over at the same time, there is a clear and much more obvious sense in which a purple object is neither red nor blue – in which I would simply be lying if I told someone that a particular object that I know to be purple in color is red. And nothing in Hardin's discussion seems to me to provide any reason for rejecting the view that in this latter sense both the proposition that nothing can be red all over and green all over at the same time and the analogous proposition involving red and blue are justified *a priori*. I have no space here to consider other such attempts, but can only report that none of them seem to me to possess any serious degree of plausibility.

figuration of properties and relations that its words mean or stand for or convey (and also, perhaps, that this fact can be self-evidently grasped).[6] Such a characterization is entirely unobjectionable in itself. The mistake is to think that it conveys any epistemological insight into *how* the truth of the proposition in question is seen or grasped or apprehended which differs from that offered by the rationalist, especially any insight of the reductive sort that at least seems to be promised by other conceptions of analyticity; or that it shows the justification or knowledge that results to be in any significant way dependent on language. The sentence in question is necessarily true because it expresses a necessary relation between certain properties, and it is of course in virtue of its meaning that it does this; but the status of that relational fact as necessary and its cognitive accessibility are in no obvious way dependent on its linguistic formulation, or even, so far as I can see, on whether it happens to be linguistically formulated or formulable at all.

It is common to refer to the intellectual act in which the necessity of such a proposition is seen or grasped or apprehended as an act of *rational insight* or *rational intuition* (or, sometimes, *a priori* insight or intuition), where these phrases are mainly a way of stressing that such an act is seemingly (a) direct or immediate, non-discursive, and yet also (b) intellectual or reason-governed, anything but arbitrary or brute in character. Here I will mostly prefer the former term, in order to avoid potential confusion stemming from other meanings of the term 'intuition'.[7] Since this justification or evidence apparently depends on nothing beyond an understanding of the propositional content itself, a proposition whose necessity is apprehended in this way (or, sometimes, whose necessity is *capable* of being apprehended in this way) may be correlatively characterized as *rationally self-evident*: its very content provides, for one who grasps it properly, an immediately accessible reason for thinking that it is true.

As a second example, consider the proposition that if a certain person A

---

6 Compare the account offered by Lewis, discussed above in chapter 2, of the *a priori* justification of the principle of contradiction. What is wrong with Lewis's account is his failure to recognize that an apprehension of the elements of meaning or content that he lists can only provide the necessary precondition for the intuitive judgment of necessity, rather than somehow eliminating the need for it.

7 A second sense of the term 'intuition' is that involved in saying that the discussion of this section is being conducted on an *intuitive* level. By this, I intend only the vague but useful sense of 'intuition' that is philosophically current, that which pertains to judgments and convictions that, though considered and reflective, are not arrived at via an explicit discursive process and thus are (hopefully) uncontaminated by theoretical or dialectical considerations. Yet a third use of 'intuition', discussed later in the text, is that employed by Kant.

is taller than a second person B and person B is taller than a third person C, then person A is taller than person C. Here again the natural view from an intuitive or phenomenological standpoint is that one who understands the elements of this proposition and the way in which they are combined, including most centrally the relational property of one thing being taller than another, will on that basis be able to see or grasp or apprehend directly and immediately that the proposition in question must be true: that there is no possible way in which both of the propositions conjoined in the antecedent of the conditional could be true without the consequent proposition being true as well. In this case it is easier than in the previous one to offer an abstract logical characterization of the basic rationale, namely that the relational property of x being taller than y is *transitive*, and that it is upon that transitivity alone that the necessary truth of the proposition in question depends. And this might tempt someone to attempt a reductive account of the *a priori* insight at issue. Thus Quinton, for example, would presumably argue that an explicit statement of the transitivity of the taller than relation constitutes a partial "implicit definition" of the term 'tall'.[8] The general deficiencies of this sort of approach have already been discussed (§2.5). Here it is enough to point out that from a purely intuitive standpoint, it is clearly my grasp or understanding of the relational property of one thing being taller than another that justifies the claim of transitivity, not the other way around.[9]

As a third example, consider the proposition that there are no round squares, that is, that no surface or demarcated part of a surface that is round can also be square. My justification for accepting this proposition appears to be entirely parallel to that in the red-green case. I understand the properties of roundness and squareness and on the basis of that understanding am able to see or grasp or apprehend directly and immediately that nothing can simultaneously satisfy them both, that anything which possesses the property of roundness must fail to possess the property of squareness and vice versa. To be sure, in this case at least a partial discursive account is potentially available. There are obvious definitions of roundness and squareness from which, together with some simple axioms of geometry, it is possible to demonstrate the truth of the proposition in question by

---

8 See Quinton, op. cit., p. 105, for such a claim in relation to a parallel example.
9 Attempts have been made to provide a similar abstract logical characterization of the underlying principle governing the red-green case, for example in terms of the contrast between determinables and determinates, but it is even more obvious in that case that any such principle is secondary in the order of justification to more specific claims like the one discussed.

showing that its denial leads to a formal contradiction. Moreover, in this case, unlike some others, it is reasonably plausible to suppose that the requisite definitions and other apparatus are at least implicitly familiar to anyone who understands the proposition in question. All this notwithstanding, however, it also seems abundantly clear at the intuitive level at which we are so far operating that my justification for accepting the original proposition need not and in general will not appeal to such a discursive demonstration, but will instead be just as direct and immediate as in the red–green case. And once it is realized that any such reduction to discursive reasoning will inevitably be only partial, appealing ultimately to axioms and inferences for which such an account is not in turn available, there seems to be no particular reason to deny that this more immediate justification can be entirely adequate by itself from an epistemic standpoint, even though the partially discursive one is also potentially available.

Something very similar can also be said about simple propositions of arithmetic, for example, the proposition that two plus three equals five. Here again, though a claim of general familiarity would be much more dubious, it is clear that a partial discursive account is available. But here again too, there is no apparent reason for thinking that an appeal to such an account is in any way essential from an epistemic standpoint. On the contrary, it once again seems abundantly clear at the intuitive level that one who understands the various ingredients of this proposition and the way in which they are structurally combined will be able to see or grasp or apprehend directly that the proposition has to be true: that any collection of exactly two entities (of whatever kind) together with exactly three more distinct entities must contain five entities altogether. (This is not to deny, of course, that the deductive systematization and unification of claims of this kind in an axiomatic system of arithmetic may have considerable epistemic significance and indeed may enhance the justification of the various propositions involved[10]; the point is merely that there is no reason to think that appeal to such an account is required in order for the acceptance of propositions like the one originally in question to be epistemically justified.)

In addition to being examples of rational intuition or rational insight, it is noteworthy that some or perhaps even all of the examples considered so far might be said to appeal to intuition in the more specific sense, at least

---

10 This assumes of course that it is possible for the justification of a proposition that is justified *a priori* to be enhanced, that *a priori* justification does not automatically confer the highest possible degree of justification. This point will be considered below in our discussion of the issue of the corrigibility of *a priori* justification (§4.5).

analogous to that which occurs in Kant, of involving something like mental pictures or images; and it will be worthwhile to look at an example that highlights this feature. Consider, then, the proposition that all cubes have twelve edges. As in the previous two cases, this claim is obviously capable of being justified in a partially discursive way, though again there is no reason to regard that sort of justification as essential. But in this case especially, even the more direct sort of justification would normally involve something that might be described as an intuitive process, with distinguishable stages or steps. Given an understanding of the various properties and relations involved in the proposition, the obvious way to think about the claim in question is to do something that it is natural to describe as picturing a cube "in my mind's eye" and counting the edges. I have no way of showing that this sort of process is essential, and indeed I suspect that it is not. But the important point is that there is no reason to think that the occurrence of such an essentially non-empirical process, even supposing that it were essential for the justification of this claim, renders that justification any less *a priori* or opens the door to any interesting reductive account.[11]

Consider, finally, a logical example, which it will be more perspicuous to put in the explicit form of an inference. I am invited to assess the cogency of inferring the conclusion that David ate the last piece of cake from the premises, first, that either David ate the last piece of cake or else Jennifer ate it and, second, that Jennifer did not eat it (perhaps because she was at work for the entire time in question). In a way that is parallel to the earlier examples, the obvious construal of this case from an intuitive standpoint is that if I understand the three propositions involved, I will be able to see or grasp or apprehend directly and immediately that the indicated conclusion follows from the indicated premises, that is, that there is no way for the premises to be true without the conclusion being true as well. It is obvious, of course, that I might appeal in this case to a formal rule of inference, namely the rule of disjunctive syllogism. But there is no reason to think that any such appeal is required in order for my acceptance of the inference as valid to be epistemically justified. Nor, in light of our earlier discussion, is there any reason to think that such a rule would not itself have to be justified either by appeal to the same sort of apparent *a priori* insight at

11 There are, however, empirical preconditions for the successful occurrence of such a process and thus for my access to the resulting justification: I must picture the correct geometrical shape (part of understanding the claim correctly); and I must count the edges correctly. For a discussion of why the need for such empirical preconditions does not prevent the resulting discussion from being fully *a priori*, see below, §4.7.

a more abstract level or else to other rules or propositions for which an analogous sort of justification would be required.

Examples of these and similar kinds could obviously be multiplied more or less without limit, but the foregoing will suffice for the moment. It is worth mentioning, however, that I am not at all concerned in this section with the important issue of the *scope* of *a priori* justification. It is obvious that the examples considered so far are relatively unexciting from a philosophical standpoint: if our capacity for *a priori* knowledge was limited to examples of these specific kinds, it would arguably have little philosophical importance outside of the philosophy of mathematics and of logic. But it is abundantly clear that the central issue from a historical and dialectical standpoint is not how widely *a priori* justification extends, but simply whether such justification, as understood by the rationalist, genuinely exists at all. Thus it is appropriate to focus initially on the thesis that such justification genuinely exists in at least some cases, without worrying for the moment about how widely it extends.

My own belief is that a rationalist conception of *a priori* justification is important and indeed essential for dealing with most or all philosophical issues, that philosophy is *a priori* if it has any intellectual standing at all. While the main argument for such a view was already implicit in the discussion of §1.1, a consideration and illustration of how it applies to the whole range of philosophical issues is obviously beyond the scope of the present book. In Chapter 7, however, I will consider the specific issue that is perhaps most relevant to the main argument of the book, arguing (i) that only a rationalist appeal to the *a priori* has any chance at all of solving the problem of induction, and (ii) that such an approach to induction is quite plausible and seems likely to succeed.

§4.3. RATIONALISM: AN INITIAL FORMULATION

At this point, we are in a position to give a more general, though initially still quite intuitive statement of the rationalist view, drawing on the examples just discussed. From an intuitive standpoint, as we have seen, what happens in cases of the kinds in question is this: when I carefully and reflectively consider the proposition (or inference) in question, I am able simply to see or grasp or apprehend that the proposition is *necessary*, that it must be true in any possible world or situation (or alternatively that the conclusion of the inference must be true if the premises are true). Such a rational insight, as I have chosen to call it, does not seem in general to depend on any particular sort of criterion or on any further discursive or ratiocinative process, but is instead direct and immediate (though in some cases, as we have seen, there are possible discursive processes of reasoning, beginning from other insights of essentially the same kind, that could have yielded that claim as a conclusion).

The occurrence of such an insight does obviously depend on a correct understanding of the claim in question, which requires in turn an adequate grasp or comprehension of the various properties and relations involved and how they are connected. As noted in Chapter 1, such a comprehension may itself depend on having had experiences of some specific sort – for example, comprehending the properties of redness and greenness involved in our initial example may well require having had experiences involving these two colors. But once the requisite understanding is achieved, the insight in question does not seem to depend on experience in any further way, thus allowing it to be the basis for *a priori* justification and *a priori* knowledge.

From an intuitive standpoint, such an apparent rational insight purports to be nothing less than a direct insight into the necessary character of reality, albeit, in the cases discussed so far, a relatively restricted aspect of reality. When I see or grasp or apprehend the necessary truth of the claim, for example, that nothing can be red and green all over at the same time, I am seemingly apprehending the way that reality *must* be in this respect, as contrasted with other ways that it could not be. If taken at face value, as the rationalist claims that in general it should be, such a rational or *a priori* insight seems to provide an entirely adequate epistemic justification for believing or accepting the proposition in question. What, after all, could be a better reason for thinking that a particular proposition is true than that one sees clearly and after careful reflection that it reflects a necessary feature that reality could not fail to possess?

As observed above, the idea of such insight has been widely rejected in recent epistemology. It will strike many, perhaps most, contemporary philosophers as unreasonably extravagant, a kind of epistemological *hubris* that should be eschewed by any sober and hard-headed philosophy. Once it is accepted that this sort of insight cannot be accounted for in any epistemologically useful way by appeal to the allegedly unproblematic apparatus of definitions or linguistic conventions, a standard reaction is to disparage it as objectionably mysterious, perhaps even somehow occult, in character, and hence as incapable of being accepted at face value – no matter how compelling the intuitive or phenomenological appearances may be, or how unavailing the search for an alternative epistemological account.

This sort of reaction is not entirely unrelated to the more articulated epistemological and metaphysical objections that will be considered in later chapters, especially the first of the epistemological objections (see §5.1). Taken in itself on an intuitive level, however, it seems very hard to take seriously. There is, to be sure, one reasonably clear sense in which many alleged rational or *a priori* insights are, if not necessarily *mysterious,* at least *inexplicable* in the sense of being apparently *irreducible:* they are apparently incapable of being reduced to or constituted out of some constellation of discursive steps or simpler cognitive elements of some other kind. But once it is realized that any such reduction would have to appeal to other apparent insights of a similar sort and thus ultimately, if an infinite regress is ruled out, to irreducible ones – and this is the essential upshot of our previous discussion of reductive conceptions of analyticity – it is hard to see why this admitted irreducibility should be thought to justify the charge of objectionable mysteriousness or lack of intelligibility.

Moreover, if the implicit demand for reducibility is set aside as unwarranted and the alleged rational or *a priori* insight is examined for intelligibility on its own merits, it is extremely difficult, I submit, to see any serious basis for the charge of mysteriousness. Returning to our initial example, it is not as though I somehow just find myself thinking willy-nilly, for no apparent reason, that nothing can be red all over and green all over at the same time, not as though this conviction were somehow a product of something analogous to revelation or oracular prophecy.[12] On the contrary, I at least seem to myself to see with perfect clarity just *why* this proposition holds and even to be able to articulate this insight to some extent, though not in a way that lends itself to discursive reduction: it is in the nature of both redness and greenness to exclusively occupy the surface or area that instantiates them, so that once one of these qualities is in place, there is no room for the other; since there is no way for the two qualities to co-exist in the same part of a surface or area, a red item can become green only if the green replaces the red. And analogous, though often more complicated, accounts could be given for the other examples. Contrary to the claim of mysteriousness, it is hard to see that there is anything in our cognitive experience that is, at first glance at least, any more transparently and pellucidly intelligible, any *less* mysterious than this.[13]

12 Nor is it, as Plantinga seems to suggest, a matter of a conviction of necessity accompanied by some peculiar, indescribable phenomenology. (See Plantinga 1993b, pp. 105–6.)
13 In one of the best recent discussions of *a priori* knowledge, Butchvarov suggests that what really happens in such a case is that the subject finds it *unthinkable* (or inconceivable or unintelligible) that a judgment whose content is the proposition in question could be

A further issue in the same general vicinity that is sometimes raised is whether rational insight of the sort in question requires a cognitive *faculty* that is either objectionably mysterious or empirically questionable.[14] Clearly and trivially, a capacity or ability is involved, but that this must involve a distinct psychological faculty in any more interesting sense is anything but obvious. While talk of faculties may have a reasonably clear meaning in relation to, for example, modes of perception, it is not clear that it has any but the vaguest and most metaphorical application to thought in general and *a priori* insight in particular. There the faculty involved is simply the ability to understand and think, without which no intellectual process of any kind would be possible. In any case, faculty psychology has long been discredited, and it is very hard to take seriously this attempt, by otherwise "hard-headed" empiricists, to revive it.[15]

As will emerge more fully later but is probably obvious enough even now, there is no way to *prove* that such apparent insights are ever, let alone always, what they purport to be.[16] But there are two further things that can be said at this point. First, if current philosophical fashions are set aside, and pending the consideration of more developed objections, there is nothing obviously unreasonable about the idea of such insight. If the proposition in question is, sheerly in virtue of its content, necessarily true, true in all possible worlds, why should this fact not be at least sometimes apparent to

mistaken. (See Butchvarov 1970, pp. 76–88.) This way of putting the matter has the virtue of emphasizing that *a priori* justification is of course a product of the individual person's psychological processes, but it is misleading in that it could be taken to suggest that the unthinkability in question is just a brute fact: I try to entertain falsehood of the proposition in question and simply find that I cannot do so. On the contrary, as Butchvarov himself acknowledges, for me to find mistake unthinkable is not for it to be the case that I literally cannot understand the supposition that the proposition in question is false; rather I do understand what is claimed by such a supposition, but am unable to *think* it (p. 81). What this seems to mean is that I cannot think this supposition to be *true*, that I find it *impossible*, not merely unthinkable, which is of course equivalent to finding the original proposition to be necessary. This is not to deny that what *seems* impossible or necessary may not really be impossible or necessary (see the discussion of fallibility in the next section), only to insist that the semblance in question is one of impossibility or necessity, not merely of unthinkability.

14 For a version of this objection, see Kitcher (1983), pp. 26–7.

15 It seems likely that those who raise this issue are merely raising somewhat obliquely the issue, to be considered below in chapter 6, of the compatibility of rationalism with materialist theories of mind.

16 It is an interesting question whether such a result can ever be proved or even independently justified for fundamental sources of epistemic justification such as sense perception, memory, and of course *a priori* insight. For a discussion of this issue, see Alston (1991) and Alston (1993), the latter an extended discussion of the case of sense perception.

an intelligence that understands that content? That we have cognitive abilities at all is perhaps in some sense mysterious or miraculous, but it is hard to see why our possession of this one is especially so. Second, it is at least arguable that some such capacity of insight is in fact required for any sort of rational intelligence. Here I am basically just reiterating the basic point made about reasoning in §1.1: if one never in fact grasps any necessary connections between anything, it is difficult to see what reasoning could possibly amount to. There is thus a way in which our very ability to dispute issues of this kind, if it genuinely has the rational character that it seems to have, shows that we do possess such a capacity.

The foregoing account is, however, still too simple in one crucial respect. It assumes or at least suggests that rational insight is always genuine, that is, that the claim that is apprehended to be necessary always is in fact necessary, so that an apparent insight of this kind would guarantee truth. But such a thesis, though it was in fact held or strongly suggested by virtually all of the historical proponents of rationalism, turns out to be extremely difficult, indeed impossible, to defend. And this, as we shall see in the next section, forces a major and somewhat troublesome revision of the rationalist view.

§4.4. THE FALLIBILITY OF RATIONAL INSIGHT

It is a familiar fact that an overwhelming majority of the historical proponents of rationalist conceptions of *a priori* justification and knowledge regarded such knowledge as *certain* – where the primary content of the notion of certainty was that a proposition that is justified *a priori*, via rational insight, cannot fail to be true, that *a priori* justification is *infallible*.[17] (In the Platonic tradition, notoriously, it was the contrast between the alleged infallibility of *a priori* justification and the fallibility of empirical justification that provided the main argument for downgrading or even dismissing the latter in favor of the former.)

Despite this almost exceptionless historical consensus, however, there is no immediately obvious way in which infallibility is a consequence of the minimal conception of *a priori* justification specified in Chapter 1: that of

17 This, at least, is what their most explicit statements on the subject seem to convey. At the same time, it must be noted that such a claim of infallibility is pretty obviously not compatible with much of their actual practice: most obviously with the fact that views of competing philosophers, put forward on allegedly *a priori* grounds, were obviously often rejected as mistaken. (As discussed further below, to resolve this conflict by saying that the mistaken claims did not reflect *genuine* instances of rational insight threatens to trivialize the claim of infallibility.)

having a reason for thinking something to be true that does not derive from sensory or introspective or analogous kinds of experience, but rather from reason or pure thought alone. Indeed, once the question is explicitly raised, it is not at all easy to see what the rationale for the historical belief in infallibility might have been. The most obvious suggestion is that it was the perceived *necessity* of the claims that are the objects of rational insight which led to the conviction that such insights could not be mistaken. The fallacy that this would involve is rather gross: a necessary proposition cannot, of course, be mistaken, but one *perceived* or *apprehended* as necessary could still be neither necessary nor true – unless, of course, the perception of necessity is itself taken to be infallible. Such an explanation of a deeply entrenched historical claim is unsatisfying, but I have no better account to offer.

In any case, the immediate issue is whether such a view of rational insight is correct, and here the answer is much more straightforward and indisputable. It is as clear as anything philosophical could be that the claim of infallibility, if not trivialized in a way to be noted shortly, is false and completely indefensible. There are simply too many compelling examples of propositions and inferences that were claimed to be objects of rational insight, and hence to be justified *a priori*, but that subsequently turned out to be false or mistaken. And although some of these examples were not available to most of the proponents of the infallibility thesis, many of them were. (It should also be stressed, however, that while identifiable mistakes of these kinds are clear enough and frequent enough to undeniably refute the thesis of infallibility, they are at the same time extremely rare in relation to the overall body of claims that are, if the rationalist is correct, accepted on an *a priori* basis.)

At least three classes of counterexamples to the infallibility thesis suggest themselves. In the first place, there are claims in mathematics and logic which though universally regarded as self-evident by the leading minds in the field in question at a particular time have subsequently proved to be false. The most historically salient example here is Euclidean geometry, regarded for centuries as describing the necessary character of space, but apparently refuted under that interpretation, indeed apparently *empirically* refuted, by the use of non-Euclidean geometry in the theory of General Relativity.[18] A further, somewhat more esoteric example is provided by

---

18 For a brief attempt to sort out the tangled issues in the vicinity of geometry and General Relativity, see the Appendix. As argued there, the standard understanding of the situation, as described in the text, is at the very least much too simple.

the fate of naive set theory in light of the Russell paradox and other similar paradoxes. And there are a few other examples of the same general kind, though their number should not be exaggerated.

Second, there are the various allegedly *a priori* claims of rationalist metaphysicians, from Plato and Aristotle through Spinoza and Leibniz down to philosophers of the present century such as McTaggart and Blanshard. Without pausing to list specific cases, it is obvious that all such claims cannot be true, and thus cannot be infallible, if only because of the great extent to which they conflict with each other. For example, reality cannot consist both of a system of timeless, windowless monads and also of one indivisible absolute mind. As contrasted with the mathematicians and scientists whose views provided the first set of counterexamples, it is rather more reasonable to doubt whether all of the philosophers in question genuinely found their claims self-evident after careful reflection, but it would be unreasonably optimistic to assume that all such conflicts can be dealt with in this way.

Third, and perhaps most obvious, there are the routine errors in calculation, proof, and reasoning that are familiar to anyone who has ever engaged in such processes. Notoriously, even the most powerful minds are susceptible to such slips. As we will see more fully in the next section, the exercise of a reasonable degree of care in the consideration of a claim is a requirement for the resulting judgment to even count as an apparent rational insight, so some errors of this kind, those produced by inattention, the use of rote procedures, or sheer sloppiness, can be dismissed as irrelevant. But there is no reason to think that a degree of care that would ordinarily be taken to be adequate will make mistake impossible. And even if there were a degree of care and attention that would avoid all such mistakes, there would obviously be no way to be sure that it has in fact been exercised in a particular case and thus no reason to regard any particular case of alleged rational insight as infallible.

What these kinds of examples seem to show is that it is quite possible for a proposition (or inference) that *seems* necessary and self-evident to a particular person, even after careful reflection, and thus that *seems* to be the object of a rational insight, to turn out nonetheless to be false. Neither does there appear in general to be any further, subjectively accessible criterion that would serve to weed out the cases where mistake is possible, leaving only insights that are genuinely infallible. Since the existence of such cases must be admitted, the only possible defense of the thesis of the infallibility of rational insight would be to deny that *genuine* rational insights are involved in cases of these kinds, insisting that a genuine rational insight must involve an insight into necessity that is not capable of being mistaken. In the absence of a workable criterion of genuineness, however, this response safeguards the infallibility of rational insight only by refusing to call a state of mind a genuine rational insight if it turns out to be mistaken, no matter how subjectively or intuitively compelling it may have been. It is thus best regarded as a mere terminological or conceptual stipulation: an apparent rational insight will count as genuine only if it actually involves the sort of authentic grasp of the necessary character of reality that ensures truth.[19] When understood in this way, such a stipulation is useful for clarification and will indeed be adopted here. But it does nothing at all to establish that any particular case of apparent insight that we may be interested in is in this sense genuine and thus fails to secure infallibility in any epistemologically useful sense. (This is the trivialization of the claim of infallibility noted earlier.)

The implication of all this is that the rationalist view considered so far must be modified in a major way. To insist that *a priori* epistemic justification requires a *genuine* rational insight, in the sense just specified, would make it impossible to tell whether a given claim was justified in this way or not without knowing independently whether or not the claim of necessity was correct[20] – thus making the appeal to rational insight entirely useless as an independent and self-contained basis for justification. Thus, I suggest, a moderate rationalism that abandons the indefensible claim of infallibility should hold instead that, subject to certain further conditions to be discussed below, it is *apparent* rational insight (and, correlatively, apparent self-evidence) that provides the basis for *a priori* epistemic justification. Such justification will thus, in common with all or virtually all other kinds of justification, be fallible, since it will be possible that the apparent insight that justifies a particular claim is not genuine. The moderate rationalist's main thesis is that such an apparent insight still yields a reason, albeit a fallible one, for thinking that the proposition in question is true.[21]

19 There is a further possibility that should be noticed here: an apparent insight might fail to be genuine in the sense specified, i.e., might fail to be a genuine perception of the necessary character of reality, and yet might have as its content a proposition that is in fact true and necessary. Such a situation could result from mere chance or from some more complicated explanation – e.g., influence from someone who does have a genuine insight. (Such a case would be something like an *a priori* version of a Gettier case.)

20 And even this would not really be enough, because of the possibility of the sort of case discussed in the previous footnote.

21 I will not worry very much here about how strong such justification might be, as opposed to whether it exists at all. It is common to speak in terms of the degree of justification required to satisfy the justification requirement for knowledge, it being standardly (if not quite universally) assumed that there is a specific degree of justification that fits this

It is crucially important, however, to stress that the idea of an apparent rational insight must not be construed too weakly. Even an apparent rational insight (i) must be considered with a reasonable degree of care[22] (which obviously includes a clear and careful understanding of precisely which claim is at issue); and also (ii) must involve a genuine awareness by the person in question of the necessity or apparent necessity of the proposition in something like the strong logical or metaphysical sense, not merely a more generic belief that it is in some way obvious – thus requiring at least an approximate (though perhaps, in some cases, very implicit) grasp of that very demanding concept of necessity. An instance that fails to satisfy these requirements will not even count as an apparent rational insight in the sense that is of interest to the rationalist, however the person in question might describe it.[23]

Pending a consideration of the various objections, such an intellectual conviction still seems at an intuitive level a more than adequate reason, *ceteris paribus,* for accepting the claim in question as true. The *ceteris paribus* clause reflects at least two possibilities: a person's apparent rational insights might conflict internally in a way that would force him to give at least some of them up, with something like coherence determining the choice (see the next section for further discussion); or it might be clear on simple inductive grounds that apparent insights of a particular sort were frequently mistaken and hence not to be trusted. But both of these bases for doubt

description and that it is not so high as to guarantee the truth of the claim in question. I am doubtful that there is any definite level of justification that fits this characterization (certainly attempts to specify it have been unsuccessful). But if such a level of justification does indeed exist, I can see no reason for doubting that *a priori* justification, if it exists at all, is capable of reaching it – but also no reason to deny that there may be genuine instances of *a priori* justification that fall short of it.

22 As suggested in the preceding footnote and discussed more fully below (and contrary to what has often been assumed), an adequate conception of *a priori* justification will admit, indeed insist, that it comes in degrees. A recognition of this fact will make it possible to say, what in any case seems obvious, that more sustained or careful consideration may result in a greater degree of justification. But there will still be something like a minimum threshold in this respect, beneath which no justification results.

23 Suppose that a relatively unsophisticated person accepts a proposition because it seems overwhelmingly obvious, where the proposition is in fact one that would seem logically or metaphysically necessary to a more sophisticated subject, and where the seeming obviousness is in fact a response to the apparent necessity of the proposition, albeit not conceptualized as such due to the lack of any reasonable understanding on that person's part of the relevant concept of necessity. I see no need to deny that some significant degree of epistemic justification results, even though this is not, on the present account, a full-fledged case of apparent rational insight. For present purposes, however, it will suffice to limit our attention to cases of the more fully developed sort. (I am indebted to the referee for calling my attention to this point.)

about particular apparent insights would rely essentially on other such insights and hence could not constitute a reason for being skeptical about apparent rational insight in general. We have already seen that there is ultimately no alternative to reliance on *a priori* insight, if reasoned thinking that goes beyond mere perception or observation is to be possible. On a more specific level, it is equally hard to see what the general intellectual alternative to accepting a claim that is the content of such an apparent rational insight might be. One could, of course, adopt the rather drastic alternative of refusing to think about the particular issue in question at all. But it is very hard to see how any serious effort at reflective thought about that issue could fail to reflect an apparent perception of necessity, unless that apparent perception had been undermined in one of the ways mentioned in the preceding paragraph. Thus, in the context of a particular issue as well, repudiation of the reliance on *a priori* insight seems to amount to intellectual suicide.

None of this shows, of course, that there may not be other, more compelling grounds for skepticism about the *a priori,* and we will examine the most important possibilities in the subsequent chapters. The point for the moment is that the fallibility of *a priori* insight is in no obvious way an adequate justification for such skepticism, however frequently it may have provided a motive for the skeptic. Fallibility appears indeed to be an unavoidable aspect of the human condition in all or virtually all areas of cognition. But no one seriously proposes to give up reliance on sense perception because of its fallibility, and such a course seems equally extreme, unnecessary, and quixotic in the area of *a priori* insight. The simple fact is that fallible *a priori* insight, while perhaps not all that we might have hoped for, is vastly better than no insight at all.

§4.5. THE CORRIGIBILITY OF RATIONAL INSIGHT

If rational insight is indeed fallible, then it is natural to think that some further, epistemically prior criterion or standard is needed in order to distinguish genuine rational insights from merely apparent ones, with any epistemic justification that results from such insight depending essentially on the fact that this criterion is satisfied.[24] We have already noticed that the

24 It is the last clause here that makes the appeal to such a criterion problematic. There can obviously be no objection to an attempt to distinguish genuine from merely apparent insights on whatever basis, nor to an argument that such insights or some specified subset thereof are likely to be true, as long as such a distinction or such an argument is not construed as a necessary condition for apparent *a priori* insight to yield justification. (I owe

need to appeal to such a criterion would deprive *a priori* insight of most or all of its cognitive value. But, at a deeper level, such an approach is in any case inherently futile: any such criterion or standard would itself have to be somehow justified; and only a little reflection will show that there is no possible way in which it could be justified without either impugning the *a priori* status of the claims that are justified by appeal to it (if it is justified empirically) or else being guilty of obvious circularity (if it is justified *a priori*). This point will be elaborated, in a somewhat more general context, in §5.5. For now, however, I will attempt to mitigate it somewhat by considering in this section two complementary ways in which it is possible to correct mistakes in apparent rational insight without appealing to any general criterion of this sort.

First. In thinking about this issue, it is useful to distinguish two significantly different sorts of mistakes to which a cognitive process may be vulnerable. On the one hand, there is the sort of mistake, typical of at least many kinds of sensory illusions, hallucinations, and misperceptions, in which there is nothing internal to the cognitive state or process that provides any clue as to its erroneous character. If, for example, I am the victim of sufficiently complete and detailed perceptual hallucinations, it is futile for me to try to decide whether a given apparent state of perception is hallucinatory or veridical by reflecting, however carefully, on that state alone, no matter how long it may persist and how clear its content may be; instead I will have to identify such a hallucination, if at all, by appealing to some kind of criterion or standard that is external to the state itself (which may, of course, involve a comparison of many such states). We may say that a mistake of this sort is only *externally correctable*.

Other sorts of cognitive mistakes, in contrast, are *internally correctable*: further reflection on the very state or process that led to the mistaken result is capable of revealing that it was a mistake and of replacing it with the correct result. At least some perceptual mistakes, those due to carelessness or inattention, seem to fall into this latter category. Thus, for example, my snap judgment that a certain tree is a pine may upon focusing more carefully on its sharp, unbundled needles be corrected to the judgment that it is a spruce.

It seems apparent that at least many of the mistakes that are involved in states of apparent rational insight are of the internally correctable kind. This is obviously true, for example, of at least most routine mistakes of

this point to the referee, though I am unsure whether he will be entirely satisfied with my way of handling it.)

116

reasoning or calculation, which yield to equally routine corrections. For catching and correcting mistakes of this sort, no external criterion is required (however helpful one might be), since it is always possible to avoid error by further consideration of the initial judgment itself.[25] There is, of course, no way to guarantee that this process of internal correction will succeed in any specified length of time, but it nonetheless provides a way in which any particular mistake of this kind can eventually be rectified.

The important question is whether *all* mistakes of apparent rational insight, all cases in which something seems necessary that is not really necessary, are mistakes that are internally correctable in this sense.[26] Such a thesis seems plausible enough on an intuitive basis, though there is no apparent way to argue for it – even if it were not the case, as it obviously is, that such an argument would be self-referential in an objectionable way. There is also, however, no compelling argument, so far as I can see, for an opposing view such as that of Kant, according to which certain kinds of *a priori* illusion are so essentially built into the nature of human reason that we can never escape them, at least not via internal reflection.[27]

Thus one solution to the problem of how to distinguish genuine rational insights from mistaken ones is to appeal to the fact that many such errors, and perhaps all of them, are correctable "from the inside" via further reflection. There is still obviously room here for skepticism as to just how widespread this possibility of internal correction actually is, but we have so far seen no particular reason that supports such skepticism.

Second. A further, complementary approach to the problem of eliminating errors in apparent rational insight is to appeal to *coherence:* to the ways in which such apparent insights may fit together or fail to fit together. Thus, for example, errors in calculation or argument are often uncovered

25 There is obviously an issue here as to when a situation of this kind involves further reflection on the same cognitive state or process and when it involves replacing the original state or process with a different one. I doubt that there is any one obviously correct way of drawing this distinction. But what matters for present purposes is that the later state be closely enough related to the original one that it is capable of illuminating and correcting the mistake involved, as opposed to simply juxtaposing a second state involving a conflicting claim.

26 There is also the possibility noticed in note 18, above: a proposition that seems necessary may actually be necessary, but not, so to speak, in the way or for the reason that is involved in the apparent rational insight. But it seems reasonable to suppose that mistakes of this other kind can be handled in the same general way as those discussed in the text, and giving explicit consideration to them would greatly complicate the discussion.

27 See the "Transcendental Dialectic" in the *Critique of Pure Reason* (Kant 1787). Notice that any argument for a view like Kant's that did not have specific exceptions built into it would be self-defeating, in that there would be no way to exclude the possibility that the apparent cogency of the argument was itself an illusion of the sort in question.

via various kinds of checking procedures that lead to contradictions or conflicts when an error has been committed.

Such an appeal to coherence has limitations that must be clearly understood. There are various conceptions of coherence, ranging from simple logical consistency to more elaborate appeals to mutual inferability or to relations of explanation. But any conception of coherence, however restricted, will presuppose certain fundamental premises or principles that define the conception in question and thus cannot be assessed by appeal to it. Thus in the case of simply logical consistency, at least the principle of non-contradiction (the principle that contradictions are false) and enough logical machinery to make implicit contradictions explicit must be treated as in effect immune to challenge in order to apply the test to other claims. And if the application of the coherence test is to yield genuinely *a priori* justification, then these presupposed fundamental premises or principles must themselves be justified *a priori*.

It is for this reason that a thoroughgoing coherence theory of *a priori* justification and knowledge is impossible, so that a theory of *a priori* justification must be, like the present one, essentially foundationalist in character. But an appeal to coherence can still play the derivative role already suggested of providing one means for catching and correcting mistakes in apparent rational insight. For this to work, two conditions must be satisfied: (i) The *prima facie a priori* justification of the fundamental premises or principles that underlie the conception of coherence in question must be stronger than that of the other claims whose justification is being assessed, so that there is *a priori* justification for thinking that in a case of incoherence, it is some among those other claims, rather than the fundamental premises or principles of coherence themselves, that are mistaken. (ii) There must be some epistemically relevant, *a priori* basis for choosing one of the various ways in which some *prima facie* claims can be rejected and coherence restored as epistemically preferable to the others; this might again involve relative strengths of *prima facie a priori* justification, but it might perhaps also involve something like preserving the greater number of claims whose justificatory strength is equal. While a full account of all these matters would no doubt be very complicated, it seems highly plausible from an intuitive standpoint that these two conditions are frequently satisfied. (It is common to assume that *a priori* justification must take the form of either direct insight or deductive inference. But I can see no reason why the outcome of starting with claims that are putatively justified *a priori* and then reconciling conflicts via principles of coherence whose warrant is also *a priori* should not also count as a form of *a priori* justification.)

Thus, even without an external criterion to distinguish genuine from mistaken rational insights, there is no reason to think that such mistakes are somehow impossible or in general even especially difficult to correct. One further important possibility that appears to be frequently realized is that these two methods of error correction in effect work together and reinforce each other: a likely candidate for a mistake is initially identified via coherence considerations, following which an internal reassessment of the apparent insight reveals the mistake. (Having devoted this much space to ways in which mistakes in rational insights might be corrected, it is worthwhile to reiterate once more that even though it cannot be denied that such mistakes are possible and do occur, the cases in which we have reason to think that mistakes have actually occurred represent an extremely tiny fraction of the cases in which, according to the rationalist view, apparent rational insights are involved.)

One ingredient of the foregoing account was the idea that *a priori* justification can vary in degree, an idea that is sufficiently at odds with the historical tradition to require some further discussion. Both proponents and opponents of the *a priori* often write as though all claims justified in this way would automatically have equal degrees of justification, perhaps because all are found to be (apparently) necessary. Only a little reflection, however, will make clear that this is not so. For example, when I consider the claim that $2 + 2 = 4$, I have an apparent rational insight that this claim is necessarily true, that there is no possible world in which it fails to hold. Similarly, when I consider the claim that $2^5 - 5 = 3^3$, I have a second rational insight that this claim too is necessary. Thus, I do not understand how either claim could fail to be true in any possible situation. But all this is quite compatible with saying that if I were somehow convinced that one of these two claims had to be false, I would have no hesitation about choosing the latter as the one that is more likely to be mistaken. Though mistake in either case appears impossible, the intuitive justification, though surely strong enough in either case to yield strong *prima facie* justification, is slightly weaker in the latter case than in the former, due to the greater complexity of the latter claim. And this in turn seems to provide an epistemically rational basis for preferring the former claim, should it somehow become necessary to choose between them (which, of course, itself appears impossible).[28]

In this case, the difference in the two degrees of *a priori* justification

28 For a good discussion of this point and some further examples, see Plantinga (1993b), pp. 109–10.

results from the relative complexity of the two claims. But it is also possible, as mentioned earlier, that such a difference might be produced by a factor of some other sort, for example, the relative degree of time and care that the person has devoted to the two issues in question. Here I do not mean to suggest that the empirical fact that less time or care was employed in one case as compared to the other would play a direct epistemic role (though this may also be a possible case – see the next section); the suggestion is instead that the two insights might, as a causal result of this empirical fact, possess different degrees of internal clarity and firmness, and that different degrees of justification might result directly from this internal difference.

§4.6. CAN *A PRIORI* JUSTIFICATION BE REFUTED BY EXPERIENCE?

The recognition of the fallibility of rational insight, together with the appreciation that *a priori* justification can come in degrees, also lends increased urgency to a further issue about *a priori* justification that was deferred earlier: the issue of whether such justification, though not requiring the positive support of favorable experience, is nonetheless capable of being negatively undermined or overridden by unfavorable experience. We may approach this issue – in a somewhat oblique, but still useful way – by considering a line of argument, rather freely extrapolated from Philip Kitcher's discussion of apriorism in the philosophy of mathematics,[29] that challenges the compatibility of *a priori* justification and fallibility. In effect, Kitcher claims that infallibility is a necessary condition for *a priori* justification (24), so that one who abandons the thesis of infallibility as indefensible must abandon the idea of *a priori* justification as well. If this were correct, the moderate rationalism being developed here would of course be untenable.

Kitcher's initial rationale for this view is that only an infallible basis for

29 Kitcher's presentation of this objection, in Kitcher (1983), is explicitly directed only at mathematical claims, but there is no reason to think that he regards its force as limited to that context. It is also formulated in a way that is not immediately applicable to the version of rationalism offered here, because Kitcher, for reasons that seem to me quite uncompelling, eschews the concept of justification in favor of what amounts to a process reliabilism. For present purposes, I will simply reconstruct the objection so that it applies to a conception of *a priori* justification like that developed here and also extends beyond mathematics. (Parenthesized references in the remainder of this section will be to the pages of Kitcher 1983.)

selecting which beliefs to accept, that is, an infallible mode of justification, can be allowed to override experience:

> if a person is entitled to ignore empirical information about the type of world she inhabits, then that must be because she has at her disposal a method that guarantees *true* belief. (30)

There are, however, two difficulties with this argument. The first and more obvious is that, as already noted in Chapter 1, it is in no obvious way a requirement for a significant conception of *a priori* justification that such justification be allowed to override experience. Rather it is enough that such justification be capable of warranting belief where experience is silent. Such a moderate conception of *a priori* justification may not measure up to the more grandiose historical claims made on behalf of the *a priori*, but it would still arguably have enormous epistemological importance – in particular, by providing a possible answer to the otherwise completely intractable problem of how both inference beyond direct experience and reasoning generally are to be justified.

Though it is hard to be sure, I suspect that Kitcher's response to this first difficulty might be to concede the tenability of the moderate conception of *a priori* justification, but insist that its applicability is so limited, because of the pervasiveness of potential empirical challenges, as to render it epistemologically insignificant.[30] To evaluate this point and to get a better idea of the problems that experience might pose for *a priori* justification, it will be useful to consider his catalog of the different kinds of experiential challenges which a claim that is allegedly justified *a priori* might face.

Kitcher identifies three sorts of experiential challenges, which he does not claim to be sharply distinguished from each other (55). First, there are *direct challenges,* in which perceptual experience directly contradicts the allegedly *a priori* statement or claim. Second, there are *theoretical challenges,* involving, for example, "a sequence of experiences which suggest that a physics-cum-geometry which does not include this statement will provide a simpler total description of the phenomena than a physics-cum-geometry which does." Third, there are *social challenges,* consisting of "a sequence of experiences in which apparently reliable experts deny the

---

30 It is worth noting that Kitcher himself, though without much in the way of explanation, seems to accept the idea of "nonempirical processes which actually warrant belief" (59). This suggests that the issue between him and the moderate rationalist may be partly terminological.

statement, offer hypotheses about errors we have made in coming to believe it, and so forth."

Do direct challenges to serious *a priori* claims ever in fact occur? Is a claim that seems rationally self-evident ever flatly and unambiguously contradicted by experience? No examples spring readily to mind, though the question is admittedly rendered somewhat vague by a familiar uncertainty, which there is plainly no space to resolve here, as to just how the direct upshot of perceptual experience should be construed. But it seems pretty clear that such direct challenges, if they occur at all, are very rare indeed, much too rare to lend any significant support to the present line of objection. Indeed, while he does not say so explicitly, it may well be that Kitcher himself would also concede this point, for his main emphasis in discussing the vulnerability of *a priori* claims to experiential challenge is on challenges of the other two kinds, that is, on theoretical and social challenges (55–6).

In assessing the threat to *a priori* justification and to rationalism posed by the possibility of these latter sorts of challenges, however, it is crucial to make clearer than Kitcher ever does exactly how the experiences in each case are supposed to pose a challenge to the *a priori* claim in question, given that they do not contradict it directly. The only available answer seems to be this: in each case, though the experiences do not contradict the *a priori* claim, it is possible to *infer* from those experiences, or perhaps a description thereof, to a conflicting or contradictory claim in a way that yields a suitably strong reason for thinking that the contradictory claim is true. Only if such an inference exists will the experiences in question genuinely provide a reason for thinking that the *a priori* claim is false and hence that the *a priori* justification in question is mistaken. But any such inference would have to rely, tacitly if not explicitly, on some underlying premises or principles of inference connecting the experiences in question with this further result: premises or principles having to do, roughly, with the likely truth of an account possessing theoretical virtues such as simplicity or with the likely truth of the testimony of experts of the kinds in question. And the obvious question that leaps to mind on the basis of this formulation is: what sort of reason do we or could we have for thinking that such connecting premises are true or at least reasonably likely to be true (or that such principles are conducive to finding the truth)? That is, what form might the epistemic justification of such premises or principles take?

Here we are back in the vicinity of the original argument for the indispensability of *a priori* justification offered in §1.1, above. Since direct experience cannot by itself justify an inference that goes beyond direct experience and since premises or principles of the sorts in question are plainly not themselves matters of direct experience, there are only three possible answers to the foregoing question. Either (i) such premises or principles are themselves justified *a priori,* or (ii) they are justified by appeal to an *a priori* justified inference from some further set of empirical claims (perhaps via several stages of inference), or (iii) they are not justified at all, so that the supposed challenge collapses. Taken as the basis for a general objection to *a priori* justification, therefore, the appeal to theoretical and social challenges is self-defeating, because such challenges can be cogent only if they are themselves justified, directly or indirectly, in the very way that they are supposed to call into question.

It is this point that constitutes the second and more important difficulty for Kitcher's original argument. If a significant experiential challenge to an *a priori* claim requires, in virtually all cases, appeal to one or more further *a priori* claims, then the whole issue of whether *a priori* justification can be refuted by experience or whether, on the contrary, it warrants ignoring conflicting experience simply does not arise in any straightforward way. The upshot of all this is not, of course, that the appeal to theoretical or social considerations of the sorts indicated cannot generate a challenge to particular *a priori* claims, but rather that any such challenge must itself rest partly on *a priori* considerations. In such a case, therefore, the situation is not that experience by itself conflicts with an *a priori* claim, but rather that certain experiences taken together with *a priori* premises or principles conflict with some further *a priori* claim; assuming (as we shall) that the experiences in question are themselves epistemologically unproblematic, this then amounts to a situation in which two or more *a priori* claims conflict with each other.

How such conflicts are to be resolved is an issue yet to be fully considered, though the discussion of the preceding section is relevant (see §5.4). Thus the possibility still exists that our inability to resolve them in a rationally acceptable way might by itself impugn the whole idea of *a priori* justification. But however that may turn out, the objection we have extrapolated from Kitcher, that is, that once *a priori* justification is recognized as fallible, instances of such justification will be virtually non-existent unless pervasive experiential challenges are illegitimately ignored, turns out to have little force in itself. And the indicated response to the issue posed in the title of this section is that *a priori* justification, if we set aside the rare or non-existent case of direct experiential challenge, is incapable of being undermined or overridden by experience alone.

Admittedly, the foregoing argument is at a very high level of abstraction and ignores the more specific features of the kinds of cases in question. Thus, for all that has been said, it remains possible that there are cases where an experiential challenge to a particular *a priori* claim requires only the support of other *a priori* premises that are entirely unproblematic and that may be, in the context in question, taken for granted. In such a case, the occurrence of the right sort of experience would in effect refute the original *a priori* claim, simply because there would be no question of abandoning the supporting *a priori* premises instead. But while there would be a point to putting things in this way, this does not alter the fact that the ultimate outcome of such a case depends primarily on a choice between two conflicting *a priori* claims, with experience serving only to create the conflict but playing no real role in resolving it.

Our initial account of the moderate rationalist view is now largely complete, pending a consideration of the various objections in the next two chapters. Before turning to the objections, however, it will be useful to say something about a somewhat tangential issue, but one that has an important bearing on the question of the scope of *a priori* justification and that will also, albeit a bit less directly, shed light on a further important aspect of the moderate rationalist position and on some of the objections to be considered later.

§4.7. DEMONSTRATION AND MEMORY

Our focus so far has been more or less exclusively on cases of intuitive *a priori* justification, cases in which the putatively justified claim is seen or apprehended to be necessary, and therefore true, in one direct act of apparent rational insight. But traditional rationalism also recognizes, of course, a second species of *a priori* justification: *demonstrative* justification, in which a proposition is arrived at via several steps of reasoning from specified premises, the justification of each step being direct or intuitive in the way already discussed. Here the initial premises themselves may be either: (i) justified by intuitive *a priori* insight, in which case both the justification for the overall inference and that for the resulting conclusion are also claimed to be *a priori*; (ii) justified empirically, in which case the justification for the overall inference is still claimed to be *a priori*, but that for the resulting conclusion by itself is classified as empirical (in that sense of 'empirical', explained in Chapter 1, in which a proposition whose justification appeals to both *a priori* and empirical considerations is classified as being justified empirically); or else (iii) mere assumptions, in which case the overall inference is claimed to be justified *a priori*, but the conclusion by itself is not thereby justified at all. The main question to be considered in this section is whether the justification that is common to these three cases, that of the overall, stepwise inference, is genuinely *a priori* in character.

The reason for doubting the *a priori* status of the justification of such a stepwise inference is that such justification appears to rely essentially on the empirical faculty of memory. As one works through a chain of reasoning, each particular step is putatively certified by *a priori* insight, but at each stage only memory certifies that the previous steps, upon which the present step depends, were genuinely apprehended to be valid. Thus when one reaches the final step, only the transition from the penultimate step to the conclusion is directly seen to be valid, while the perceived validity of all the earlier transitions is merely remembered. In some cases, of course, it may be possible after some effort to get a relatively simple argument all before one's mind at the same time, so that all of the steps are grasped intuitively at one moment. But in the far more common case in which this result is not achieved, it is argued, the justification for the conclusion depends on memory in a way that makes it (partly) empirical rather than purely *a priori*. Chisholm puts the point as follows:

> But if, in the course of a demonstration, we must rely upon memory at various stages, *thus using as premises contingent propositions about what we happen to remember,* then, although we might be said to have "demonstrative knowledge" of our conclusion, in a somewhat broad sense of the expression "demonstrative knowledge," we cannot be said to have an *a priori* demonstration of the conclusion.[31]

There can be no doubt that memory does play a role in demonstrative reasoning: if I were utterly unable to remember earlier steps, then I would clearly be unable to engage in such reasoning. But has Chisholm given an accurate account of the precise role played by memory? If I am concerned with a strictly deductive argument involving, for example, purely logical or mathematical subject matter, is it really true that I must employ as premises "contingent propositions about what [I] happen to remember"? Does the justification for the eventual conclusion really depend on such premises?

In a valuable discussion of this point, Tyler Burge argues that Chisholm's view (shared by many others) of the role of memory in demonstrative reasoning is mistaken.[32] In Burge's terminology, the role of memory in demonstrative reasoning is normally *preservative,* rather than *substantive:*

---

31 Chisholm (1989), p. 30 (my italics, except for "*a priori*").
32 Burge (1993). The following discussion is greatly indebted to this paper.

Memory does not supply for the demonstration propositions about memory or about the reasoner or about past events. It supplies the propositions that serve as links in the demonstration itself. Or rather, it *preserves* those propositions, together with their judgmental force, and makes them available for use at later times.[33]

Burge's suggestion, in effect, is that in a normal case of demonstrative reasoning, while memory may indeed play an essential role in my *access* to the demonstrative argument in question and so also in my *access* to the justification for the conclusion, it need play no role in the argument or justification themselves – so that the justification may still be entirely *a priori*.

As a useful, albeit imperfect, comparison, consider the role of consciousness itself in immediate *a priori* insight. Clearly my ability to grasp a self-evident claim depends upon the contingent fact that I am conscious. Obviously if I were not conscious, I would have no access to the nature of, for example, redness and greenness nor, consequently, to the necessity and truth of the claim that nothing can be red all over and green all over at the same time. But, equally clearly, this does not make the obviously contingent proposition that I am conscious part of the intuitive reason for the necessity and truth of this claim. The idea of *a priori* justification may, despite all that has been said here, still turn out to be somehow incoherent, but it is surely not incoherent in the simple way that it would be if the plainly contingent and empirical fact that I am conscious constituted part of the reason for an allegedly *a priori* claim.

Burge's suggestion, which I believe to be correct, is that something similar should be said about the role of memory in demonstration: though I could not grasp a deductive argument if I did not remember the earlier steps, this does not make the fact that I remember those steps part of the reason for the eventual conclusion. To be sure, the situation with memory is more complicated: there are more ways that memory can fail and it is obviously harder to be sure that it is working properly than it is to be sure merely that I am conscious. But this does not remove the distinction between, as Burge nicely puts it, a background condition for the functioning of reason and the propositions that constitute the actual content with which reason is concerned. In deductive reasoning, the content of the reasoning is a series of propositions having to do with whatever subject matter is in question, and the reason for the eventual conclusion is the person's understanding of those various propositions and of the relations

33 Ibid., p. 462.

among them.[34] These propositions will usually have nothing whatsoever to do with memory.

Having made this point about memory, it may be added that something closely similar should be said about the requirements mentioned above (§4.4) for a state to constitute even an apparent *a priori* insight: that the proposition in question be considered with a reasonable degree of care and that the person in question have at least an approximate understanding of the concept of logical or metaphysical necessity. The satisfaction of these obviously contingent requirements is necessary for a person to have the right sort of access to *a priori* reasons, but that these requirements are satisfied is not in any way a part of the reason that results.

This account of the requirements for access to *a priori* justification has far-reaching and at least somewhat disturbing implications, about which it is important to be completely clear. Suppose, however unlikely this may seem, that a certain person believes himself to have demonstrative *a priori* justification because he mistakenly believes that he has gone through a series of valid steps leading from the premises to the conclusion of the argument in question, where the mistake in question pertains to the memory of having gone through an adequately connected series of steps, rather than to the assessment of validity at any particular step. Or suppose that in a putative case of intuitive *a priori* justification, the person in question either believes mistakenly that he has carefully reflected on the claim in question or else has a clearly mistaken understanding of the relevant concept of necessity.[35] On the present account, such a person does not in fact genuinely possess an *a priori* reason for thinking that the relevant claim is true (or that the relevant argument is deductively cogent), because the conditions for access to such a reason are not satisfied. In the latter, intuitive case, he fails to have even an apparent rational insight, his own subjective impression of the situation notwithstanding.

There is obviously a whole spectrum of possible cases here, depending on the degree to which the mistake in question is *internally correctable* in

34 As Burge notes (ibid., pp. 464–5) this standard situation does not always obtain. In cases where memory has proved to be unreliable in certain specific ways, reference to memories of procedures designed to avoid the resulting sorts of error may indeed be essential to the justification. But this would no longer be a simple case of demonstrative reasoning.
35 We need not worry here about the case where the person simply misunderstands the main claim (or claims) in question. Such a person is confused about his epistemic situation in a way that may well lead to a false or misleading verbal expression of it, but there is pretty clearly no reason to say that he is genuinely justified on this basis in accepting the claim that he fails to understand.

approximately the sense explained in §4.4. At one end are cases where the degree of additional scrutiny required to uncover the mistake is quite moderate. In these cases, which seem obviously to be by far the most common, even a thoroughgoing internalist about justification, one who holds that the factors relevant to justification must be grasped by or at least directly accessible to the believer, may find it at least reasonably acceptable to say that such a person is not justified *a priori* in accepting the proposition (or inference) in question, the rationale being that what seems to him to be an *a priori* reason is undercut by his epistemic failure in not subjecting the mistaken background belief or assumption to a degree of scrutiny that was clearly within his power. As the degree of scrutiny required to discover the mistake increases, however, the strict internalist will become increasingly uneasy. The other end of the spectrum is the extreme but still apparently possible case where the mistaken background belief or assumption is not internally correctable at all. In this case a thoroughgoing internalist will presumably want to say that his acceptance of the claim (or inference) in question is epistemically justified, because he has an apparent reason for thinking that the claim is true which survives any degree of internal scrutiny. But this result seems wrong, both intuitively and from the stand-point of the account of the requirements for access to *a priori* justification offered above. Though such a person seems to himself to be justified, his grasp of what is really going on is simply too defective to have any genuine epistemic force; in effect, he fails to pass what might be regarded as a condition of cognitive sanity.

If the foregoing suggestion is correct, then both demonstrative and intuitive *a priori* justification turn out after all to have an *externalist* dimension: it is possible to believe oneself to be justified *a priori* in either of these ways and still not be thus justified, where the reason for the failure of justification is something that is, at least at the time in question and perhaps in extremely rare cases even permanently, outside one's subjective grasp. This is a stronger concession to externalism than I have heretofore been willing to make, but one that seems required by the facts of the situation.[36]

36 There are two reasons, however, why such a view is still not externalist in the strong sense that pertains to, e.g., recent versions of reliabilism: First, where the external undermining factor or condition is in fact not present, the person can still have an adequate internal grasp of the reason why the proposition in question is likely to be true. His access to that reason depends on the undermining factor being absent, or rather on the contrary condition being present; but, as argued earlier in this section, the absence of such a factor or condition (or the presence of the contrary condition) is still not part of the *a priori* reason. The present view is thus still quite different from those in which the external element is itself an essential part of the reason for thinking that the belief is true. Second,

128

My conclusion in this section is that the traditional rationalists were correct in recognizing demonstration as a basis for genuinely *a priori* justification. Although for both demonstrative and intuitive *a priori* justification, there are empirical conditions that must be satisfied if a particular person is to have access to such justification, the satisfaction of these conditions does not thereby become part of the justification in question and hence does not prevent that justification from being genuinely *a priori*.

This chapter has offered an initial statement of a moderate rationalist conception of *a priori* justification. On this conception, such justification derives from direct or immediate rational insights or apparent insights, insights that purport to be direct apprehensions of the necessary character of reality. It is clear, in light of the undeniable (albeit rare) mistakes that do occur, that not all apparent rational insights are genuine apprehensions of this kind and that there is accordingly no reason for regarding apparent rational insight as infallible and indeed much reason to the contrary. The claim of the moderate rationalist is that such fallibility does not prevent such an apparent rational insight from being an adequate, albeit defeasible reason for thinking that the proposition in question is true. In addition, while there are plausible ways in which mistaken apparent rational insights can be corrected, such insights do not appear to be vulnerable to strictly empirical refutation.

Such a conception of *a priori* justification seems to me to possess enormous initial plausibility in light of examples such as those considered above. But, as already noted, it has been the object of a number of allegedly compelling objections, both epistemological and metaphysical in character, objections that are frequently claimed to be decisive. The next two chapters will be devoted to a consideration of those objections, one which will also help to refine the view and develop it further.

even though an apparent *a priori* reason may be undermined by a factor or condition of which the person is unaware, there is no general reason why he could not come to be aware of this factor or condition, even though it is possible that such an awareness may not in fact be achievable in a particular case. Neither of these things is true, *mutatis mutandis*, for standard versions of reliabilism.

5

Epistemological objections to rationalism

§5.1. INTRODUCTION

This chapter will consider a number of epistemological objections to the moderate rationalism outlined in the previous chapter. What qualifies these objections as distinctively epistemological in character is their underlying concern with whether and why rational insight, as characterized in the preceding chapter, can provide *epistemic* justification for a belief, in the sense specified in §1.1 above: that is, can yield a compelling reason for thinking that the belief in question is *true*. There can be little doubt that an apparent rational insight provides *some* sort of reason for believing the proposition in question. A belief arrived at in this way is certainly not merely arbitrary or capricious and may indeed be psychologically compelling to the point of being inescapable. But none of this shows that the believer in question possesses a genuinely *epistemic* reason for his belief, and it is this that the objections to be considered attempt to call into question.

I have already remarked that despite the widespread conviction that rationalism is untenable, fully developed and articulated objections to rationalism are difficult to find. This is especially true of the epistemological objections that are the subject of this chapter. Thus, while it is unlikely that anyone who has thought very much about the issue of *a priori* justification will find the general drift of these objections to be utterly unfamiliar, the specific presentations offered here are largely my own attempts to tease out and develop lines of thought that are usually only briefly hinted at in the literature or, more often, in oral discussion (thus the relative dearth of specific citations). I believe nonetheless that the objections that will be discussed here are in fact the strongest and most important epistemological objections to moderate rationalism. If they can be adequately answered, then it seems most unlikely that any further objection of this general kind will pose a serious problem. (As will be seen, there is some overlap between the various objections. But I believe that their main emphases are distinct enough to warrant separate consideration.)

§5.2. THE VERY IDEA OF RATIONAL INSIGHT

The central focus of the first objection to be discussed is the *directness* or *immediacy*, the essentially non-discursive character of rational insight, as contrasted with other sorts of intellectual operations or processes. The basic suggestion, often left fairly implicit, is that while intellectual processes that appeal to criteria or rules or to articulated steps of some kind are thereby rendered intellectually transparent and hence capable of possessing rational force in a comprehensible and plausibly objective way, allegedly direct intellectual insights that involve no such appeal are fundamentally opaque and unacceptably subjective in character. How, it may be asked, can a supposed insight count as rational when it is arrived at on the basis of no intelligible process or objective criterion, no reason that is independently statable, but seemingly amounts merely to a brute subjective conviction? Is not the appeal to such an immediate and not further articulable insight essentially foreign to the very idea of rationality? Such seeming insights may no doubt be subjectively compelling, but, precisely because of their unarticulated character, there can be, it is alleged, no genuine basis for ascribing rational cogency to them – and in particular no reason to think that beliefs adopted in accordance with them are likely to be true.

What the proponents of the objection do not seem to have noticed, however, is that the application of any sort of criterion or the employment of any discursive, stepwise process must ultimately rely on immediate insights of the very same kind that the objection is designed to impugn. In the first place, any criterion or rule itself requires justification, and an eventual appeal to immediate insight is the only alternative to an infinite and vicious regress. Second, less obviously but even more fundamentally, criteria or rules do not, after all, somehow apply themselves. They must be judged or intellectually seen to apply or not to apply, and this judging or seeing can in the end appeal only to the very same sort of rational insight or intuition that the rationalist is advocating.

Though a full discussion of the issues surrounding logical formalism is impossible here, I submit that this is true of the application of even the most severely formal rule of inference. Even to apply as straightforward and seemingly unproblematic a rule as *modus ponens,* I must see or grasp in an immediate, not further reducible way that the three propositions comprising the premises and conclusion are of the right forms and are related in the right way: that, for example, the two simpler propositions in question are in fact identical with the antecedent and consequent of the conditional proposition is as much a necessary, *a priori* knowable truth as anything else. Contrary to the view that seems to be assumed in many discussions, perhaps most commonly in elementary logic books, there is no way to somehow replace this act of insight with a purely mechanical appeal to linguistic forms and linguistic templates without utterly destroying the claim of the inference in question to be genuinely cogent. In many cases, of course, the requisite insight is extremely simple and obvious, making it all too easy to fail to notice that it is required. But the objection that we are presently considering makes no exception for simple and obvious insights, and could not do so without abandoning its central thrust.

The same is even more obviously true for the appeal to discursive, stepwise processes of inference. While it is frequently possible to interpose a series of steps between the premise and conclusion of a previously direct or immediate inference, or similarly to replace a simple propositional insight with a more extended inference involving a number of steps, the cogency of each of the steps must in the end still be recognized or apprehended by immediate insight, as must the new premise or premises in the case where a discursive inference replaces a previous propositional insight. In many such cases, still further steps can be interposed; but although this may be of value in relation to some more specific problem or interest, it clearly does not avoid the general need for rational or intellectual insight to certify each newly added step or premise.

In this way it may be seen that the demand that is implicit in the present objection, namely to somehow find a mode of intellectual process that is entirely a function of criteria, rules, or steps, that is somehow purely discursive in character, requiring no immediate insight or judgment of any kind – in effect, to find a mode of thought that does not require thinking – is futile in principle. As even some moderate empiricists, for example, Quinton,[1] have recognized, this would be true even if the thesis that all *a priori* justified claims are analytic could after all be defended. Indeed, it would be true even if the appeal to *a priori* justification in the sense advocated here were abandoned, so long as any theses going beyond direct observation or any kind of inference or reasoning or allegedly rational transition from one claim or proposition (or set of claims or propositions) to another continued to be accepted. Renouncing the idea of *a priori* justification makes the credentials of such theses or inferences obscure, but

1 See Quinton, "The *a Priori* and the Analytic," in Sleigh (1972), p. 90.

132

as long as some are regarded as acceptable and others not, there will ultimately have to be an appeal to immediate, non-discursive acts of intellectual insight or judgment to distinguish between the two categories.

The upshot is that the present objection, if cogent, would impugn *all* varieties of reasoning or non-observational judgment, including, of course, those that lie behind this very objection itself. This is enough to show that a general skepticism about direct or immediate insight cannot be grounded on the contrast between such insight and supposedly more secure or respectable discursive intellectual processes. Indeed, the conviction that these rule-governed or stepwise intellectual processes are at least sometimes intellectually compelling and conducive to arriving at the truth should seemingly tell in favor of, not against, according the same status to the rational insights that are their essential preconditions.

What emerges from the discussion of this initial objection is that there is no apparent alternative to the reliance on immediate, non-discursive insights of some sort as long as any sort of reasoning or thinking that goes beyond the bounds of direct observation is to be countenanced. This being the case, the immediate and non-discursive character of rational insight cannot by itself provide the basis for a cogent objection to moderate rationalism. But the indispensability of rational insight does not by itself show, of course, that such insights are genuinely cogent or truth-conducive. This underlying skeptical concern is taken up, in somewhat different ways, by the succeeding objections.

§5.3. DOGMATISM AND BIAS

The next objection (or related pair of objections) argues that the moderate rationalist conception of *a priori* justification incorporates insufficient safeguards against abuse, specifically against the dangers of bias and dogmatism. What, the objection asks, is to prevent any person who is emotionally biased or intellectually dogmatic from regarding a claim that seems subjectively compelling to him as a product of such insight? In this way, it is alleged, a would-be rationalism in fact opens the door to the most obvious and blatant kinds of *irrationalism,* and the suggestion is that this risk of abuse makes it unacceptable to regard an apparent rational insight as a genuine reason for thinking that the belief in question is true.

There are two preliminary points that need to be made about this objection. First: It should be noted at the outset that the present objection is arguably dependent for at least much of its perceived force on the previous one. Any sort of intellectual process or method can, after all, be applied in a biased or dogmatic way, and at least part of the reason that this danger is perceived as more threatening here is that in other kinds of cases there is apparently something further to appeal to in seeking to eliminate the influence of bias or dogmatism: one can recheck the steps in the reasoning or re-apply the relevant criteria or rules, and this may seem to provide a kind of rational court of appeal that is lacking in the case of rational insight. We have already seen in the previous section, however, that any such invidious distinction between immediate intellectual insights and more discursive sorts of intellectual processes is ultimately self-defeating, because the latter rely essentially on the former and cannot exist without them. But although this reflection weakens the force of the present objection, something more specific still needs to be said.

Second: In dealing with the problem of bias and dogmatism, it is crucially important to get the issue into clearer focus than is sometimes achieved. Those who raise this problem commonly formulate their objections in relation to an imagined public context of dialogue or argument. What, it is asked, is to prevent an emotionally biased or intellectually dogmatic person from *claiming* in an argumentative context that his favorite view is a product of rational insight and consequently in need of no further defense? It is of course quite true that such a person might make such a claim, and that this would be obviously objectionable, but it is unclear why this fact is supposed to constitute an objection to the idea of rational insight itself. There is, after all, no mode of cognition that is immune to perverse or frivolous claims of this kind. A person may certainly claim to have the rational insight that 2 plus 2 equals 5, but he may also of course claim to have seen a flying saucer or to have discursively proved a theorem that is in fact invalid. Such claims may be highly troublesome and annoying from a practical standpoint, and it may be difficult to deal with them in a way that does not threaten to disrupt the social fabric of argument or communication in which they occur. But it may nonetheless be perfectly clear in a given context that they are insincere, ill-considered, or both, and hence need not be taken seriously from an epistemological standpoint; and there is no apparent reason for thinking that this is somehow less true for claims of rational insight than for cognitive claims of other kinds. And even where the insincerity or frivolousness of the claim is not thus apparent, it would take a highly dubious verificationism or behaviorism to turn this fact into an epistemological objection to the central rationalist thesis.

Thus the sort of case that would pose a genuine epistemological problem would be, not one in which a biased or dogmatic person merely *claims* to have a particular rational insight, but rather one in which such a person sincerely *believes* that he has such an insight, even though the seeming insight in question is in fact merely a product of his bias or dogmatism.

The first thing to note about this sort of possibility is that it is much less pervasively realized than it is often claimed to be. Many, probably most, of the biased or dogmatic claims that someone might be tempted to make will not from the standpoint of the person in question even seem to fit the foregoing specification: despite seeming clearly and obviously true, they will not seem *necessary* in the relevant sense even to him. It is simply not the case that bias and dogmatism typically or even very often take the form of what would amount to hallucinations of necessity. Thus, for example, while a mother's emotional bias may lead her to regard her own child as better-behaved than other children, she is extremely unlikely to regard this fact as metaphysically necessary, if indeed this latter claim even makes clear sense. Similarly, a dogmatic historian can scarcely regard his favorite historical hypothesis as metaphysically necessary; indeed, to do so would prevent it from having the very status that he wants to ascribe to it, that of a well-established historical claim.

But although these observations serve to limit the scope of the problem even further, they do not remove it entirely. It remains possible that bias or dogmatism may on rare occasions take the form in question: one in which they make a claim seem subjectively to be necessary in the relevant sense, even after reasonably careful reflection by the person in question. Such a person, perhaps a mathematician or philosopher whose main subject of inquiry involves judgments of necessity, would thus have an apparent rational insight that was in fact cognitively valueless. And it is thus at least tempting to suppose that apparent rational insights cannot be rationally trusted unless they are somehow certified in advance as unbiased and non-dogmatic by appeal to an independent criterion of some sort, with the satisfaction of that criterion thereby constituting an essential part of the justification of the supposed *a priori* claim.

We have already briefly noticed the general difficulties that arise for such appeal to further criteria (§4.5), and these difficulties will be re-examined later in the present chapter (§5.5). But even apart from those concerns, it is clear that any criterion for the presence or absence of bias or dogmatism in a particular psychological subject would have to be empirical in character, so that construing the appeal to such a criterion as an essential part of the main justifying reason would mean that the justification in question was no longer (fully) *a priori*. Thus a rationalist view of *a priori* justification plainly cannot appeal in this way to an independent criterion in order to solve the present problem. Indeed, we have already seen yet a further reason why such an appeal would be inherently futile: since neither the justification of such a criterion nor its application to a particular case could conceivably be a matter of direct observation, both would have to involve reasoning or non-observational judgment and thus would have to appeal to non-discursive, *a priori* insights of precisely the sort that raise the concern about bias and dogmatism in the first place. And to appeal to that same criterion to resolve these new worries would be both circular (as regards its justification) and viciously regressive (as regards its application). In fact these difficulties are hardly surprising: it is doubtful if there is any cognitive process of at least approximately this level of generality that can be certified as free of bias and dogmatism by appeal to other, entirely independent cognitive processes.

The obvious response here is to appeal, not to external criteria, but to internal correctability: to the possibility and indeed the likelihood that the biased or dogmatic apparent insight can be recognized as such via further reflection and appropriately corrected. A suggestion of bias or dogmatism, whether raised by others or by the very person to whom the proposition appears self-evident, is thus to be viewed as a challenge to the apparent self-evidence in question, a challenge that can be dealt with only by carefully re-examining the proposition to see if it continues to appear self-evident. Coherence can also play an important role here (see the discussion in §4.5), though it clearly does not provide a general solution. Such re-examination is merely one dimension of the careful reflection that is demanded by the very idea of rational insight.

As far as I can see, however, there is no guarantee that all cases of apparent *a priori* insight that result from bias or dogmatism can be discovered and corrected in this way. It is at least possible that a person might have what seems to him to be an apparent rational insight that is in fact a product of bias or dogmatism, but for which the mistake in question is so deeply entrenched in his thinking as to be in practice immune to reflective disclosure. It seems wrong to regard such a person as being justified, *a priori* or otherwise, in holding the resulting belief, in spite of the fact that he will seem to himself to be justified and will not be in any clear sense epistemically blameworthy in making this assessment. I can see no reason to think that such cases are at all common, and it is hard to be very confident that they occur at all. But as long as they cannot be definitively ruled out, we need to ask what a moderate rationalist view should say about them.

It seems to me helpful to regard such cases as at least somewhat analogous to those considered at the end of §4.7, in which apparent rational insights fail to yield justification because, in Burge's phrase, a background condition for the functioning of reason is not satisfied. In a similar way, I suggest, the requirement that one's reason not be irreparably clouded by bias or dogmatism or both, that one be capable of attending in an unbiased and non-dogmatic way to the rational credentials of the claim (or inference) in question, can be viewed as such a background condition, albeit perhaps a somewhat less central one than those discussed earlier. In these terms we can then say that in the rare case where this further condition is not satisfied, the putative justificatory force of the apparent insight in question is again defeated, and no genuine *a priori* justification results, the person's subjective impression to the contrary notwithstanding. As in the other sorts of cases, this requirement of freedom from irreparable bias and dogmatism should not be construed to mean that the satisfaction of this plainly empirical condition is part of the *a priori* reason for a proposition (or inference). When I have the apparent rational insight that nothing can be red all over and green all over at the same time, the cogency of the *a priori* justification that results depends on the fact that the putative insight is not a product of irreparable bias or dogmatism. But the *a priori* justification to which I thus have access still has only to do with the natures of red and green, and not at all with empirical facts about my existence, my consciousness, my grasp of the concept of logical or metaphysical necessity, or my freedom from bias or dogmatism.

It might happen that some particular kind of seeming *a priori* insight turns out to be especially susceptible to this kind of error, something that might be established on the basis of empirical evidence.[2] This would be a reason for no longer accepting apparent insights of the kind in question at face value, for scrutinizing them more carefully, and perhaps even, depending on the further details of the situation, for according them no epistemic weight at all. This is a further way in which the justification provided by rational insight is empirically defeasible (a possibility that we have already acknowledged at a general level).

We have thus seen no reason why the mere possibility of bias and dogmatism should be taken to impugn all claims of rational insight or self-evidence, any more than the possibility of biased perception impugns all perceptual claims. At most it is a reason for additional care and scrutiny, especially in cases where there is reason to think that errors of this kind are especially common.

---

2 Supplemented, as we have seen that it would have to be, by *a priori* reasoning of some sort, probably the sort that underlies induction (see Chapter 7).

The next objection begins from the seemingly undeniable fact that disparities of rational insight, or at least of apparent rational insight, do occur: situations in which a proposition P that seems rationally self-evident to one person either (a) fails to seem rationally self-evident to a second person or else (b) is in clear conflict with something that does seem rationally self-evident to the second person – where the conflicting claim that seems rationally self-evident to the second person might be either *not-P,* the denial or contradictory of the original proposition, or else merely the weaker thesis that *not-P* is possible.[3] How, the objection asks, are such conflicts to be resolved, given the immediate and non-discursive nature of the alleged insight, except via essentially irrational or arational processes like coercion or non-rational persuasion? And if only such non-rational means of persuasion are available to the parties in such a disparity, how can apparent rational insights be taken as good reasons for thinking that the beliefs in question are true? In this way, it is argued, the moderate rationalist view, far from being the embodiment of reason, threatens again to lead to irrationality and intellectual chaos.

Though some historical proponents of rationalism may perhaps have wanted to deny that conflicts of this sort genuinely occur, it seems clear that this is not an adequate response to the problem. Given our earlier terminological stipulation that a genuine rational insight must be a grasp of the necessity of a proposition that really is necessary, it indeed follows (given the principle of contradiction) that at least one of any conflicting pair of alleged rational insights must automatically fail to be genuine. But this sort of terminological legislation obviously provides no way to distinguish genuine insights from merely apparent ones[4] and in any case says nothing about the case where one person has an apparent insight that the other simply fails to share. Thus it does not really speak to the main problem raised by the objection, namely that of how to resolve such

---

3 Or analogously for an inference. The tenability of the distinction between case (a) and case (b) obviously depends on not construing every case in which a person fails to find a claim necessary as one in which he has a conflicting apparent rational insight into the *possibility* of its denial, for on this construal any case where one person has an insight that another fails to share would be a case of conflicting insights. It seems clear enough from an intuitive standpoint, however, that the distinction is genuine, that there are cases of sort (a) that are not cases of sort (b).

4 I assume that the spurious insights which result from uncorrected bias or dogmatism can be dealt with in the way discussed in the previous section.

conflicts in a rational way and what to say about cases where they cannot be thus resolved.

In some cases, of course, it may be possible to resolve an apparent disparity of insight by appeal to an argument whose premises and inferential steps are certified by shared rational insights, or perhaps by appeal to a version of coherence that is grounded in such shared insights. But there is no very apparent reason for thinking that such a resolution will always be available in the sort of case in question, and still less for thinking that it somehow *must* be available. The moderate rationalist must thus concede that disparities of the sort needed to pose the problem may and very likely do occur: cases where each of two (or more) people sincerely and reflectively differ, in one of the ways we have distinguished, on an issue of rational insight, and where the conflict is ultimate in the sense of not being resolvable by appeal to further rational insights that are shared.[5]

To say that the disparity is in this sense ultimate, however, is not yet to say that rational means of resolving it have been exhausted, so that only flattery, threats of violence, and the like remain available as means of persuasion. One obvious possibility in such a case is that the individuals in question have failed to adequately understand the claim or claims in question and that there is some way of clarifying or refining the contents of the insight or insights that will remove the appearance of disparity or conflict. This familiar possibility is often spoken of as "clarification of meaning." But although the elimination of strictly linguistic ambiguity or vagueness may occasionally be involved, it is unlikely to be central. The main sort of clarification at issue will instead involve refining and distinguishing subtleties and nuances of content that have little essential relation to language, though language must of course be involved in conveying them. There can be little doubt that apparent disparities of insight are often eliminated in this way.

A further possibility in the same general vicinity is what might be called "talking around" the issue: attempting through rephrasing, examples, analogies, contrasting cases, and similar devices to display the alleged insight or insights more fully or present problems for a competing insight. Such discussion may of course lead to the discovery of a relevant discursive

---

5 It is of course also possible, though perhaps less common, for one person to have conflicting apparent insights, either at the same time or at different times, or to have an insight at one time and fail to have it at a later time (the opposite case is obviously less troubling). But these sorts of cases are closely enough parallel to the multi-person cases not to require separate consideration.

argument, but its helpfulness in resolving the disparity is not confined to the cases where this occurs. What may happen instead is that as the parties to the dispute are led in this way to think in further and different ways about the issue, the original apparent insight or insights that were the basis of the disparity either dissolve entirely or come to have a significantly different content, so that the disparity is once again resolved. Here we have what amounts to a multi-person version of the sort of rational re-examination that was discussed earlier as a means of eliminating errors among a single person's apparent rational insights.

There is obviously once again no guarantee that such a solution will emerge. But reflection on actual cases seems to suggest strongly that if both parties enter into this process seriously and in good faith, it is quite unlikely that the apparent insight or insights in question will emerge sufficiently unscathed to preserve the conflict. Thus it is simply not true that the absence of relevant shared premises must result in either stalemate or the employment of non-rational means of persuasion.

Suppose, however, at least for the sake of the argument, that despite the best efforts of both parties, none of these possible ways of eliminating a given disparity of insight actually succeeds. Suppose, that is, that after all reasonable efforts toward such a resolution have been made, the two parties still find themselves either (a) with a clear and unshaken apparent insight on the part of one that the other is not able to see or (b) with two clear and unshaken apparent insights into the necessity of seemingly incompatible claims. Cases of the former sort seem relatively rare, and those of the latter sort, rarer still. But there is no apparent way to rule them out entirely, and thus we need to consider how the rationalist might deal with them.

It is clear that these cases are not to be assimilated to those considered earlier in this chapter and in Chapter 4 in which a background condition for the functioning of reason may fail to be satisfied. That other people do or do not agree is surely not a necessary condition for the proper functioning of my reason. But the failure of others, in these different ways, to agree may constitute evidence against the genuineness of my apparent rational insight, evidence that might in some cases be strong enough to defeat it. Whether this is so will depend substantially on the further circumstances of the case.

Consider first cases of sort (a), which we may refer to as cases of *mere disparity:* cases where one person has an apparent insight that the second person fails to share but without the second person having a conflicting apparent insight. Is the person who has the apparent insight still justified *a priori* in accepting the claim (or inference) in question?

It is a familiar, albeit perhaps not entirely satisfactorily explained fact that rational insights are not easily arrived at and are often easy to miss. Especially with regard to claims or inferences of substantial complexity, it seems intuitively to be often the case that one person grasps or apprehends a necessary connection that eludes others, at least for a time. This is less common where serious efforts of the sorts discussed earlier in this section to elucidate the claim in question have been made, but still seemingly common enough. For this reason, the fact that another person fails to share an insight that I believe myself to have is not in itself a very strong reason for thinking that my insight is not genuine. Such a situation is surely a reason for re-examination, but if the insight in question continues to seem clear and solid, the failure of another person to share it does not seem in general sufficient to defeat it. (One obviously relevant factor here is the extent to which a plausible explanation for the other person's failure to agree is available.)

On the other hand, the longer the situation persists (given continued effort and examination by the dissenting person) or the more people that are involved (given adequate understanding and effort on their part), the more serious the challenge to the apparent rational insight becomes. Also, the simpler the apparent insight, the harder it becomes to understand how it could be missed, and again the more serious the challenge. And so the point may be reached at which the presence of dissenting opinions meeting these various conditions makes it empirically more likely than not that the original apparent insight is mistaken, thus defeating the justification that it would otherwise have provided.[6] But such a situation is inherently problematic and unstable so long as the original insight continues to appear clear and unshaken: how can one reject a claim that continues to seem clearly and plainly self-evident without thereby impugning rational insights generally – including those that, as we have seen, are inevitably needed to undergird the empirical counter-argument? About the only thing one can do is to "bracket" the issue and hope for some further development. Fortunately, such situations are in general quite rare.

Something analogous should also be said about cases of sort (b), cases of *actual conflict*, the difference being that the presence of a conflicting insight presents a much more serious challenge, since the possibility that the second person has simply failed to notice the point is no longer available. In such a case, each of the two knows: (i) that at least one of them is

---

6 As noted several times before, the justification for such a non-observational claim would itself have to be partially *a priori* in character.

mistaken (assuming that the rational insights according to which the competing claims are incompatible are not themselves in doubt); and (ii) that each of them has what seems to him a compelling reason for thinking that it is the other person that is mistaken. This surely constitutes a significant empirical reason for each of them to believe that he himself may well be the mistaken one, thus tending to defeat the justificatory force of his own insight. Where the situation is as described above, that is, where all possible efforts at clarification, elucidation, and re-examination have been made, the correct result seems to be that neither of the competing claims emerges as justified. Again, the situation is inherently unstable and problematic until some further resolution is reached. And again, such situations are extremely rare, albeit quite conspicuous when they do occur.[7]

Such situations of unresolved disparity or conflict are thus quite unsatisfactory from an epistemological standpoint, and it is fortunate that they are quite uncommon. The crucial point, however, is that there is no clear reason why the possibility or even the very occasional actuality of such cases should be taken to destroy the justificatory force of apparent rational insight in general, even in the multitude of cases where no such conflict is present – especially since, as we have already seen, the empirical challenge that they present must inevitably depend on other apparent rational insights. The mere possibility of such cases shows beyond question that rational insight cannot be regarded as infallible and would therefore constitute a decisive objection against those strong versions of rationalism that made such a claim. But it provides no clear basis for an objection to the more moderate form of rationalism being advocated here. (There is again a useful analogy with the status of sensory observation: while such observation is by no means immune to conflicts of an analogous sort, presumably no one takes this as a reason for a general denial of its epistemic force.[8])

§5.5. THE DEMAND FOR METAJUSTIFICATION

The penultimate epistemological objection is also the most straightforward, and can be seen to underlie several of those considered so far. It

---

7 The referee suggests that they are not rare in philosophy. I think that this is wrong, that even in philosophy cases of the sort described occur against the backdrop of an enormously larger number of cases in which rational insights agree. But I do agree that such cases and also the previously discussed sort of case where one person has an apparent insight that another fails to have are substantially more common in philosophy than in many other areas – and of course it is the issues where such disagreement exists that are the most widely discussed.
8 Tony Anderson suggested making this comparison.

challenges the moderate rationalist to offer a second-order reason or justification for thinking that accepting beliefs on the basis of apparent rational insight or apparent self-evidence is likely at least to lead to believing the truth. Without such a reason, it is claimed, the supposed *a priori* justification that results from rational insight will simply not count as justification in the relevant epistemic sense, and accepting beliefs on that basis will accordingly be quite irrational from an epistemic standpoint. To adopt a term that I have employed elsewhere, what is being demanded is a *metajustification* for accepting *a priori* insight as a source of epistemic justification.[9]

The demand for a metajustification is in effect a demand for an overarching premise or principle to the effect that beliefs which are the contents of apparent *a priori* insights – and perhaps which also meet some specifiable set of further criteria intended to distinguish genuine rational insights from merely apparent ones – are likely to be true. The implicit suggestion is that one who accepts a claim on the basis of such insight must be appealing, at least tacitly, to a premise of this sort as an essential part of the alleged justifying reason in order for a justification that is genuinely epistemic in character to even putatively result. And the obvious problem posed by such a view, already briefly noticed earlier, is that there is clearly no way in which the rationalist can hope to provide justification for such a premise itself. To construe it as justified empirically, for example, by finding that claims that are the contents of apparent rational insights are mostly true and generalizing inductively, is to abandon any claim to *a priori* justification: if it is essentially dependent in this way on an empirically justified premise, the justification of the original claim would be empirical as well. But to argue that the metajustificatory premise is justified *a priori* results in obvious circularity, since that premise would then in effect have to be appealed to for its own justification. Thus, if such a premise is indeed necessary in the way alleged, the rationalist view collapses.[10]

9 See *SEK*, §§1.3 and 8.1. One objection that is frequently leveled against the overall argument of *SEK* is that the argument offered there against foundationalism for empirical knowledge (chapters 2–4) is inconsistent with the subsequent acceptance of foundationalism in the case of *a priori* knowledge (appendix A), in that the metajustification that is demanded in the former case is not demanded in the latter. This objection has never seemed to me very compelling in itself, since the two kinds of knowledge are different enough that what holds for one need not hold for the other. But see note 11 for some further discussion of this issue.

10 As I have tried to make clear in the foregoing discussion, this problem arises only if the appeal to the metajustificatory premise is construed as an essential part of the original, first-order justification for the supposedly *a priori* claim. There is no problem with a metajustificatory premise or argument (for which the term 'metajustification' would in

Before speaking to this objection directly, it is worth noticing how strong, perhaps implausibly strong, the demand for metajustification really is. It might be thought, for example, that the traditional rationalist view that claimed infallibility for *a priori* insight could at least have met this demand, however vulnerable it may have been from other directions, but this would be a mistake. It is true that the premise that rational insight is infallible, that is, that every apparent rational insight is a genuine one, would, if somehow established, provide an excellent, indeed a conclusive metajustificatory reason for regarding the contents of such apparent insights as true. But the same problem would arise as to how this version of the metajustificatory premise is itself to be justified, and the available alternatives would be no more palatable to the rationalist than before.

Indeed, even if worries about circularity are put aside, it is very hard to see how the thesis of infallibility could have been claimed with any plausibility to be justified *a priori*, at least as long as *a priori* insight is something that we are supposed to be able to recognize from a subjective standpoint. How, after all, could it plausibly be regarded as a metaphysically necessary truth that finite beings of a specified kind, operating in a subjectively recognizable way, never make mistakes? And since this sort of reflection is by no means obviously restricted in its application to the strong claim of infallibility, it suggests an even deeper way in which, if such a metajustificatory premise is indeed required as a part of the original supposedly *a priori* justification, the rationalist conception of *a priori* justification verges on total incoherence: that beings like ourselves have rational insights that are even generally correct or, weaker still, correct more often than not (which seems the least that a claim of epistemic justification can tolerate) does not appear to be even an initially plausible candidate for the status of metaphysical necessity. Indeed, this would still be true even if the objects of *a priori* insight were required to be (apparently) analytic, as a fallibilist version of moderate empiricism would have to say: even claims of analyticity can be mistaken; and that beings like ourselves are more often correct than mistaken in making them would once again seemingly have to be a contingent and thus an empirical claim, albeit perhaps, on a such a view, an extremely plausible one.

The upshot of these reflections is that if a metajustification is indeed essential to the original *a priori* justification in the way alleged by the

fact be more appropriate) that is not claimed to have this status. I am indebted to the referee for firmly insisting on this point, though he may still not be satisfied with all that I say here.

present objection, then the very idea of *a priori* justification, whether given a rationalist (moderate or immoderate) or moderate empiricist construal, turns out to be impossible or incoherent in a simple and extremely straightforward way: supposedly *a priori* claims would require for their justification a supplementary premise that could only be empirical. But even a convinced radical empiricist should, I think, be dissatisfied with a victory that comes as cheaply and easily as this. While we can perhaps understand how the idea of *a priori* justification might turn out to be incoherent in some relatively deep or complicated way, it seems difficult or impossible to believe that there is not even a *prima facie* coherent concept that generations of rationalists and moderate empiricists could have had in mind. And this in turn is a powerful, albeit indirect reason for doubting the legitimacy of the demand for metajustification that underlies the present objection.

In addition, there is a more direct reason for regarding the demand for a metajustification of the appeal to rational insight as misconceived, and indeed as ultimately question-begging, when employed as the basis for an objection to rationalism. The dialectical picture that such a demand in effect assumes is one in which apparent rational insight has no epistemic value in itself, but instead functions merely as a kind of earmark or symptom for picking out a class of believed propositions that the supposedly required metajustificatory premise then tells us are, on some independent ground, likely to be true. That the earmark in question consists, in whole or in part, in the believed proposition seeming, after careful consideration, to be logically or metaphysically necessary plays no essential role in the envisaged justification. The ultimate reason for accepting such a proposition, on this view, is not that it seems to be necessary, but just that it has a feature (any subjectively identifiable feature would do) that there is some independent metajustificatory ground for regarding as a reliable index of truth.

But from the standpoint depicted in the previous chapter, this is obviously the wrong picture and amounts simply and obviously to a refusal to take rational insight seriously as a basis for justification: a refusal for which the present objection can offer no further rationale, and which is thus question-begging. As discussed above, when I consider, for example, the proposition that nothing can be red and green all over at the same time, my intuitively apparent reason for accepting this proposition as true is that I see or grasp or apprehend, or at least seem to myself to see or grasp or apprehend, that it must be true in any possible world or situation – or, equivalently, that I am unable to understand how it could be false, unable

145

to make intelligible sense of a falsifying situation. As remarked earlier, this seems intuitively to be in itself an excellent reason for accepting such a claim, one that does not in any obvious way need to be supplemented by an overarching metajustificatory premise of the sort being considered in the present section. This intuitive assessment may, of course, be mistaken. But this must be shown rather than simply being assumed, which is what in effect occurs when it is claimed without further defense that a meta-justificatory premise of this sort is required.

This amounts to saying that according to the moderate rationalist position, each instance of apparent rational insight or apparent self-evidence, each alleged case of *a priori* justification, should be construed as *epistemically autonomous,* as dependent on nothing beyond itself for its justification.[11] We have already conceded that such justification is fallible. In addition, we have seen, in §§4.5 and 4.6, that it may be only initial or *prima facie* in the sense that it is capable of being overturned by further *a priori* reflection, by considerations of coherence, or by (partly) empirical considerations. But this does not alter the fact that apparent rational insight is, according to the moderate rationalist, sufficient by itself to justify the claim so long as these sorts of countervailing considerations do not arise. Such a view of the epistemic status of rational insight is at least *prima facie* plausible in light of

11 Might a similar claim be made on behalf of the empirically basic beliefs advocated by empirical foundationalism, contrary to the criticism of foundationalist views that I offered in *SEK*? Such basic beliefs result from my coming to believe, presumably as a result of perceptual or introspective or some other sort of experience, that some contingent claim is true. My earlier argument was that being contingent, the claim in question cannot be genuinely *self*-evident (though that term is sometimes, misleadingly, employed): its content cannot offer, by itself, any intellectually accessible reason for thinking that it is true or likely to be true. Therefore, there must be some further feature of the belief in question that indicates that this claim, as contrasted with others having analogous sorts of content, is true or likely to be true. And hence, it was claimed, some reason is needed for thinking that beliefs with that feature embody claims that are true or likely to be true, thus leading to the need for a metajustification. In particular, if the appeal is to the experience that produces or motivates the belief, then some reason is needed for thinking that believing on the basis of such an experience is likely to lead to the truth. And thus, it was claimed, no contingent, empirical belief is capable of being epistemically autonomous.

I still believe this argument to be correct, and indeed decisive, for most versions of empirical foundationalism. But there is one version that now seems to me to escape its force: the version in which the allegedly basic beliefs are simply reports that conscious experiences of various sorts have occurred. In that case, and in that case only, the experiences themselves seem to provide good, indeed the best possible, reasons for thinking that the beliefs are true, reasons of which I am aware simply by virtue of having those experiences, and which do not in any apparent way require the support of a further metajustification. But a development and assessment of this view is obviously a task for another occasion.

examples like those discussed in the previous chapter, and we have so far seen no compelling reason for giving it up. And if such a thesis of epistemic autonomy is correct, then there is no legitimacy to the demand for a metajustification.

Thus the present objection fails because the demand for metajustification that underlies it turns out to simply beg the question of whether rational insight or self-evidence can constitute, as the rationalist claims, a genuine and autonomous basis for epistemic justification.

§5.6. THE EPISTEMOLOGICAL CASE FOR RATIONALISM: OVERVIEW AND SUMMARY

There is one final objection to be discussed in the present chapter, one which although possessing an obvious epistemological dimension is less narrowly epistemological than those considered so far. Before turning to this last objection, however, I want to reflect a bit further on those that have been discussed up to this point and on the character of the responses that have been offered. This will lead to some further reflections on both the nature and inherent limitations of the argument for moderate rationalism.

Each of the objections discussed so far questions whether the existence of an apparent rational insight really provides, as claimed by the moderate rationalist, a good reason for thinking that the proposition that is its content is true. Several initially different reasons were offered for doubting that this is so: the immediate, non-discursive character of the alleged reason; the threat of bias and/or dogmatism and the absence of an independent criterion for excluding them; the absence of an independent standard for resolving conflicts; and, most fundamentally, the absence and indeed impossibility of a non-question-begging metajustificatory argument. My response to these objections has been essentially defensive and dialectical in character, with the core point being that the demand, explicit in the final objection but implicit to some degree in each of the others, for the inclusion as an essential element in the supposed *a priori* justification of an independent criterion or standard or metajustificatory premise for determining when and why an apparent rational insight should be accepted is itself unjustified and ultimately question-begging against the rationalist. A second theme has been the invocation of various conditions, themselves empirical and contingent in character, under which seeming *a priori* justification would be defeated, even though the absence of those conditions is not to be regarded as part of the *a priori* justification in question.

But though this response and the more detailed discussions that embody it seem to me correct as far as they go, they may appear unsatisfying in a way that still needs to be addressed. Even if there is no conceivable alternative to reasons of an immediate non-discursive sort, and even if it is both futile and illegitimate to demand as a part of the original *a priori* justification a further independent standard or criterion for excluding bias and dogmatism, for resolving conflicts, or for providing a metajustification, it still seems possible to simply question or doubt whether accepting apparent rational insights is indeed conducive to arriving at the truth and to point out that no clear positive reason, over and above appeal to intuitions about particular cases, has yet been offered for an affirmative answer. Even if the demand for including in this way a further criterion or standard is indeed dialectically illegitimate, this essentially negative point does not constitute such a positive reason.

What the foregoing considerations seem to me to show, in first approximation, is that the appeal to apparent rational insight is epistemologically so basic and fundamental as not to admit of any sort of independent justification. But while I believe that there is a correct and important point to be made here, it is one that needs to be carefully focused and clarified if it is not to be misleading. It seems obvious that some mode of justification (perhaps more than one) must have this status, that it is impossible for each mode to be justified by appeal to others.[12] It also seems clear that the appeal to apparent rational insight is a plausible candidate for such a role, both intuitively and dialectically, and indeed that it has no apparent rival for this status.

The foregoing is not intended as an argument (which would of course be question-begging) to show that conferring this foundational status on apparent rational insight is likely to lead to believing the truth. What it does show, I believe, is something like this: apart perhaps from direct observation, narrowly construed, we have no conception at all of what a standard of epistemic justification that did not appeal to apparent rational insight would even look like. This is also not intended to be an instance of the long-discredited paradigm case argument. A skepticism that holds that the only standard of epistemic justification that we can understand is nonetheless incorrect, not conducive to finding the truth, remains dialectically tenable. But a fundamental standard of justification that is intuitively

---

12 Some may want to appeal to coherence at this point, but this overlooks the fact that coherence depends essentially on principles, such as the principle of non-contradiction and others, that must be justified in some other way.

plausible, dialectically defensible, and to which there is no apparent alternative, though it may not be all that we could ask for, is almost certainly all that we can ever hope to have. My claim is that the standard advocated by the moderate rationalist view has this status.

§5.7. CONCEPTS AND REALITY

There is one more broadly epistemological objection to moderate rationalism, or at least one more anti-rationalist line of thought, that needs to be discussed, one that could perhaps be advanced on either epistemological or metaphysical grounds. I hesitate to call it an objection, because that label suggests more specificity, both of content and of argument, than is usually present. What is at issue is rather more like a vague background assumption or attitude regarding *a priori* justification, one that may indeed in some cases amount to little more than a favored manner of formulating more specific issues. But the assumption or attitude in question nonetheless amounts, if taken seriously, to a thorough repudiation of rationalism, no less threatening for being relatively unarticulated and undefended.

I offer two samples of the assumption or attitude in question, chosen almost at random from the large number available in the recent philosophical literature. In *A Treatise on Space and Time*, J. R. Lucas, in discussing the issue of the direction of time, formulates one sub-issue as follows:

we might wonder whether our temporal experience might not differ in other, more radical, ways from person to person, and in particular, whether its direction might not be different for different people. Could we not, in a looking-glass land, meet people whose temporal experience ran in the opposite direction to ours? We know that in practice we do not, but it is not immediately obvious whether this is just a brute empirical fact, or a conceptual necessity of some sort.[13]

My concern is with the final sentence of this passage. The obvious issue is whether the two alternatives offered are genuinely exhaustive – or perhaps instead whether the latter alternative means what it seems to mean. Lucas's question about time is plainly metaphysical in character: might the direction of experiential time be different for different people? Thus it is surely natural and initially plausible to construe the necessity in question as a *metaphysical* necessity pertaining to the nature either of time or of temporal experience. Lucas's formulation in terms of *conceptual* necessity suggests on the contrary, without quite saying, that the necessity pertains *solely* to our concepts, rather than to the metaphysical reality itself. To be sure, the employment of this sort of phrasing (which pervades Lucas's generally

13 Lucas (1973), pp. 44–5.

excellent book) may not be intended to be taken so seriously, and indeed there is some evidence that it is not so intended, that it represents more an almost unconscious mannerism of formulation than a considered conviction. But this does not alter the suggestion that his words convey: that *a priori* arguments of the sort that he proceeds to offer tell us only about our *concepts* and not about reality.

For a more considered and explicit version of the same idea, we may turn to Michael Dummett. At the very beginning of his William James Lectures, he remarks, almost in passing:

> although we [contemporary analytic philosophers] no longer regard the traditional questions of philosophy as pseudo-questions to which no meaningful answer can be given, we have not returned to the belief that a priori reasoning can afford us substantive knowledge of fundamental features of the world. Philosophy can take us no further than enabling us to command a clear view of the concepts by means of which we think about the world, and by doing so, to attain a firmer grasp of the way we represent the world in our thought.[14]

Here the view in question is quite clear and unmistakable: *a priori* philosophical argument cannot tell us about independent *reality*, but only about our subjective (though for Dummett necessarily shared) *concepts*.

Anyone who has read at all widely in recent analytic philosophy will have no trouble coming up with further examples of this assumption or attitude, which indeed seems very often to be regarded as a mere truism. What needs to be asked is what the rationale for this pervasive view is supposed to be and, even more urgently, what the view in question really amounts to. But I should confess in advance that I am able to find no very satisfying answer to either of these questions.

The view in question could be construed as a lingering relic of moderate empiricism: if *a priori* claims are justified merely by appeal to our definitions or linguistic conventions, then it is plausible enough, as we have seen, to think that they tell us nothing about metaphysically independent reality. But we have seen that such a general view of *a priori* justification is thoroughly untenable. Moreover, it is a striking fact that the assumption or attitude with which we are presently concerned is often held by philosophers who make no very specific appeal to analyticity.

Clearly the main difficulty in trying to understand and assess such a view is to get clearer about what sort of thing a *concept* is supposed to be. While it is clear enough that concepts are at least roughly the philosophical descendants of the *ideas* invoked by earlier philosophers like Locke, and also that

14 Dummett (1991), p. 1.

talk of concepts (or ideas or notions) often seems virtually unavoidable in philosophical discourse, none of that helps in any very immediate way to clarify exactly what such talk is about. Perhaps the clearest point of agreement is that the possession of the concept of an X by a person is to be identified with that person's having a certain cluster of intellectual abilities: the ability to think of X's, to classify things as X's, and, in some cases at least, to recognize X's in appropriate circumstances. But none of this makes it very clear how a concept can be itself an object of knowledge in a way that makes knowledge of concepts an alternative to knowledge of the world.

I am inclined to think that there is no very clear sense to be made of this idea. To have a concept is, as the foregoing suggests, to have the ability to represent and think about a certain property, relation, kind of thing, or whatever – where the item in question is usually represented as a feature or aspect of the objective world, of *an sich* reality. Thus if I have the concept of red, I have therewith the ability to think of things as red, to reflect on the property redness, and normally at least to recognize things as red. There is nothing wrong with saying that my rational insight or justified belief that, for example, nothing can be red all over and green all over at the same time pertains to my concept of red (or redness), but this means merely, I suggest, that it pertains to the putatively objective property that I represent, not that it pertains to some distinct subjective entity, whose nature and metaphysical status would be extremely puzzling.

It is possible, of course, either: (a) that the property that I represent is not in fact instantiated at all in the world; or, less drastically, (b) that although it is instantiated, I misrepresent it in some significant way. (I am not suggesting that the distinction between these two possibilities is sharp.) In case (a), my *a priori* justification still pertains to the world, albeit hypothetically: I am still justified *a priori* in thinking that no world can contain something that is red and green all over at the same time, and hence that this one does not. In case (b), if the misrepresentation affects the claim in question, then my claim is mistaken (though perhaps still justified if carefully arrived at, etc.); but this has no tendency, as far as I can see, to show that it is in any interesting sense a claim merely about my concept and not about the world. And, more importantly, even if someone insisted on characterizing either of these sorts of cases in this misleading way, there would be no justification at all for generalizing this to all cases of *a priori* justification and knowledge.

The foregoing is the best that I am presently able to do in trying to make sense of the idea that *a priori* justification pertains only to concepts and not to the world. Such justification, like all epistemic justification, pertains to properties, relations, and perhaps other sorts of features or elements that I represent the world as containing, and the possibility always exists that my representations are either inaccurate or entirely mistaken. But there is no apparent reason for thinking that the existence of this skeptical possibility shows that *a priori* justification, even in cases where no such misrepresentation is involved, pertains to something other than the world – even if we could figure out what that other something is supposed to be. (It is worth noting that while these possibilities of misrepresentation affect empirical justification at least as much, this produces no apparent tendency to say that empirical justification really pertains to concepts rather than to independent reality.)[15]

My conclusion is that a moderate rationalism of the sort described here does not face any insuperable objections of an epistemological kind. It is, to be sure, unfortunate that our apparent rational insights are not infallible (as it is similarly unfortunate that our capacities are limited in numerous other respects). But the fact that our powers of rational thought are imperfect and do not guarantee success is hardly a reason for giving up rational thought altogether, which is what the rejection of rationalism, if consistently carried through (even in the absence of any reason to be consistent!) would arguably amount to.

There are still, however, the distinctively metaphysical objections to rationalism to be considered. These will be the subject of the next chapter.

15 Another idea lurking in the vicinity, though one that is unlikely to be shared by all proponents of the view or attitude that is my concern in the text, is the quasi-Kantian idea that concepts *necessarily* falsify the reality that they attempt to depict, i.e., that any thinking being (or perhaps any such being at all like us) will inevitably misrepresent in certain pervasive ways the features of the world that he attempts to represent. I will only say here that I can find no intelligible rationale of any sort for such a view.

6

Metaphysical objections to rationalism

§6.1. INTRODUCTION

The main conclusion of the preceding chapter was that the distinctively epistemological objections to rationalism, while perhaps not entirely without force, are very far from being decisive. Indeed, it is more natural to construe the epistemological objections, taken as a group, as merely revealing various limitations of our *a priori* capacities. These limitations are no doubt unfortunate, but they cannot plausibly be construed as serious reasons for taking the quixotic step of abandoning rational thought altogether, or at least any claim of cogency on its behalf – which is what we have seen that the rejection of rationalism would amount to.

In any case, though such a conjecture would be impossible to verify, it seems to me likely that the reasons for the widespread dismissal of rationalism lie on the metaphysical rather than the epistemological side of the ledger. I have already voiced the suspicion that the intellectual motives for the rejection of rationalism lie more in the realm of fashion than of argument, but even the relevant fashions seem primarily metaphysical in character. My purpose in this chapter is to examine and evaluate some of these metaphysical fashions and objections.

As was the case with the epistemological objections, the metaphysical objections to rationalism are only rarely spelled out and developed in any detail. It is clear, however, that most of them can be viewed as specific instances of one general claim: that rationalism is incompatible with allegedly well-established theses about the nature and limitations of human beings and human intellectual processes. These theses may take the form of sweeping, general claims, such as the vaunted theses of materialism (or physicalism) and naturalism, or they may be much more specific in character.

There are three general difficulties, worth noting at the outset, that apply in varying degrees to most of these objections. First, the characterizations of many of the supposedly incompatible theses are seriously vague or obscure (or both), making it difficult to be very sure what they really amount to. This is true of materialism and even more of naturalism, views which, despite their widespread acceptance or at least apparent acceptance, are very difficult to define clearly. Materialism presumably says that everything that exists is material or physical in character, but the precise boundaries of the material or physical are rendered seriously obscure by the expectation of continued progress in physics and related sciences: if some radically new kind of entity or process is discovered in the future, one that stands to physical reality as presently conceived in something like the way that electromagnetic waves stood to the seventeenth-century corpuscular conception of physical reality, what exactly will decide whether or not an acceptance of these new items is compatible with materialism? And naturalism is even more vague and diffuse, so much so as to make it doubtful that there is one central thesis that the various supposed proponents of naturalism could all agree upon.

Second, it is often unclear just how and why the allegedly well-established theses in question are supposed to be incompatible with rationalism, making it often very hard to assess the force of the supposed objections, even if the theses themselves were to be accepted. This is in part a result of the vagueness and obscurity already alluded to, but it is also attributable in part, it must be admitted, to a good deal of uncertainty about what precisely the metaphysical commitments of rationalism might be. Like the preceding difficulty, and in large part as a result of it, this second difficulty also applies most obviously to the objections that are based on the more sweeping and general of the supposedly conflicting theses.

Third, though the theses in question are often treated as though they were obvious and unproblematic, the precise nature of the evidence or other basis for accepting them is often very uncertain. Not surprisingly, this also tends once again to be especially true of the more sweeping and general ones.

Most of this chapter will be devoted to a detailed consideration of two specific objections of this sort. But there is no space here for a detailed discussion of materialism or naturalism in general, and thus it is fortunate that there is a general rejoinder available, growing out of the third of the foregoing problems, that applies to all objections of this general form, a rejoinder that seems to me to be in fact completely decisive by itself.

The rejoinder in question is essentially just a specific application of the general argument for *a priori* justification that was offered in §1.1. The first thing to note is that the various theses in question are all both clearly synthetic in character and also sufficiently abstract and general to preclude any possibility of construing them as a product of direct experience or direct observation. Thus, if we ask what reason there is to think that these theses are true, there are apparently only three possible answers: The first is that there is no such reason, in which case the objection collapses because its central premise is unsupported. The second answer is that the claims in question are justified via inference from experiential or observational premises. But, as we saw in the earlier discussion, any such inference must rely, at least implicitly, on some premise or principle connecting the relevant observations with the intended conclusion. This premise or principle will not itself be a matter of direct experience or observation, so it will have to be justified *a priori* if there is to be any reason for accepting it. The third possible answer, of course, is that the claims in question are themselves justified *a priori*. On either of the last two alternatives, therefore, the claims in question cannot provide reasons for ruling out *a priori* justification without entirely undercutting their own alleged justification. If the objection in question is otherwise forceful, it becomes in effect impossible that there could be a good reason for thinking that the allegedly factual premise to which it appeals is true: to suppose that there is such a reason leads, via the argument of the objection itself, to the conclusion that the reason in question was not a good one after all.

This general line of argument may seem entirely too easy, and proponents of the views in question are likely to be annoyed rather than persuaded by it in much the same way that the early positivists were annoyed by questions about the verifiability of the verification principle. I make no apology for this. It is a conspicuous feature of the contemporary philosophical scene that claims are made in metaphysics and other areas without giving adequate attention to the epistemological issue of how they might be justified, and that this uncritical practice makes the rejection of many traditional views and especially of rationalism seem enormously more palatable than it otherwise would. The line of argument just appealed to is the best corrective to this pervasive tendency and should, I believe, be invoked as often as necessary to do the job. Moreover, in addition to being an expression of the third of the general problems with metaphysical objections to rationalism outlined above, it also has the virtue of making an assessment of the other two far less urgent. Once we see on these general grounds that the theses that fuel the objections to rationalism cannot be both well-established and genuinely in conflict with rationalism, it becomes far less pressing to decide what they really amount to or whether the alleged objections would be cogent if the theses in question were known to be true.

But although my own view is that the foregoing counterobjection is in fact decisive against all metaphysical objections to rationalism, it would be unwise to rely on it exclusively. Moreover, a more specific consideration of two of the metaphysical objections will also contribute toward a better understanding of the moderate rationalist view itself. The first of these two objections will be considered in the next section and the second in the balance of the chapter.

§6.2. THE CAUSAL OBJECTION

One of the most influential and widely discussed of the specific objections to rationalism grows out of an argument offered by Paul Benacerraf, in his paper "Mathematical Truth."[1] As the title of the article suggests, Benacerraf's concern is with mathematics specifically, rather than *a priori* knowledge generally. Moreover, he is concerned not so much with rationalism for its own sake, but rather with rationalism as the presumptive epistemological adjunct of something like Platonism as an account of mathematical truth. But the objection that he makes to mathematical rationalism, that is, to the appeal to mathematical intuition, can be extended to rationalist *a priori* knowledge and justification generally, and it has frequently been invoked in this broader form by others. Thus I will focus here on the more general version of the objection.

Construed in this broader way, the objection in question involves two main components, each of which will require some preliminary elucidation. The first is the idea that a necessary condition for knowledge or even for justification is the existence of a causal connection between the belief in question and the object or situation to which the supposed knowledge pertains; while the second is the idea that the objects of the rational insight advocated by the rationalist must be construed as abstract, Platonistic entities, and hence as incapable of entering into causal relations. The indicated conclusion is then that rationalist-style *a priori* insight could not possibly yield knowledge or justification.

We may begin with the first of these components. Why should it be thought that knowledge and justification require such a causal connection? There are many possible ways of defending this claim. Some of these would invoke epistemological views like externalism or reliabilism, while

1 Reprinted in Benacerraf & Putnam (1983), pp. 403–20.

156

others would appeal once again to general metaphysical views like materialism or naturalism. Most of these views seem to me highly questionable, but a full discussion of them is impossible here.[2] Fortunately, however, there is a more general and substantially less problematic line of argument available for a somewhat weakened version of this requirement, one which has the virtue of making the requirement directly applicable to justification, thus allowing us to largely circumvent the difficult further issues raised by the concept of knowledge.

To approach this argument, suppose that there is a person who holds a belief that is at least putatively about some specifiable element or region of reality, for reasons or evidence that seem initially substantial and compelling, but where neither the specific content of the belief nor the person's reasons for holding it are in fact causally shaped or otherwise influenced, directly or indirectly, by the element or region of reality in question. In such a situation, though the belief might still be true, it seems clear that its truth could only be accidental, a cognitive coincidence. One suggestive way to put the matter is to say that in the absence of such influence, the character of the reality in question could just as well have been different in such a way as to make the belief false without either the belief or its supporting reasons being affected in any way, showing that the existence of the belief and the presence of those reasons is entirely compatible, logically and even probabilistically, with the belief's being false.[3] It is arguable, for the sorts of reasons displayed in the Gettier problem,[4] that such a person would not have knowledge, even if the belief were in fact true and no matter how apparently compelling the reasons or evidence might seem. But it is sufficient for our purposes to point out that if the person himself were aware of this situation, that is, aware that there was no relation of influence between the element or region of reality in question and his belief and reasons, the belief would no longer be epistemically justified for him because his apparent reasons would no longer constitute for him a genuine basis for thinking that it was true.[5] This does not show that a

---

2 See the items mentioned in note 1 of Chapter 1 for further discussion of these views.
3 Admittedly, this formulation is not really applicable in the case of *a priori* justification where the belief, if true, will normally be necessary and hence incapable of having been false; but it is still heuristically valuable in clarifying the point at issue.
4 I am thinking here especially of Peter Unger's solution to the Gettier problem: adding the requirement, as a fourth condition for knowledge, that it not be an *accident* that the belief is true. See Unger (1968).
5 This argument seems to me to capture what Benacerraf is getting at, admittedly none too clearly, in his account of the intuition that favors a causal requirement. See Benacerraf, op. cit., pp. 413–14.

genuine relation of influence between a belief and its object is required for justification, since it would be possible for such a relation to be absent even though the believer still believed and even had good reasons for believing it to be present. But it does show that if such a relation is *known* to be absent or impossible, as is allegedly the case for beliefs about Platonistic entities, then justification is ruled out as well.

I have spoken here of the belief or reasons being "causally shaped or otherwise influenced," leaving it deliberately vague just what form such influence might take. Eventually, we shall have to see if a more specific claim is defensible here. But before tackling that question, we need to have a look at the second main component of the objection, the claim that rationalism essentially involves a Platonism that would (allegedly) exclude any sort of causal relation between the supposedly *a priori* belief and its putative object. As already noted, Benacerraf's main concern is with a Platonistic view of mathematical truth, with what amounts to a restricted version of rationalism entering the picture merely as the only apparent possibility for an epistemological accompaniment to such a metaphysical view. My concern here is in effect the opposite of his: with the thesis that Platonism is a metaphysical corollary of rationalism, rather than with the thesis that rationalism is an epistemological corollary of Platonism.

Certainly it is often assumed, without much discussion, that rationalism is committed to Platonism. Moreover, intuitive presentations of rationalism, like that offered in §§4.2 and 4.3, surely seem on the surface to support such an assumption: such accounts are naturally formulated in terms of propositions and the properties, relations, and perhaps other metaphysical items that are their ingredients, and it is at least plausible to construe these things as abstract entities of a Platonistic sort. But while such a construal of the rationalist picture is natural, it is by no means obviously inevitable. Rationalism requires at most only that propositions, properties, relations, etc., exist and be capable of being objects of thought and reflection; it requires Platonism only if Platonism is the only possible account of how this could be so. If, on the contrary, there is an alternative metaphysical account that can accommodate the seemingly undeniable fact that we do genuinely think about such things, then the rationalist could almost certainly accept it as well. My own inclination is to think that Platonism is in fact the only tenable account of these matters, and thus I will proceed here on that assumption. But it is worth reiterating that it is not rationalism by itself that yields this result.[6]

6 In addition to ill-defined and highly dubious views such as conceptualism and nominalism,

Given this assumption of Platonism, the remaining issue is then whether, as alleged by Benacerraf and others, the combined rationalist-Platonist view is untenable because Platonism makes it impossible that there could be a relation of influence between *a priori* justified beliefs and the corresponding reality. The idea here, apparently,[7] is that abstract, unchangeable entities, such as propositions, properties, and relations when Platonistically construed, are causally inert. They do nothing, nothing happens to them, and accordingly they are unable to figure in causal regularities.

If this is the argument, however, it is not at all compelling. It is quite true that abstract entities cannot, by definition, figure in the spatio-temporal events that make up causal regularities or chains in the way that concrete objects do: they are not objects or substances that act or are affected in the way that trees, tables, and people are. But it is very far from obvious that a relation of influence between the object of justified belief (or knowledge) and the state of believing, the possibility of which was shown above to be necessary, requires that the object figure *in this way* in the events of a causal regularity or chain. If, to recur to our earlier example, I am to be justified on the basis of rational insight in believing that nothing can be red and green all over at the same time, then the properties redness and greenness must be capable of influencing or affecting my state of mind: what I think must be at least potentially responsive to the actual character of these properties.[8] But it simply does not follow that redness and greenness

discussions of the problem of universals often distinguish between two supposedly different versions of realism: a Platonistic form which says that universals exist apart from the things that instantiate them (*ante rem*); and a form, usually attributed to Aristotle, according to which universals exist only in their instances (*in rem*). But it is very hard to attach any solid content to this distinction. I am inclined to think that the only clear implication of saying that universals exist only in their instances and not apart, so that they would not exist if there were no instances, is that there are no truths about universals that never have been and never will be instantiated. E.g., if there are two very specific shades of color, C_1 and C_2, that fortuitously have never been and will never be instantiated in the history of the universe, then on the Aristotelian view it would not be true that nothing can be C_1 and C_2 all over at the same time. But such a conclusion seems obviously mistaken, making it doubtful whether this supposed alternative version of realism is a really a tenable position. If it is tenable, however, there is no apparent reason why it could not equally well serve the needs of the rationalist. This would render inappropriate the term "Platonism," as it is employed in the text, but would, I believe, affect nothing of substance.

7 Benacerraf's own discussion of the point (op. cit., p. 414) is quite unspecific. But the account in the text is the way in which his argument is standardly, and I believe correctly, interpreted.

8 "Capable of influencing" and "potentially responsible" because our concern is justification, not knowledge: there is nothing in the earlier argument to show that the failure of actual influence in a particular case defeats justification, though it might rule out knowl-

themselves must be concretely involved in a causal chain of events connected to my state of mind. The obvious alternative is that such influence involves instead the presence in such a causal chain of an event or events involving concrete objects that *instantiate* these properties, where the fact that it is just those specific properties that are instantiated and not others affects the overall result. This seems to be a perfectly intelligible way in which the nature of redness and greenness could influence a subsequent occurrence, such as a certain state of mind in me, without redness and greenness themselves acting or being affected.

A useful comparison here is with the abstractive theories of concept acquisition typical of concept empiricism. On such accounts of concept acquisition, the concept acquired is certainly influenced by the instantiated property: it is in virtue of such influence that encountering a red object allows someone to acquire the concept of red, rather than the concept of some other property. But this influence does not seem to require that the property itself, as opposed to the object instantiating it, do anything or be affected in any way.[9] I have no desire to endorse any particular view of this kind, and at least the most standard versions seem to me to be problematic on other grounds. My point here is that if such a view is even intelligible, as it certainly seems to be, then the idea that abstract, Platonistic entities, simply in virtue of their abstractness, must be regarded incapable in principle of influencing minds cannot be correct.[10]

Whether such influence should be described as causal is less clear: it may be correct to say that causation *per se* obtains only between concrete objects or events, so that there can be no strictly *causal* relations or *causal* influence

edge for the reason noted there.

9 An issue worth taking brief note of is whether the suggested alternative is ruled out, at least for the example in question, by the familiar account of colors as secondary qualities that are not in fact instantiated in the world. A full discussion of this problem is not possible here, but obviously it would affect only a limited range of examples, examples that are in no way essential to the overall case for rationalism, despite the very extended use that I have made of one of them. I would suggest, however, that what the secondary qualities analysis, if correct, shows is only that colors are not instantiated in the physical world, not that they are not instantiated at all.

10 To be fair to Benacerraf, I should repeat that his primary concern is with mathematical entities such as numbers. For that specific case, the fact that numbers are standardly regarded as particular entities rather than properties (as either reflected in or perhaps resulting from the fact that number words are grammatically singular terms), may seem to make alternative modes of influence like that suggested above unavailable. I think that this would be a mistake, roughly on the Fregean grounds that, whatever exactly the correct account of numbers as entities may be, they must turn out to be closely connected with the correlative properties of sets or collections (e.g., the property of being 3-membered) – closely enough to allow a treatment analogous to that suggested in the text.

between abstract entities and minds. But we have seen no argument to show that influence of this more specific sort is required for either knowledge or justification, nor, I believe, is any compelling argument to this effect to be had. The upshot is that there is no reason to think that Platonic entities are incapable of influencing minds in the only way that justification and knowledge require – and thus nothing to prevent the rationalist from accepting as a requirement for justification that such influence be possible, while denying that this requirement must be satisfied in a way that would be ruled out by Platonism. On this basis, I conclude that the overall objection to rationalism, as formulated above, does not succeed.

There is, however, one further possibility that needs to be considered. Someone, perhaps even Benacerraf himself, might want to advocate a more specific sort of causal requirement that would genuinely conflict with Platonism, not on the grounds discussed above, but by insisting on the construal of rational insight as a process that requires or involves a perception or quasi-perception of abstract entities that is closely analogous to sense perception. Such a construal is surely suggested by many intuitive presentations of rationalism, including the one offered in §4.2, which speak of grasping or apprehending properties and relations and of seeing or apprehending on this basis that various propositions are true. These descriptions, though extremely natural, are obviously metaphorical in character. But if they suggest explicitly anything non-metaphorical, it is surely some sort of perceptual or quasi-perceptual account. And if the analogy with sense-perception is taken sufficiently seriously, then it would seem to require that the abstract entities in question be after all involved in the causal chain in a way analogous to that in which ordinary objects are involved in the causal chains that occur in ordinary cases of perception – a requirement that is indeed incompatible with their abstract character.

To this argument, the short answer is that the analogy with perception cannot and should not be taken that seriously. To say this, however, only raises the legitimate question of what the alternative to a perceptual or quasi-perceptual account of the apprehensions on which rational insight is supposed to be based, and indeed of the apprehension of thought content in general, might be. This is arguably the main question that an account of the metaphysics of rationalism must confront, and it will accordingly be the central focus of the balance of the present chapter – though a substantial part of the discussion will be devoted to refuting a related and widely accepted metaphysical claim that would, if correct, make rationalism untenable.

§6.3. THE NATURE OF THOUGHT

A partial answer to the question just posed, though hardly one that removes all of the mystery, is that the grasping or apprehending in question is simply that which is involved in thought in general. It is a basic and obvious fact about human beings that we are able to think about, consciously represent to ourselves, a wide variety of entities and properties and relations and states of affairs that are external to our cognitive processes.[11] But while it is abundantly clear that we do possess such a capacity, it is much less obvious how it works, how we are able to do this puzzling and supremely valuable thing. Thus what is really at issue here is what is perhaps the deepest and most difficult of all philosophical problems: that of the nature of intentional thought or mental representation itself.

It might be supposed, at first glance, that while a general account of the intentionality of thought would be very desirable for epistemology and indeed for philosophy in general, there is no reason why the moderate rationalist in particular is under any special obligation to provide one. What alters the dialectical situation, however, is the existence of a certain general view of the nature of thought, one which is regarded by many not only as correct, but in fact as virtually the only conceivable account: the view that thought is essentially a symbolic or linguistic process that employs a representational system at least strongly analogous to a natural language (a view that has a good claim to be the defining thesis of the linguistic or analytic school of philosophy).

Such a view of thought appears to be seriously incompatible with even moderate rationalism. To appreciate the incompatibility, reflect once again on the intuitive picture of rational insight offered above. A person apprehends or grasps, for example, the properties redness and greenness, and supposedly "sees" on the basis of this apprehension that they cannot be jointly instantiated. Such a picture clearly seems to presuppose that as a result of this apprehension or grasping, the properties of redness and greenness are themselves before the mind in a way that allows their natures and mutual incompatibility to be apparent. But according to the symbolic view of thought, what happens when I think about redness and greenness is only that either the English *words* 'red' and 'green'[12] or close analogues of these words in a "language of thought" occur in my mind or brain. Here it is

11 We are also, of course, able to represent much about those cognitive processes themselves, but even then the process represented seems to be necessarily external to the state that represents it.
12 Or perhaps rather the words 'redness' and 'greenness'.

important to be very clear about the precise content of the view in question: it is not merely the view that these linguistic or quasi-linguistic elements are one element among others in thought, but rather, as explained further below, the much more radical view that the occurrence of such items is all there is to the internal, subjective aspect of thought. No doubt there is some further story to be told (though proponents of the view differ fairly widely as to how it goes) about how and why such mental words have the particular meaning or content that they do, rather than meaning something entirely different or being mere uninterpreted symbols. (The favorite story here seems to be some version of the causal theory of meaning.) But whatever else such a story may involve, it cannot involve any sort of additional thoughtlike element, any sort of internal awareness of meaning or content that is attached to or associated with, but yet distinct from the symbols: to adopt any such account would be to abandon the very core of the symbolic view, since any such further awareness would be precisely the sort of non-symbolic thought that the theory rejects.

It should now be apparent how the symbolic view of thought, thus understood, is incompatible with the moderate rationalist account of *a priori* justification. For when I am aware of redness and greenness, I do not according to the symbolic view have thereby any direct access to the properties themselves of the sort that would be needed in order for me to see directly that they are incompatible. Since the words are the sole internal vehicle of my thought, they are also my sole access to the correlative properties. But nothing about the words in themselves can be the basis for a genuine rational insight – as though I were to attempt through simply inspecting the words 'red' and 'green' (e.g., as written on a real blackboard) to determine that nothing could have both properties.

To be sure, if I *understand* the words on the blackboard, whether mental or otherwise, then I can do this; and, as we have seen, there is, according to the symbolic view, some further account to be given of what it is in virtue of which the mental words mean one thing rather than another, which seemingly could be used to explain how I understand them. The problem is that whatever this understanding might amount to, it cannot, as we have seen, involve any further awareness of content that is distinct from, albeit perhaps closely associated with, the occurrence of the symbols. Thus no account of what it is to understand the mental symbols that is consistent with the symbolic view seems to allow the sort of awareness of the properties themselves that rationalism demands.

This problem will become clearer in the subsequent discussion. I will argue, in the next three sections, that the symbolic view of thought is unacceptable, for a reason that is closely related to the problem that it would pose for moderate rationalism: because it is unable to provide for a genuine awareness of content, it is also unable to do justice to the fundamental fact that the content of our thoughts is, to some significant degree at least, apparent to us, that is, we are aware "from the inside" of what we are thinking. The development of this objection to the symbolic view represents something of a digression from the main argument of the present book. But it is important to see clearly why this popular view of the nature of thought is untenable, and hence cannot provide the basis for a cogent objection to moderate rationalism – and also to appreciate clearly the implications for the nature of thought of rejecting it.

§6.4. A BASIC PROBLEM FOR THE SYMBOLIC CONCEPTION OF THOUGHT

Though the objection to be developed is intended to apply to a symbolic view of representational mental states generally, all states that can be *about* some external intentional object or property or state of affairs, it may be helpful to focus initially on one particular kind of state where the phenomenon of awareness of content appears without distracting accompaniments: the mental state of simply contemplating or envisaging such an object or property or state of affairs – of, as one says, having it in mind.[13]

Here is a very partial and unordered list of things that I am able to contemplate or think about: cats, telephones, basketball, there being cherry trees in the quad, redness, triangularity, one thing being longer than another, Napoleon's having lost the Battle of Waterloo, New York City, justice, seven, multiplication, Immanuel Kant, Ronald Reagan. Moreover, in each of these cases and in indefinitely many others, I am aware, simply by virtue of having the thought in question, of what it is that I am thinking about, of the content of the thought. (Indeed, though this does not matter for my present argument, it seems plain that such awareness of content is in fact essential to the ordinary concept of thought: a being who represented

---

13 Such a focus differs significantly from much recent work in the philosophy of mind, which tends in the main to concentrate on states of belief and to rely heavily on our linguistic practices of belief attribution. In my judgment, this is unfortunate, for reasons that are too complicated to go into in detail here, but which can be summed up by saying that what counts as a correct belief attribution appears to be heavily dependent on a wide variety of contextual and social factors, factors that are largely independent of what is actually going on in the mind of the person in question.

the world in some fashion but who was not thus aware of the content of his representative states would simply not count as thinking.[14])

But how is it that I am able to think about such things? In virtue of what is a mental state or act of mind about, for example, triangularity? The answer to this question that is offered by the symbolic conception of thought is that I am able to think about triangularity by having a token of the word 'triangular'[15] or its translation into some other language present in an appropriate way in my cognitive operations – inscribed on my mental blackboard, as proponents of the view like to put it. It is such a token that constitutes the internal vehicle of my thought. On some views, the language in question is either identical with or very closely related to some natural language like English; while on other views, it is a distinct "language of thought," sometimes argued to be innate and commonly referred to as "mentalese." (For the sake of expository convenience, I will assume for the most part that the latter of these views is to be preferred and will formulate my discussion accordingly; but, as far as I can tell, this will affect nothing of any substance.)

What all such views have in common, the defining thesis of the symbolic or linguistic conception of thought, is the idea that the tokens in question are symbols in essentially the way that the ordinary word 'triangular' is a symbol: that their representative capacity or content is not somehow fixed by their intrinsic character, but is instead imposed upon them from the outside by relations of some sort in which they are involved. Just as the word 'triangular' could, given its intrinsic character, have represented anything else or nothing at all instead of representing the property that it actually does represent, so is it also allegedly the case with the corresponding thought-symbol.

The symbolic view is thus a species of what Fodor calls "the representative theory of the mind": it holds that propositional attitudes (and other representative states) are relations to internal representations, in this case to the appropriate linguistic or quasi-linguistic tokens.[16] But it is important to realize, as Fodor does not always seem to, that the claim that the internal representations are, in the way just explained, symbolic in character is a

---

14 This is not to say that the idea of a thought whose content is not thus apparent or perhaps even accessible, as is presumably the case with subconscious mental states (if such states exist), is unintelligible – only that such states are, from the standpoint of the ordinary conception of thought, necessarily exceptional.

15 Or, perhaps, 'triangularity'.

16 See, e.g., "Propositional Attitudes" and "Methodological Solipsism Considered as a Research Strategy in Cognitive Science" (hereafter abbreviated as "Methodological Solipsism"), in Fodor (1981), pp. 177–203, 225–53.

further thesis that does not follow from the representative theory of the mind simpliciter. There may be insuperable objections of some sort to the idea of representations whose representative content is somehow intrinsic to them, not dependent on external relations of any sort; but such states, if otherwise possible, would seemingly be quite capable of satisfying the main considerations that Fodor adduces on behalf of the representative theory[17]: they could provide a mediating mechanism between the person and abstract propositions, account for the phenomenon of opacity, endow mental representations with logical form, and even allow for a substantial degree of structural parallelism between thought and language.[18]

There are two related problems that any version of the symbolic theory must face. The first is obvious enough: If the representative content of a thought-symbol is not a result of its intrinsic properties, how then is it fixed or determined? What makes the mental word 'triangular' represent that particular property, rather than one of the indefinitely many other things that it might have represented (or perhaps nothing at all)? But this first problem, already difficult enough for the ordinary English word 'triangular', is seriously aggravated in the case of the thought-symbol by the second problem, that of explaining how the representative content is accessible to the thinker in question, that is, of explaining how it is possible for him to be aware of the representative content of his thought-symbols. This problem does not arise in quite the same way for ordinary linguistic symbols, where the obvious (though currently unfashionable) account of understanding is an appeal to the thoughts with which the symbol is conventionally associated.

Someone may want to ask at this point what exactly it means for a person to be aware of the content of his thought, to grasp or understand what he is thinking about. At one level, the answer is easy enough: for me

---

17 See "Propositional Attitudes" and "Methodological Solipsism."
18 The view of mental representations as possessing intrinsic content (together with the assumption that such content is internally accessible – and thus presumably would play a role in explaining linguistic and other behavior) does, of course, conflict with a further thesis endorsed by Fodor: the thesis that psychological processes are purely *computational* in character, that it is only the "formal-syntactic" features of the internal representations that play any psychological role, a thesis that is more or less equivalent to the symbolic conception of thought itself. But Fodor's attempts to argue for this further thesis seem to involve a confusion between the plausible claim that external relations to the world, such as truth and reference, play no direct role in psychological processes and the much less obvious claim that internally represented content, understood in a way that leaves issues of truth and successful reference open, plays no such role. See, e.g., "Methodological Solipsism," where these two very different kinds of things are lumped together under the heading of "semantical properties."

to be aware of what I am thinking about is simply for me to have an intelligible idea or conception of the object of my thought. Thus if I think that there is a dead crab on the beach, I am aware of having in mind a certain distinctive sort of marine animal and not, for example, a furry mammal or a red fruit or a motor vehicle[19]; I grasp what it means for it to be dead rather than alive; and I have a conception of the beach as a distinctive location that differs from the fish counter or the backyard. What a deeper account of this phenomenon would look like is a vastly more difficult issue. But that such a phenomenon genuinely and pervasively exists and that it involves more than the contemplating of bare symbols to whose interpretation I have no direct or automatic access seems to me completely undeniable. Thus the urgent question is whether the symbolic conception can account for it. Can the view explain what it is for mentalese symbols to have a particular meaning or interpretation or content in a way that makes that meaning or interpretation or content something of which the person who allegedly thinks by means of them is aware simply by virtue of having the thought?[20]

It is easy to think of views of how the content of mentalese symbols is determined that clearly fail to satisfy the requirement that the content be thus directly available to the person having the thought. Consider, for example, a view according to which a thought-symbol's having a certain representative content is determined entirely by some external causal or causal-historical relation between tokens of that symbol and whatever it thereby comes to represent. If tokens of the mentalese word corresponding to 'triangular' have the representative content that they do entirely by virtue of standing in such an external relation to triangular things (or even to the abstract universal triangularity), then the person having the thought, trapped as it were on one end of this relation and having direct access only to the tokens themselves, would have no way of being aware of what the

---

19 Though, as we shall see in the next section, not necessarily that I am thinking about an Earth crab as opposed to a Twin Earth crab. This is an important qualification, no doubt, but (as argued more fully below) it has no tendency at all to show that I do not have a substantial, though still incomplete, grasp of what I am thinking about – which is quite enough for the present argument.

20 This awareness of content should not be thought of as involving an apperceptive second-level thought that is about the first-level thought and its content, but rather as a feature or aspect, indeed the essential feature or aspect, of the first-level thought itself. For otherwise we would have the absurdity that to understand or grasp the content of a first-level thought would require a second-level thought, the understanding of which would require a third-level thought, and so on, *infinitum*. For pointing out to me the need for clarity on this point, which was not clear in an earlier version of this argument (BonJour 1991), I am indebted to my colleague Cass Weller.

symbol thus represents, no way of having any inkling at all of what he is thinking about by virtue of the presence of the symbol in his mental economy – a result that is, I submit, plainly absurd.[21] (A crude but perhaps helpful analogy: Seattle is north of Portland, but not by virtue of any intrinsic characteristic of Seattle. Thus someone who was aware only of Seattle and its intrinsic characteristics would not thereby have access to its relational property of being north of Portland, nor to any further fact that depended on that relational property.[22])

Here it is important to be clear about the exact claim being made by the symbolic conception. The connection between the obtaining of the causal-historical relation and the content that allegedly results is *not* supposed to itself be a causal connection: the view is *not* that the obtaining of such a relation somehow infuses the symbol with content that is realized or embodied in some form other than the bare symbol itself, and which might then be accessible to the believer. (And the symbolic conception could in any case give no account of what form the result of such a process might take: to appeal to further, accompanying symbols would only raise the same issue again with respect to them, while to admit any other kind of content-bearing state or non-relational feature would, as we have seen, be a repudiation of the symbolic conception.) Rather the claim is and must be that the existence of the appropriate causal-historical relation *constitutes* the symbol's having a certain content, so that the content is realized only in the entire complex situation that includes the obtaining of the relation, but not in any of its components by themselves – and in particular not in the symbol alone. From this it follows that one can have access to the content only by having access to that entire situation, an access that is obviously not in general available to a user of mentalese.

Essentially the same problem also arises for other analogous views that appeal to relations external to mind as constitutive of content, for example,

21 Fodor's account in Fodor (1987), chapter 4, is one example of such a view. Lest this dismissal of causal theories seem too fast, it may be useful to restate the essential point and generalize it a bit. Causal relations may play a derivative role in our *ascriptions* of content: e.g., in the Twin Earth cases discussed later in §6.5, the fact that a certain internally accessible descriptive content (roughly, that of the locally familiar liquid that appears in lakes and rivers, falls from the sky at times, and is good to drink) is causally related to H_2O may account for our saying that the person in question is thinking about H_2O, even if he or she is unaware of the chemical composition. But despite the enormous recent popularity of theories of this kind, no appeal to causal relations can by itself account for thought content in general: the mere existence of a causal relation between me or my state of mind and some object or property is obviously not sufficient to bring that object or property before the mind in a way that allows it to be thought about.
22 Ann Baker suggested this analogy.

the view according to which the meaning of my thought-symbols is constituted entirely by its relation to practices and conventions in my linguistic community and perhaps especially to the practices of the relevant experts. Here again, since the user of the symbol will not in general have access to this entire social complex or even to very much of it, there is no apparent way in which the content of his thought can on this view be accessible to him. (This is not to deny that relations of these sorts could play some more complicated role in a defensible view, only to insist that they cannot be the whole story about how representative content is constituted, as long as the requirement that such content must be something of which the person can thereby be internally aware is maintained.)

Thus, by relying on considerations of this kind, it is possible to mount a simple and yet completely general argument against the symbolic account of thought: According to that conception, *all* that is present in my mind (or brain) when I think contentful thoughts is symbols of the appropriate sorts; these symbols are meaningful or contentful by virtue of standing in relations of some sort to something lying outside the mind in which they stand, but this meaning or content is represented in the mind only by the symbols themselves, not by any further content-bearing element or feature. Thus, merely having such thought-symbols present in my mind (or brain) in itself gives me no awareness of their content, and there is apparently nothing else that the symbolic theory can appeal to in order to account in general for such awareness.[23] Therefore the acceptance of the symbolic conception seems to lead inexorably to the conclusion that I have no awareness of the content of my thought, no internal grasp or understanding at all of what I am thinking. But this is surely an absurd result, and so the symbolic conception must be mistaken. (Thus, as already noted above, it is the very feature of the symbolic conception that is incompatible with moderate rationalism that also makes it independently unacceptable.)

I can think of only two lines of response to the foregoing argument. One is to appeal to recent work in the philosophy of language, centering around the idea of "direct reference," in an attempt to undercut the claim that representative content is internally accessible in the way that the argument assumes. The other is to attempt to account for the representa-

---

23 Merely employing the symbols correctly could not constitute understanding in the sense at issue here, the behaviorist views of Wittgenstein and many others to the contrary not withstanding. Such employment would either be a consequence of an independent understanding, which would then still have to be accounted for, or, if it could somehow occur on its own, would be simply irrelevant to our present concerns (in addition to being extremely puzzling).

tive content of thought-symbols on the basis of the relations in which such symbols stand to each other by virtue of the ongoing functioning of the person's internal mental-linguistic system, thus perhaps making such content internally accessible in the required way. The next two sections will be devoted to these two responses.

§6.5. THE APPEAL TO DIRECT REFERENCE

The key premise in the foregoing argument against the symbolic conception of thought is the premise that the content of our mental representations is something of which we are internally aware. But there are many who would hold that such a premise is simply false, that recent work by Putnam, Burge, Kaplan, Perry, Kripke, and others has shown, in Putnam's phrase, that content or meaning "just ain't in the head"[24] and thus need not be internally accessible.[25] I believe, however, that the degree to which the work in question supports this conclusion has been greatly exaggerated, that the genuine insights of the philosophers in question can be accommodated while still retaining a thesis of the internal accessibility of content that is more than sufficient for the requirements of the present argument. I have no space here for a detailed consideration of these issues, but a brief look at them will nonetheless prove useful in clarifying the claim of accessibility and indicating the qualifications that I have already suggested that it requires. I will look first at the most famous and widely discussed of Putnam's examples and then briefly consider the somewhat different issues raised by indexicals.

Consider, then, Putnam's now famous Twin Earth example. We are to suppose that there is somewhere a planet, Twin Earth, that is, with one important exception, exactly like Earth in every respect: apart from that exception, Twin Earth contains the same kinds of things as Earth, including most importantly people, some of whom speak a language that is superficially indiscernible from English. The exception is that whereas the liquid called "water" on Earth is, of course, composed of H_2O molecules, the superficially indiscernible liquid called "water" in Twin Earth English is in fact composed of molecules that are quite different in chemical composition, XYZ molecules.

Consider now a time on Earth prior to the discovery of the chemical composition of water and the corresponding time on Twin Earth. Con-

---

24 Hilary Putnam, "The Meaning of 'Meaning'," in Putnam (1975), p. 227.
25 Perhaps the most explicit published version of such an argument is LePore and Loewer (1986).

sider also an Earthian speaker of English, $Oscar_1$, who has the thought that he would express by using the Earth English sentence 'water is wet', and a corresponding Twin Earthian speaker of Twin Earth English, $Oscar_2$, who has the thought that he would express by using the Twin Earth English sentence 'water is wet'. We may even suppose that $Oscar_2$ is an exact Doppelgänger of $Oscar_1$ in every respect, both physical and mental (if these are in fact distinct) – except, of course, that whereas a large portion of $Oscar_1$'s body is made up of H_2O molecules, the corresponding portion of $Oscar_2$'s body is made up of XYZ molecules.

What should we say about the content of the thoughts had by the two Oscars? Putnam's claim is that while $Oscar_1$'s sentence and the corresponding thought are about H_2O and assert that H_2O is wet, $Oscar_2$'s sentence and the corresponding thought are about XYZ and assert that XYZ is wet. The two thoughts thus have quite different contents. But in the situation as described there is presumably no difference at all in what the two Oscars are internally aware of (it is surely plausible that the difference between H_2O molecules and XYZ molecules would make no difference at this level) and thus no way in which this difference of content is internally accessible to them. In a clear sense, neither Oscar is aware "from the inside" of what he is thinking about.[26]

Though some have tried to resist it, I believe that Putnam's claim here is essentially correct when properly qualified: there is a dimension of the content of at least many of our thoughts that is not internally accessible, of which we are not automatically aware just by having the thoughts in question. But this is obviously very far from the claim that would be needed to defend the symbolic theory of thought against the charge that it renders the content of our thoughts completely inaccessible. For that, we would need the claim that we are not aware of our thought contents to any degree, and there is no apparent way to get anything even remotely this strong out of Putnam's argument. On the contrary, the intuitive appeal and probably even the intelligibility of the example depends on ascribing to the two Oscars accessible thought contents that are identical, perhaps roughly the content that the locally familiar liquid that appears in lakes and rivers, falls from the sky at times, is good to drink, etc., is wet. The point demonstrated by the example is only that this accessible content is unable by itself to determine the chemical composition of the liquid in question, thus leaving open the possibility that this might differ on Twin Earth.

26 Putnam's actual discussion is couched in terms of meaning rather than content, but it seems quite clear that he would accept the modified version of the argument just offered.

A useful way to put this point is to distinguish, following Fodor[27] and others, between narrow content and wide content with respect to mental representations.[28] The thoughts of the two Oscars have different wide content, in that they are about different kinds of stuff, but they have the same narrow content, that is, the two different stuffs are internally represented in precisely the same way. Wide content has to do with the semantical relation between the representation and the world and is thus partly a function of what the world actually contains, and perhaps also of other external contextual factors; in this way, it is analogous to the truth of a propositional representation, which is obviously not an internally accessible feature. It is only narrow content that can plausibly be claimed to be internally accessible, and my suggestion is that nothing in Putnam's argument does anything to call such a claim into question.[29]

An analogous objection to the premise that content is internally accessible can also be made by appeal to the discussions of indexicals by Kaplan and Perry, among others.[30] Here the point is that the content of an indexical sentence, and of the presumably analogous indexical thought, is clearly in one way a function of what is actually picked out in the relevant context, which is once again a matter of how the representation in question is related to the world and hence something that there is no reason at all to expect to be internally accessible. Thus, for example, a thought that I might express by saying "that man is very tall" might have as its content, in the sense relevant to determining its truth value, the claim that a particular passerby is tall, or the claim that I myself am tall (unbeknownst to me, I am looking in a mirror), or perhaps even no content of this sort at all (I am

27 See "Methodological Solipsism."
28 Or at least to invoke something like this distinction. Most actual attempts to explicate the notion of narrow content, including Fodor's for the most part, adhere to the standard practice in cognitive science and philosophy of language of giving little or no attention to internal accessibility or awareness. But I think that something like the view of narrow content invoked here can be glimpsed between the lines of Fodor's discussion, especially when he tries to characterize particular narrow contents like that involved in the Twin Earth case.
29 It is also often assumed in the literature that differences in wide content can never be captured in narrow content. But this seems clearly wrong, as the Twin Earth case itself illustrates: it is only because the (hypothetical) difference between H_2O and XYZ is grasped internally by us that we can see that the broad contents of the thoughts of the two Oscars are different in a way that they cannot appreciate. (This of course does not preclude the possibility that at any particular time there are further differences in broad content that we do not grasp.)
30 See David Kaplan, "Demonstratives," Almog, Perry, and Wettstein (1989); and Perry (1979).

merely hallucinating a man). But although the contents of these various possible thoughts would in this way be quite different, it is clear that this difference is not in general internally accessible, so that they might be quite indiscernible "from the inside." And this might again be taken to show that the premise that the content of thought is internally accessible is mistaken.

Once more, however, this conclusion is much too hasty. What such examples show is again that a certain important dimension or aspect of content is internally inaccessible, but they have no tendency at all to show that *all* content is thus inaccessible. On the contrary, what makes the example just given intuitively appealing is once again that there is a clear sense in which the three thoughts in question have the same internally accessible content, even though this content picks out different things in the world due to the differences in context. Here again we may invoke the distinction between narrow and wide content, saying that the narrow content of an indexical thought is internally accessible, but that the wide content, depending as it does on what the indexical element actually picks out in the world, is not. And my suggestion is that the same general strategy will also work for the examples and arguments offered by Burge, Kripke, and others in the same general vein, though there is no room here to consider those views in detail.

The foregoing discussion has been unavoidably fast and loose, and there is undoubtedly much more that could be said. In particular, it is still not clear precisely where the distinction between narrow and wide content is to be drawn. Examples of the sorts in question also show that cases where what is internally grasped is fully propositional – in the sense of having by itself, unsupplemented by context, a definite truth value – are a good deal rarer than might have been thought, though hardly, as is sometimes suggested, that they never occur. But even where the content is not propositional, it plainly does not follow that there is no internally accessible content in a sense that poses the indicated problem for the symbolic conception of thought: even if what is internally grasped is only complexes of properties and relations, together perhaps with something like indexical elements pointing to context, that is still very far from being aware only of bare symbols. Thus even the little that has been said here is still enough to make plausible the claim, which should have been obvious enough anyway, that nothing about Twin Earth examples or indexicals can support the conclusion that the content of thought is inaccessible to the thinker in the complete and radical way that the symbolic conception of thought seems to entail.

§6.6. CONCEPTUAL ROLE SEMANTICS

Is there then any way to provide for internally accessible content while continuing to adhere to the symbolic or linguistic conception of thought? The only apparent possibility here is to attempt to account for such content solely by appeal to relations among the thought-symbols themselves, relations that hold by virtue of the person's ongoing "use" of the language of thought.[31] Views in this general direction, which have recently come to be known as "conceptual role semantics," have been held by a wide range of philosophers, though they have not always been specifically applied to a language of thought and are often not developed in such a way as to speak clearly to the issue that concerns us here.[32] For this reason, and also for reasons of space, I will develop a schematic version of such a view rather than discussing any particular author.

The basic idea of conceptual role semantics as applied to the language of thought is that the meaning or content of a sentence in mentalese (and thus the content of the various thoughts that I may have by using tokens of that sentence) derives from the role that sentences of that type play in various kinds of inference, both deductive and inductive. For any given mentalese sentence, there will be certain patterns of inference (involving other mentalese sentences) in which it functions as the conclusion and others in which it functions as a premise; and the suggestion is that if these patterns are fully spelled out, they will exactly fix the distinctive (narrow) content of that sentence. Thus, although the individual representations of men-

---

31 One could, of course, appeal to relations between the thought-symbols and other sorts of internally accessible states, e.g., perceptual experiences or images of some sort. But such a view could apparently succeed in accounting for the accessibility of content only if either (i) the other states were themselves contentful in a way that would amount to a rejection of the linguistic theory, or (ii) the relation to such states led to the appropriate content being somehow encapsulated, in an accessible way, within the thought-symbols themselves – in which case we still need an account of how that is supposed to work. A view that rejected both of these alternatives and simply said that the obtaining of the content is *constituted* by the thought-symbols standing in this complex of relations to these other internally accessible states would still be subject to the third and fourth objections, developed below, to the view discussed in the text.

32 A recent paper by Ned Block (Block 1986) offers a very detailed presentation of the view; but while Block is attempting to give an account of narrow content specifically, he, like most philosophers of psychology and cognitive scientists, has little to say about the problem of the internal accessibility of content. Earlier proponents of the view include: various of the absolute idealists (who held what might be called a coherence theory of meaning as one part of the complex of views usually referred to as "the coherence theory of truth"); C. I. Lewis (1929) (*Mind and the World Order*), chapter 2; and Wilfrid Sellars (especially Sellars 1953).

talese, taken apart from their actual functioning in the person's cognitive processes, could have meant many things other than what they actually mean, the claim is that when these representations are taken together in the context of the overall pattern of inferences, their specific content is precisely fixed, because for them to have that specific content just *is* for them to stand in that specific network of inferential relations.[33]

But why should it be thought that the pattern or network of inference relations will fix content in this way? What exactly is the connection between inferential pattern and content supposed to be? Fodor, though he does not accept the view, offers a useful account of its underlying rationale[34]: Propositions, abstract contents of assertive thoughts, stand in various sorts of entailment and probability relations to each other, thus forming a sort of logical network. The sentences of the mentalese stand in causal-inferential relations to each other, by virtue of the various inferences that the user of mentalese makes or is disposed to make, thus forming a causal-inferential network. Suppose that the two networks are isomorphic to each other, thus establishing a correlation between them. The claim is then that a given item in mentalese has as its content the proposition with which it is correlated by this isomorphism.[35]

Before attempting to assess the plausibility of this suggestion, there are some important points of clarification that need to be noted. In the first place, note that the relations among propositions that are to be appealed to here cannot be merely logical or formal relations, for appeal to such relations alone would fail to distinguish terms of the same logical type. Second, to avoid presupposing the very content that is to be accounted for, the "inference relations" among the mentalese sentences must ultimately be specifiable in purely causal (i.e., non-intentional and non-semantic) terms: such a specification can appeal only to the fact, roughly, that the person in question is disposed, mutatis mutandis, to internally assert the item that is the "conclusion" whenever he is disposed to assert the items that are the "premises." Third, it is obviously crucial in thinking about the plausibility of this sort of view to keep firmly in mind that the other

33 Most versions of conceptual role semantics also appeal to external relations such as causal relations to the environment in specifying the conceptual role. But since such versions would fail, for reasons already considered, to meet the requirement of accessibility, they need not be considered here.
34 Fodor (1987), pp. 78–9.
35 In discussing this view, I will neglect the reasons discussed in the previous section for thinking that narrow content is often non-propositional in character. Presumably the rationale just discussed could be recast in terms of inference relations among indexical claims or even among concepts.

mentalese items to which a given item stands in these "inferential" relations also are supposed to have meaning or content only by virtue of the causal-inferential pattern.

There are a variety of problems and difficulties raised in the literature that would have to be solved in order to develop such an account of the content of thought in detail. There is the extremely non-trivial problem of delineating and distinguishing the various inferential patterns. There is a worry, raised by Fodor, as to whether the account of narrow content that would result from such a view can be made compatible with the further semantical ingredients needed to account for wide content.[36] And there is the notorious "collateral information problem," resulting from the fact that on this sort of view, it looks as though any further belief that has any influence on the inferences one draws will affect the meaning or content of one's representations, so that it will become virtually impossible for two people with significantly different sets of beliefs to have any belief in common.[37] But while these problems are serious enough, I will argue that when taken as a solution to the problem of the internal accessibility of content, the conceptual role view is afflicted by much more serious and less subtle difficulties, difficulties that are in fact clearly fatal.

First. Is there any plausibility at all to the idea that the isomorphism between the causal-inferential structure of mentalese inferences and the entailment-cum-probability relations of abstract propositions could ever be close enough and unique enough to fix content to a degree adequate to account for our intuitions about the internal accessibility of (narrow) content? Think, for example, of the mentalese terms CAT and DOG (I follow Block in using capitals for mentalese items). There is obviously no implausibility in supposing that mentalese sentences containing these terms are involved in two largely different sets of causal-inferential relations to other sentences. But is there any reason to think that the formal structure of the two sets of causal-inferential relations is different, that it is not the case that for each inference involving CAT there is a structurally isomorphic inference involving DOG (in which case, the structure would give no indication of which mentalese sentences to correlate with abstract propositions about cats)? One important consideration that is easy to miss

36 See Fodor (1987), pp. 82–3.
37 From a rationalist standpoint, of course, one would want to distinguish *a priori justifiable* transitions from associations of other kinds; only the former would have a genuine bearing on content and, indeed, would even deserve to be called *inferences*. But, since his allowable information is restricted to the behavioral/dispositional pattern, the proponent of conceptual role semantics appears to be unable to make such a distinction.

here is that any actual language, mentalese included, will contain terms for only a small (perhaps vanishingly small) proportion of the properties, kinds, etc., which might have been represented. Thus the entailment relations among abstract propositions will be vastly richer and more complicated than the actual causal-inferential relations among the mentalese tokens, so that any isomorphism between mentalese and the overall system of abstract propositions will be quite partial at best – making it even more likely that there is more than one such partial isomorphism that is equally close. Also, even more basically, it is unclear that there is any strong reason to think that the network of propositional entailments cannot be mapped back onto itself in more than one way, in which case for any mapping from mentalese to abstract propositions, there would automatically be others that are equally acceptable. The burden of proof in these matters is clearly on the proponent of the thesis that narrow content can be adequately determined in this way, and there is no apparent reason for thinking that he can discharge it.

Second. An even more serious difficulty is that even if the isomorphism between the mentalese inferences and the propositional entailments were exact and unique, it is extremely unclear how exactly it is supposed to follow that the mentalese statements have the same narrow content as the correlated propositions. Why couldn't there be a set of items standing in a causal structure exactly isomorphic to the abstract entailment and probability structure while still having no content at all? Having the right structure may be a *necessary* condition for being contentful in a certain way: if we knew in advance that a state was contentful and were merely trying to figure out what specific content it possessed, then it is plausible to suppose that the structure of the inferences in which that state and other similar states are involved and the relation of that structure to the entailment relations of abstract propositional contents would be highly relevant (though even here it is not clear why some of the actual inferences in question could not simply be mistaken in ways that would upset the isomorphism). But there seems to be no reason at all to take the obtaining of such an isomorphism to be a *sufficient* condition for having specific content, which is what the conceptual role view must apparently claim.

Third. Even if the network of causal-inferential relations did somehow suffice to fix content in the way suggested, it is not obvious exactly how this would speak to the issue of internal accessibility. There is no doubt that from an intuitive standpoint, our inferences and inferential inclinations are, at least in principle, accessible in a way that, for example, external causal-historical relations are not. But though the details of the causal-inferential network may be plausibly regarded as internally accessible to some degree, are they really accessible to a degree that could account for our ability to be aware of the content of our thought with the lack of effort, confidence, and freedom from uncertainty that we seem to have? It is very hard to believe that when I am aware that I am thinking about crabs, that awareness depends on a grasp of the multifarious causal-inferential relations between mentalese sentences involving the mental word CRAB that would suffice to distinguish its content from that of, for example, the mental word LOBSTER. (Here again it is important to remember that the causal-inferential pattern relates one mental word to other mental words, not to other contents, except insofar as these contents are captured by the pattern itself.)

A further related point worth noting is that from an intuitive standpoint, the inferential inclinations in question seem to depend, in large part at least, on a prior grasp of content. It is *because* my thoughts have various specific contents that I am inclined to make certain inferences among them; and my awareness of the inclinations seems, intuitively, to be derivative from my prior awareness of the content. But this suggests that if, as conceptual role semantics claims, content results from inferences, rather than the other way around, there would be no intuitive reason to expect such logically prior inferential inclinations to be internally accessible.

Fourth. Even if all the foregoing problems could be somehow solved, it is at least clear that my awareness of what I am thinking about is not an explicit awareness of the causal-inferential pattern as such, as shown by the fact that I would find it extremely hard in any particular case to say what that pattern is. But then we seem to need an independent account of how I formulate or represent to myself the content that results from or perhaps is constituted by the inferential pattern. Clearly this formulation cannot be simply identified merely with the presence of the mentalese word or sentence itself, but there is apparently nothing else that is available so long as the symbolic conception of thought is maintained.

This last objection is perhaps the most fundamental and insurmountable. It points again to one of the basic objections to the symbolic conception that was revealed by the argument at the end of §6.4: In order for the symbols of mentalese to function as vehicles of meaningful thought whose content is capable of being internally grasped, the meaning or content of those symbols must be understood. But there is nothing available to the symbolic conception in which such an understanding can consist: more symbols will not help, since the same problem recurs for them, and to allow an awareness of content that is not a further symbol is to abandon the symbolic conception. This problem will arise for *any* account of the factors that determine the content of mentalese symbols, as long as it is conceded that the awareness or understanding of the content of thought is not to be identified with an explicit awareness of those determining factors as such.

I conclude that the symbolic conception of thought is totally and indeed obviously untenable, that it is unable to deal in any way that has even an initial appearance of success with what is surely the most obvious and fundamental fact about our thought. What is startling is that this problem has scarcely been noticed, let alone seriously addressed, in the rather large literature defending this view.[38] None of this shows, of course, that a system of mental symbols might not be in some way an essential ingredient of contentful thought, only that the employment of such symbols would have to be accompanied by a further state that constitutes the understanding of those symbols, that is, by an internally accessible representation or manifestation, itself not linguistic or symbolic in character, of their meaning or content. But once the existence of such non-symbolic representations or manifestations of content is admitted, it is difficult to see any reason why they could not constitute contentful thought by themselves, without any general need to be accompanied by tokens of mentalese. (And, contrary to the claim of conceptual role semantics, it seems obviously more plausible, given the existence of such non-symbolic representations or manifestations, to suppose that the causal–inferential pattern reflected in our use of mental representations – whether construed as symbolic or not – is derivative from our awareness of their content, rather than being primary.)

It is also worth emphasizing at this point that the premise needed to derive this result is not (i) that we *always* have complete access to the contents of our thoughts, nor indeed (ii) that we ever have *complete* access to the content of any thought, nor even (iii) that we have at least partial access to the contents of *all* of our thoughts. It is enough if we have even very partial access to the contents of at least some of our thoughts, for example, some meaningful grasp or apprehension of some of the represented properties that are ingredients of that content, for even that, if the

---

38 One noteworthy exception to this general pattern is Paul Boghossian's paper "Content and Self-Knowledge" (Boghossian 1989), which argues, in a way that is roughly parallel to the argument offered here, for the superficially more general thesis that any relational account of how thought content is constituted would make it impossible for us to know reflectively what we are thinking. But while Boghossian is unwilling to accept the skeptical conclusion that we do not "know our own minds," he is also unwilling to make the seemingly obvious move of regarding his argument as a *reductio ad absurdum* of relational accounts of content.

179

rest of the argument is correct, is something that the linguistic or symbolic conception of thought cannot account for.

§6.7. TOWARD A THEORY OF MENTAL CONTENT

The conclusion we have thus arrived at is that as long as it is conceded that we have an awareness of the content of our thoughts that goes beyond an awareness of bare, uninterpreted symbols, thought cannot be merely a symbolic process, composed entirely of elements whose content is imposed upon them from the outside in some relational way. Instead, at least some of the elements of thought must be *intrinsically* meaningful or contentful, must have the particular content that they do simply by virtue of their intrinsic, non-relational character. It is still possible, of course, that symbolic elements of some sort play a role in thought, for example, that we sometimes or even often think in words (words made meaningful or contentful by associated non-symbolic thoughts). But once the existence of non-symbolic, intrinsically contentful thought elements is admitted, the role of any symbolic elements that are also involved becomes clearly secondary and derivative, albeit perhaps sometimes practically indispensable.

This result is relevant to the defense of moderate rationalism in several ways. In the first place, it eliminates the possibility of any cogent objection to moderate rationalism, along the lines suggested earlier, that takes the symbolic conception of thought as a premise. Second, because the idea of intrinsic thought content is difficult (or probably impossible) for many of the alleged theses that provide the premises for objections to moderate rationalism to accommodate, those objections are undermined in a way that supplements the general argument in §6.1. Third, and most importantly, the idea of intrinsic thought content may at least suggest how the abstract objects that are involved in *a priori* justification can be accessible to the mind, without the need for a perceptual or quasi-perceptual relation that might raise anew the causal objection. But an appreciation of this last point will require some further discussion of what intrinsic, non-symbolic thought content might be like and how it might be possible. This is obviously a very large and difficult question, far too large to be adequately dealt with in the space that can reasonably be allocated to it here. But even some quite tentative and preliminary exploration will, I believe, help to clarify both the idea of such content and its bearing on moderate rationalism.

Let me begin by enunciating two general and closely related convictions about what a satisfactory account of intrinsic content will have to look like.

The first is that such a solution will have to involve metaphysics of a pretty hard-core kind, a kind that is still relatively rare and unfashionable even in this post-positivistic age. What is needed is an intelligible account of the connection between the intrinsic features of thoughts or thought elements and such things as metaphysically independent properties or universals, in virtue of which the former can be about the latter in an internally accessible way. I can see no way to guarantee that such an account must be possible, that we may not ultimately have to take our ability to genuinely think about or conceive properties to be a primitive fact, not capable of being further explained. But such a result would mean that our search for philosophical understanding had failed in a fundamental way. The second, correlative conviction pertains to the sweeping and obscure metaphysical theses that were discussed in §6.1 as providing the basis for objections to moderate rationalism: it would be foolish in the extreme while attempting to deal with this most difficult problem to shackle ourselves in advance with the constraints of the vague theses of materialism or naturalism that have been so pervasively invoked in recent discussions in this area. The point here is very simple: That we are able to think contentfully and be aware of what we are thinking to some degree at least is far more obvious and indisputable than any doctrine like materialism or naturalism could ever be. Thus, if such a capacity indeed requires intrinsically contentful thoughts, as has been argued here, then these views can be reasonably judged to be correct only after they have succeeded in providing an account of how such thoughts are possible; and if the only available account turns out to be non-materialistic or non-naturalistic, then it will be materialism or naturalism rather than that account that is thereby refuted.

But what might such a metaphysical account actually look like? Here it will be useful to make a fairly sweeping assumption for which no adequate defense can be offered here, but which nonetheless seems to me to stand a good chance of being correct: the assumption that the contents of thought can be adequately accounted for by appeal to only two general sorts of ingredients: (a) contents representing properties (including relational properties); and (b) indexical contents of some sort or other. One reason that this is at least somewhat plausible is that one possible, though by no means generally accepted account of natural kind concepts in light of phenomena like Putnam's Twin Earth example (see §6.5) is that the content of such concepts involves an indexical element referring to something like the local environment. And one particularly neat account of how such a view might work is offered by Chisholm, on whose view all thought contents can be reduced to the attribution to oneself of various properties (including, of course, relational properties reflecting claims about other objects).[39] Given this assumption, it seems reasonable enough to focus here on the case of contents representing properties or universals as the central case, especially since it is this sort of content that seems most clearly and obviously to be internally accessible. And it is, of course, this case that is most immediately and obviously relevant to our main concern with *a priori* justification and the defense of moderate rationalism.

How then is it possible that a thought, simply by virtue of its intrinsic character, is about or has as an element of its content a particular property or universal, whether simple or complex, concrete or abstract, descriptive or evaluative? How might the intrinsic character pick out that particular property against all others, without appeal to external relations like conventions, associations, and causal connections, and also without appeal to any relation of representation or reference or apprehending or "grasping" that would require further explication? The answer to this question that I want to consider here is very radical indeed from a contemporary perspective, so much so that it would be very hard to take seriously, were it not that there is no apparent alternative. It is that in order for the intrinsic character of the thought to specify precisely *that* particular property to the exclusion of anything else, the property in question must *itself* somehow be metaphysically involved in that character. The rationale for this suggestion is the realization that no surrogate or stand-in of any sort will do, since any account of the relation between such a surrogate and the property itself would raise anew all the same difficulties that afflict the symbolic theory (of which any such view would in effect be an instance). But at the same time, of course, it will plainly not do to say that thoughts simply instantiate the properties they represent: Most properties obviously cannot literally be features of thoughts on any tenable view of thoughts, whether materialist or dualist. And, even more obviously, there is no plausibility at all to the idea that a thought's simply instantiating a particular property has any tendency to result in a relation of representation between the two.[40]

---

39 See Chisholm (1981). David Lewis defends a similar view in his paper "Attitudes De Dicto and De Se" (Lewis 1979).
40 One possible appeal here would be to images, which have sometimes been thought to possess literally at least some of the features that they in some sense depict. But the problems with such a view are well known: at best, it would apply to far too few of the cases that need to be dealt with; and, more basically, an image does not represent anything by itself, but rather needs at least to be supplemented by a content directing that it be interpreted in the right way – something analogous to a caption on a picture. Thus while images may and probably do play a derivative role of some sort in mental representation, they cannot provide the main account that we are seeking here.

Here we find ourselves in the dialectical vicinity of the venerable account of thought offered by Aristotle and his followers, especially Aquinas. In Aquinas's version, the core of the view is that when I think of something X, the form or nature of X literally occurs in, "informs," my mind. Thus if I think of something triangular, my mind is informed by the nature triangularity. But to be informed by the nature triangularity is also, of course, precisely what makes something a triangular thing, and my mind is obviously not a triangular thing, nor does it literally contain any triangular things. Thus the view is that when I think of triangular things, the form triangularity informs my mind in a special way that is different from the way in which it informs triangular things: it has *esse intentionale* as opposed to *esse naturale*.[41] It would be easy to dismiss this view as merely a restatement of the problem in more obscure terminology, but I think that such a reaction would be a serious mistake. On the contrary, the central idea of the view – namely that thinking of something as having a particular form or property involves the literal occurrence of that form or property in the mind, but not in the same way in which it occurs in its ordinary instances – seems to me very much in the right direction.

There are, however, two importantly different possible interpretations of the view, which it is important to distinguish. On the first, the property that the mind instantiates when it thinks of triangular things is the very same property that a triangular thing instantiates, the difference between the two cases lying not in the property but rather in there being two different relations of instantiation involved. Thus on this view, which I take to be the more natural interpretation of the historical philosophers in question, we are faced with the need to make sense of two distinct instantiation relations in which something can stand to the very same universal, both species of a more generic relation of instantiation. I can only say that I am extremely skeptical that there is any good way to do this.

The alternative interpretation, which I regard as less plausible as an interpretation of the historical views but more defensible philosophically, would hold that, for example, triangularity qua having *esse intentionale* and triangularity qua having *esse naturale* are distinct, though presumably intimately related universals, the latter of which is instantiated by triangular things and the former of which is instantiated by thoughts of triangular things. This would have the virtue of eliminating the need for a second

41 For some discussion of this view, see P. T. Geach, "Aquinas," in Anscombe and Geach (1961), pp. 95–7; and Peter Sheehan, "Aquinas on Intentionality," in Kenny (1969), pp. 307–21.

instantiation relation, but would obviously require that some more articulate account be given of the two universals and the relation between them, something that is not to be found in Aquinas – or, as far as I know, anywhere in that tradition.

The obvious, albeit highly schematic, suggestion to make at this point is that the universal instantiated by thoughts of triangular things is a more complex universal having the universal triangularity as one of its components, with other components pertaining to other aspects of the content, to the kind of thought in question (belief, desire, intention, contemplation, etc.), and perhaps to further matters as well. Such a complex universal would have to be so structured that a mental act could be an instance of the complex universal without it thereby being literally an instance of triangularity, indeed without anything being such an instance. The logical relations involved in the structure would thus have to be quite different from truth-functional conjunction and other similarly extensional relations. The very existence of logical relations of this sort is obviously controversial, but the argument up to this point seems to me a strong indication that they must be available.

The key claim of such a view would be that it is a necessary, quasi-logical fact that a thought instantiating a complex universal involving the universal triangularity in the appropriate way (about which much more would obviously have to be said) is about triangular things. In this way, the content of the thought would be non-contingently captured by the intrinsic character of the mental act, and could accordingly be accessible to the thinker in a way that it is not on competing views like the linguistic theory. Though such mental acts would still be representations in a broad sense, such a position would, in George Bealer's useful terminology, be a version of realism, rather than representationalism, because the properties or universals that are the constituents of reality, of the world, would be the ultimate ingredients of thoughts as well.[42]

The bearing of all this on the defensibility of moderate rationalism should be obvious enough. If having a thought whose content is, for example, the claim that nothing can be red and green all over at the same time involves being in a mental state that instantiates a complex universal

42 George Bealer, *Quality and Concept,* p. 189. My main suggestion in this last section is in effect that only a view that is realist in Bealer's sense can ultimately make sense of the internal accessibility of thought content. Bealer's own substantially more complicated view is at least in approximately the same general direction, though he says nothing at all specific about the problem of internal access. (See also Bealer 1986.)

of which the universals redness and greenness are literal constituents, then at least much of the mystery surrounding my access to those universals and my ability to intuitively apprehend the relation of incompatibility between them is removed. In particular, there is no need to regard the apprehension of properties as a perceptual relation involving some mental analogue of vision that somehow reaches out to the Platonic realm.

These conclusions, it should hardly be necessary to say, are highly tentative and exploratory in character, much more so than anything else in the present book; and many extremely difficult problems remain. Merely the fact that I am in a state that instantiates a universal in which a particular property is a constituent, though it eliminates the main metaphysical gap between mind and Platonistically construed universal, obviously does not fully explain how I am thereby able to be conscious of the nature of that universal. (Part – though only part – of the problem is that we still have no account of how consciousness of anything is possible.) Moreover, it is clear that the distinction between thinking about an instance of a property and thinking about the property itself, between thinking about a triangular thing and thinking about triangularity, would have to be somehow accounted for. (There are obvious moves to try here, but this is not the place to explore them.) Much more would have to be said to deal with these problems and others and to develop the view in adequate detail; and, despite the venerable history of this kind of view, most of the work that such a development would involve remains to be done.[43] But if there is a solution to the general issue of the nature of intentional thought that does not simply deny the obvious fact of internal accessibility of content, it seems to me pretty likely that it lies in this general direction. (It is perhaps worth adding, however, just to make the dialectical situation clear, that while such an account is very amenable to moderate rationalism, it is really essential only if it is, as argued here, the only tenable account of how thought with internally accessible content is possible – in which case, of course, we have in my view conclusive reason to think that it is correct.)

With this, I conclude the main discussion of the moderate rationalist view and the objections that it faces. I have argued that moderate rationalism, in addition to being essential if skepticism about all trans-observational claims is to be avoided, is highly plausible from an intuitive standpoint and faces

---

43 There are several philosophers whose work includes important contributions to this project, including: Bealer (see the previous footnote); Laird Addis, who defends the idea that mental representation involves "natural signs," i.e., in my terms, intrinsically intentional representations (see Addis 1989); Gustav Bergmann; and Husserl.

no compelling objections of either an epistemological or metaphysical character. Given the failure of the two empiricist views, the case for rationalism thus seems overwhelmingly strong. My aim in the final chapter of the book will be to elaborate this case and the account of the moderate rationalist view still further by considering in detail one pivotal philosophical issue where the appeal to the *a priori* is arguably essential: the venerable problem of induction.

7

The justification of induction

§7.1. INTRODUCTION

Our discussion of *a priori* justification so far has been in the main relent-lessly abstract, with only a few of the most obvious examples to enliven the way. While this seems to me appropriate where it is the very existence of non-tautological *a priori* justification that is at issue, it does leave the issue of the scope of *a priori* justification almost entirely unillumined. For all that has been argued so far, it would be possible that *a priori* justification of the rationalist kind, though genuinely existent, is confined entirely to the general kinds of examples discussed in §4.2. And if this were so, then such justification, though perhaps important in these limited areas, would have little significance for human knowledge in general and would in particular do almost nothing to solve the problem of observation-transcendent in-ference raised in §1.1. Radical empiricists would indeed be mistaken in their central claim, but their error would be of little consequence; their general epistemological position would still be closer to the truth than that of the rationalist in the ways that matter most.

My conviction is that, on the contrary, rationalistic *a priori* justification is of crucial importance for epistemology and indeed for philosophy gener-ally. While a full defense of this claim would be as large as philosophy itself and would greatly transcend the scope of this or any reasonable book, the aim of this final chapter is to make a start in this direction. In this chapter, I will offer a more specific and detailed (though still far from complete) discussion of one central epistemological problem, to the solution of which an *a priori* appeal is arguably essential: the classical Humean problem of induction.

I choose this problem for extended treatment because it is obviously central to the general issue of observation-transcendent inference. Induc-tion is the intuitively simplest example of an inference that transcends direct observation, and inductively arrived at conclusions also provide the essential basis for many inferences of more complicated sorts, including, I would argue, the inference to the external world. Thus it is plausible to suppose that any adequate non-skeptical epistemology must be able to offer a justification of induction. I will argue in this chapter, first, that only an *a priori* justification of induction has any chance of success and, second, that the prospects for such an *a priori* justification, contrary to widespread belief (or prejudice), are quite good.

§7.2. THE SHAPE OF THE PROBLEM

In a lecture on Bacon delivered in 1926, C.D. Broad describes the failure of philosophers to solve the problem of justifying inductive reasoning as "the scandal of Philosophy."[1] Broad's choice of terms is noteworthy. The failure to solve a serious intellectual problem would not in itself be *scandalous:* perhaps there simply is no solution or only one so difficult and obscure that no stigma would attach to the failure to find it. What might make the situation with regard to induction seem a *scandal* is such a failure together with the overwhelming intuitive conviction that there must be a solution and indeed a fairly obvious one, that thoroughgoing inductive skepticism is *obviously* an unreasonable position. (Broad suggests such a view by describing inductive reasoning as "the glory of Science," as well as "the scandal of Philosophy.")

One purpose of the present chapter is to suggest that the scandal of which Broad speaks (for I agree that it is a scandal) is still very much with us, despite the best efforts of recent analytic philosophy. Indeed, I shall argue, the typical analytic approaches to the problem of induction not only do not succeed in removing the scandal, but never had any chance of such success in the first place: rather than solving the central problem, they in effect concede that it cannot be solved, and then proceed to offer one or another sort of palliative.

I begin with a schematic account of the problem of induction as I shall understand it here. Suppose that there is some reasonably definite observational or experimental situation *A,* and that out of a large number of observed instances of *A,* some fraction m/n have also possessed some further, logically independent observable property or characteristic *B;* in brief, m/n of observed *A*s have also been *B*s. Suppose further that the locations and times of observation, the identity of the observers themselves, the conditions of observation, and any further background circum-

1 "The Philosophy of Francis Bacon," reprinted in Broad (1952), pp. 117–43; the passage quoted is from p. 143.

stances not specified in the description of A have been varied to a substantial degree; and also that there is no relevant background information available concerning either the incidence of Bs in the class of As or the connection, if any, between being A and being B.[2]

In the situation as described, a standard (enumerative) inductive inference would move from the premise that m/n of observed As are Bs to the conclusion that (probably),[3] within some reasonable measure of approximation, m/n of all As (observed or unobserved, past, present, or future, even hypothetical as well as actual) are (or will or would be) Bs. In the special case in which the fraction in question reduces to 1, the conclusion would be that probably all As are Bs. (An alternative conclusion would concern the likelihood of the very next observed A being a B; I shall assume that the difference between this sort of conclusion and the more general one does not affect in any important way the issues to be considered here.)

In its most basic form, the problem of induction is the problem of why inferences that satisfy this schema should be expected to lead or at least to be likely to lead to the truth about the world. Is there any sort of rationale that can be offered for thinking that conclusions reached in this way are likely to be true if the inductive premise is true – or even that the chance that such a conclusion is true is enhanced *to any degree at all* by the truth of such a premise? If we understand *epistemic justification* in the way discussed earlier in this book, that is, as justification that increases to some degree the likelihood that the justified belief is true and that is thus conducive to finding the truth, the issue is whether inductive reasoning confers any degree of epistemic justification, however small, on its conclusion.[4]

Hume's original elaboration of this problem continues, as we shall see,

2 In this chapter, I will simply stipulate that the predicates involved in such arguments are not of the sort (such as "grue" and "bleen") that are involved in Goodman's "new riddle of induction." See Goodman (1955). Contrary to the views of many philosophers, I cannot see that the issues involved in the "new riddle" have any major bearing on the classical problem of induction; but a consideration of them would in any case take more space than is available in the present chapter.

3 I take the probability qualification to apply to the inference rather than to the conclusion: the conclusion is about A's and B's, not about the proposition that m/n of all A's are B's. But there are complicated issues lurking here that I will largely ignore in the present chapter.

4 I have couched the problem in terms of epistemic justification rather than knowledge, because I do not think that the current controversy as to whether knowledge requires epistemic justification (in this sense), as opposed to something like reliability, has any bearing on the classical problem of induction; the central issue is whether we have any reason to think that the conclusion of an inductive inference is true, not whether it is knowledge in some alleged sense that involves no such reason.

to have a major and not altogether salutary influence on contemporary views, and it will be helpful to look briefly at his discussion.[5] Hume's focus is narrower in two ways: he is concerned only with cases (i) in which *all* observed cases of *A* are cases of *B*, and (ii) in which the intended conclusion is that being *A* is the *cause* of being *B*. But the nub of the problem is the same. Having argued that causal knowledge always depends on repeated experience of the putative causal sequence, Hume proceeds to ask how such repeated experience warrants or justifies the causal conclusion. What sort of *reasoning* moves from the observation of particular cases in which *A* has been followed by *B* to the general conclusion that *A* will always be followed by *B*? His initially startling thesis is that there is no such reasoning, that the conclusion in question is not based on reasoning at all but is rather the result of an ultimately arational process: *custom* or *habit*.

Besides the challenge to supply such reasoning, Hume offers an argument, specifically a dilemma, to show that no possible line of reasoning could justify the inductive conclusion. Such reasoning, he argues, would have to be either *a priori* demonstrative reasoning concerning relations of ideas or "experimental" (i.e., empirical) reasoning concerning matters of fact and existence. It cannot be the former, because all demonstrative reasoning relies on the avoidance of contradiction, and it is not a contradiction to suggest that "the course of nature may change," that sequences of events which occurred regularly in the past may not be repeated in the future. But the reasoning also cannot be based on experience since the justifiability of experimental reasoning, of generalizing from experience, is precisely what is at issue and cannot be assumed without begging the question. Hence, he concludes, there can be no such reasoning.

An alternative formulation of Hume's dilemma, in some ways clearer, may be obtained by formulating it with reference to a principle that he mentions but never focuses on very directly: the Principle of Induction, which says roughly that the future will resemble the past (or, better, that unobserved cases will resemble observed cases). The suggestion is that inductive arguments should be construed as enthymematic, with some such principle serving as the suppressed premise. Hume's argument is then that there is no way in which the Principle of Induction can itself be epistemically justified: it cannot be justified *a priori* because its denial is not a contradiction; and it cannot be justified by appeal to experience without

---

5 See David Hume, *An Inquiry Concerning Human Understanding* (Hume 1748), section IV. I will not consider here the similar but more complicated account in Hume's *Treatise of Human Nature* (Hume 1739–40).

reasoning in a circle, since an experiential argument will presumably be based on the fact that the principle has been (generally) true in the observed past and hence will ultimately depend on the very same principle. Thus inductive reasoning, being dependent on an unjustifiable principle, is itself unjustifiable.

Perhaps the best way to appreciate the destructiveness of this conclusion is to consider the skeptical view that is its apparent corollary. As Hume, along with many others, points out, the conclusion that inductive reasoning is unjustifiable appears to decisively undermine the rational credentials of both the scientific and the commonsense views of the world. Not only does it render epistemically unjustified all inductively supported beliefs in laws or regularities in the world, but since even the beliefs in a world of enduring objects and, via memory, in one's own past history seem to rely ultimately on such regularities, the unjustifiability of induction arguably leads to perhaps the most radical form of skepticism imaginable: a solipsism in which my epistemically justified beliefs are restricted entirely to my own present experience.[6] Such an extreme version of skepticism is obviously enormously implausible from an intuitive standpoint, thus providing an equally strong intuitive reason for thinking that a satisfactory justification for inductive reasoning must be available and making it seem intellectually scandalous if none can be found.

What is the contemporary response to this problem? Though there has been little explicit discussion of late, the generally received view seems to go something like this: Hume's dilemma, it is claimed, demonstrates decisively that induction cannot be epistemically justified if epistemic justification is understood in the way discussed earlier, that is, demonstrates that it is impossible to give any non-question-begging argument or reason to show that the conclusion of an inductive argument which fits the schema set out above is likely to be true or even that its chances of truth are thereby enhanced to some degree. For such an argument would have to be either deductive or inductive in character: a deductive argument could not succeed because there is no contradiction in supposing that any or all such inductive conclusions (whose truth has not been independently estab-lished) are false; while an inductive argument would beg the question. But this result, the received view continues, does not show that induction is unjustified or rationally unacceptable, so that the skeptic would prevail. Instead, it is claimed (and here the received view divides into two main versions) either (a) that induction can be adequately justified in a different,

6 Assuming that this is capable of standing epistemically on its own.

"pragmatic," way, roughly by showing that it is nonetheless our best hope for finding the truth; or (b) that the problem of induction can be "dissolved" by showing, through linguistic or conceptual analysis, that the demand for a non-trivial justification of inductive reasoning ultimately makes no sense. And in either case, it seems to be suggested (though often not very explicitly), the skeptical challenge is adequately dealt with, even if not exactly refuted.[7]

This response to the problem – one which, as we will see more clearly below, flows more or less directly from a repudiation of the rationalist view of *a priori* justification – seems to me deeply unsatisfactory. My conviction is that neither of these distinctively analytic "solutions" to the problem of induction is adequate to meet the problem or to lessen at all the force of the threatened skeptical conclusion. In a way this conclusion is partially implicit in what has already been said about the positions in question, but I will attempt to spell it out a bit more fully in the next two sections. (My concern here is with the broad outlines of the various positions and not with their detailed and often highly technical elaborations. To employ a military metaphor, I am interested in philosophical strategy rather than tactics; for it is my conviction that no amount of brilliant tactical maneuvering can save a philosophical position whose strategic conception is fundamentally flawed.)

§7.3. THE PRAGMATIC JUSTIFICATION OF INDUCTION

The first of the two positions to be considered is the so-called pragmatic justification (or "vindication") of induction, first advocated by Reichenbach and developed further by Wesley Salmon, among others. Here I will confine myself largely to Reichenbach's original presentation, in which the essential thrust of the view is perhaps clearest.[8]

7 I will not consider in this chapter a third contemporary approach to the problem of induction, that of Karl Popper. See, e.g., Popper, "Conjectural Knowledge: My Solution to the Problem of Induction," reprinted in Popper (1972), pp. 1–31. Though Popper describes his view as a solution to the problem, it seems to amount mainly to the insistence that the problem as posed here cannot be solved, i.e., that inductive evidence provides no reason at all to think that the corresponding inductive conclusions are true, thus endorsing inductive skepticism rather than even attempting to answer it. More generally, Popper's overall epistemological view is devastatingly skeptical in its implications, implications that are only lightly disguised by his use of the term 'corroboration' in a highly misleading way that departs strongly from its ordinary meaning.
8 See Reichenbach (1938), pp. 339–63; and Reichenbach (1949), pp. 469–82. References in the text are to the pages of Reichenbach (1938).

Reichenbach's basic move is to treat induction, not as a form of inference, but rather as a *method* for arriving at *"posits."* A posit is not a statement or belief, not something asserted or maintained as true. Instead, it is analogous to a bet made in a gambling situation (352). Just as a gambler who wagers on red while playing roulette is not thereby asserting and need not believe that red will be the actual result (though he may of course also have such a belief), so also the scientist in the standard inductive situation who adopts the posit that the proportion of A's that are B's is m/n is not thereby asserting and need not believe that this is even likely to be the true value in reality. His posit is an intellectual wager, nothing more. Construed in these terms, the inductive method says roughly that one should posit the observed proportion as the true proportion and then correct and continue to correct that initial posit as new information comes in.

There is, however, a fundamental disanalogy, according to Reichenbach, between the gambling situation and that in which the inductive method is employed: surprisingly enough, the gambler is in an epistemically *superior* position. In a typical gambling situation, the gambler at least knows the odds, knows what the chances are that the outcome on which he bets will actually occur. Thus the roulette player knows that the bet on red has (allowing for the house share) slightly less than a 50 percent chance of success; his bet is what Reichenbach calls an "appraised posit." The inductive bet is, however, a "blind posit": although, for reasons yet to be discussed, it is the best bet we can make in such a situation, we do not know its chances of success or indeed that it has *any likelihood at all* of succeeding (352–3). This is so because of the subject-matter of the bet. What we are gambling on when we use the inductive method is the value of a certain proportion in nature, which Reichenbach construes as the limit of the observed proportion m/n as the number of observed cases of A increases to infinity. But we have no way of knowing that there even *is* such a limit, that the proportion of A's that are B's converges in the long run on some reasonably stable value rather than simply varying at random; Reichenbach agrees with Hume that we cannot know that nature is uniform. And if we cannot know that the limit even exists, we obviously cannot know that we have any definite chance of finding it.

What we can know, according to Reichenbach, is that *if* there is a truth of this sort to be found, the method of induction will eventually find it to any degree of accuracy that might be wished. This is so simply in virtue of Reichenbach's account of what it is for such a limit to exist: to deny that the observed proportion ever converges on some definite proportion m/n and thereafter remains within the desired degree of approximation of that value no matter how many more cases are observed is to deny that there *is* any limit, which amounts to denying that there is any truth to be found concerning the proportion of *A*s that are *B*s. Thus the claim that the method of induction will find the truth in the long run if there is any truth to be found turns out to be tautologous, as indeed any such *a priori* justification must be, according to Reichenbach's moderate empiricist epistemology. And, he adds, no more than this can be established for any alternative method. The inductive method is therefore rationally justified, not by showing that it will succeed or is even likely to succeed, but rather by showing that following it gives us our best chance for success, our best gamble in a situation that is essentially unfathomable. It will succeed (eventually) if success is possible.

Reichenbach's approach to the justification of induction is problematic in a number of ways. Before turning to the objection that is most important from the standpoint of the present book, I will briefly mention two others. First, there are indefinitely many other "methods" for arriving at a posit of the sort in question for which the same sort of justification can be given. Intuitively, these are methods that say to posit the observed value m/n plus or minus some further correction factor, where this further factor is so specified that it diminishes to zero as the number of observed cases increases to infinity. Such an alternative method will obviously yield the same result as the inductive method in the infinitely long run and is thus sure to succeed eventually if induction does; but it is possible to find such an alternative that will yield any arbitrarily chosen result in the short run, no matter how far from m/n that result may be. Obviously some way must be found of excluding such alternative methods, and Salmon especially has labored in this direction. I doubt very much whether any such attempt really succeeds, but the issues surrounding such efforts are too complicated and tangential to be gone into here.[9] Second, even if success is possible, even if there is a truth of the requisite sort to be found, the method of induction is guaranteed to find it only in the indefinitely long run. Thus the guarantee of success if success is possible does not extend to any specific finite short run – and yet, of course, any actual practical application of the inductive method always takes place in such a short run. Thus the bearing of the pragmatic justification on the actual use of induction is quite problematic.

The fundamental problem, however, is that even if these other difficulties did not exist, even if there were only one method to which the

9 See, e.g., Salmon (1963), pp. 353–70.

justification in question applied and even if that justification could somehow be extended to the short run, the significance of Reichenbach's pragmatic justification in relation to the original problem remains obscure. As he himself indeed insists, that justification still yields no reason at all for thinking that inductive conclusions, or any of the myriad further beliefs that are epistemically dependent on them, are to any degree likely to be *true*. The sort of justification in question is thus not epistemic justification, as that concept was construed above; to show that beliefs are justified in this alternative way does not answer, or even purport to answer, the basic skeptical worry about induction, and is indeed quite compatible with the deepest degree of skepticism. It is thus hard to see why it should be regarded as any sort of solution to the classical problem of induction.[10]

It is clear what the response of the proponents of the pragmatic justification to this criticism would be: they would argue, following Hume, that this is the best justification that is possible for induction, with the implication being that the best we can do must be good enough. But of course the fact, if it is a fact, that the best we can do is quite compatible with extreme skepticism tells in favor of the skeptical view, not against it. The point I want to insist on, however, is the extreme intuitive implausibility of such a result, according to which the most carefully derived results of science are epistemically no better, indeed worse, than a gambler's bets. Consider Reichenbach's metaphorical description of the situation one is in when employing induction:

A blind man who has lost his way in the mountains feels a trail with his stick. He does not know where the path will lead him, or whether it may take him so close to the edge of a precipice that he will be plunged into the abyss. Yet he follows the path, groping his way step by step; for if there is any possibility of getting out of the wilderness, it is by feeling his way along the path. As blind men we face the future; but we feel a path. And we know: if we can find a way through the future it is by feeling our way along this path.[11]

We can all agree that the blind man should follow the path and that he is, in an appropriate sense, acting in a justified or rational manner in doing so. But is there any plausibility at all to the suggestion that when we reason inductively, or accept the myriad scientific and commonsensical results that ultimately depend on such inference, we have no more justification for

---

10 Salmon in effect concedes this point by redefining the problem of induction as the problem of choosing a rule for making non-demonstrative inferences concerning matters of fact out of the enormous variety of such rules that might be chosen, where it is admitted from the outset that no such rule can be shown to be even likely to yield true conclusions. See, e.g., Salmon (1972).

11 Reichenbach (1949), p. 482.

thinking that our beliefs are likely to be true than the blind man has for thinking that he has found the way out of the wilderness? Here in especially clear-cut form is the intellectual scandal of which Broad spoke. I find it hard to believe that anyone who is at all familiar with the spectacular successes of modern science or its even more conspicuous technological by-products can believe this for even a moment, and perhaps even harder to understand how such vigorous proponents of science and scientific method as Reichenbach and Salmon can accept it with apparent equanimity.

This objection does not, of course, show that the pragmatic view is mistaken in claiming that nothing more is available, for skepticism of this sort, though extremely implausible, might still turn out to be true and can be refuted only by actually finding an adequate justification for induction. At the very least, however, the massive implausibility of such a result provides abundant warrant and motivation for questioning the general epistemological views that lead to it and for seeking a better alternative.

§7.4. THE ORDINARY LANGUAGE JUSTIFICATION OF INDUCTION

The second of the two distinctively analytic responses to the problem of induction is the attempt, mainly characteristic of ordinary language philosophy, to argue that the question of whether induction is justified cannot be meaningfully raised and is thus a "pseudo-problem." Views of this general sort have been advanced by many philosophers in this general tradition, including Ayer, Edwards, and Strawson. In the present chapter, I will largely confine myself to Strawson's version, but the basic objection to be raised against his view applies just as well to the others.[12]

Strawson claims that the question of whether induction is reasonable or justified makes sense only if it tacitly involves the demand that induction be shown to meet the standards of deductive reasoning, that is, the demand that the inductive conclusion be shown to follow deductively from the inductive premise (together, perhaps, with a suppressed premise of some sort). Such a demand cannot be met, but this, according to Strawson, in no way shows that induction is unjustified or unreasonable, since the demand itself is absurd. Deduction is one kind of reasoning and induction is simply a distinct, fundamentally different kind of reasoning. Each of these kinds of reasoning possesses its own autonomous standards, and there is no reason at

12 See Ayer (1946), pp. 49–50; Edwards (1949); and Strawson (1952), chapter 9. References in the text in this section are to the pages of Strawson (1952).

all to expect one kind to meet the standards of the other nor for demanding that it do so (250). And if this error of attempting to assess induction by appeal to deductive standards is avoided, no meaningful question remains, according to Strawson, regarding the reasonableness or justifiability of induction – or at least none that cannot be easily and trivially answered.[13] For *of course* induction is reasonable if judged by inductive standards, the only ones that are appropriate.

This claim is spelled out more fully in the following pivotal passage:

> It is an analytic proposition that it is reasonable to have a degree of belief in a statement which is proportional to the strength of the evidence in its favor; and it is an analytic proposition . . . that, other things being equal, the evidence for a generalization is strong in proportion as the number of favorable instances, and the variety of circumstances in which they have been found, is great. So to ask whether it is reasonable to place reliance on inductive procedures is like asking whether it is reasonable to proportion the degree of one's belief to the strength of the evidence. Doing this is what 'being reasonable' *means* in such a context. (256–7)

If we confine our consideration to a strong sense of belief amounting to full acceptance of the proposition in question, and understand "believing in accordance with inductive standards" to mean believing, in the strong sense just specified, just in case the inductive standards roughly specified in the passage are satisfied to a high degree, we get the following, somewhat simplified, version of the argument:

(1) Believing in accordance with strong evidence is believing reasonably.
(2) Believing in accordance with inductive standards is believing in accordance with strong evidence.

Therefore, believing in accordance with inductive standards is believing reasonably.

Strawson's claim is that both of the premises of this seemingly valid argument are analytic truths, established as such by appeal to the ordinary usage of the expressions in question. In particular, premise (2) is analytic simply because inductive evidence is what we call "strong evidence" in cases of the sort in question.[14]

For this conclusion to be relevant to the problem of induction as it was formulated above, however, "believing reasonably," as it occurs in the

---

13 Strawson's initial claim is that there is no meaningful question. But he proceeds to both answer the question and argue for the correctness of the answer (see below), thus suggesting that the second formulation above is more accurate.

14 Strawson says nothing very specific about what he means by 'analytic'. Since the main problems with the argument are clear enough even without resolving that question, I will largely ignore it here. (But see the second footnote following.)

conclusion, must be construed to mean that the belief in question is *epistemically* reasonable or justified, in the sense specified earlier, that is, that there is reason to think that it is likely to be true. And if the conclusion is understood in this way, it is easy to see that something has gone seriously wrong. For if both of the premises of the argument were analytic, then the conclusion would also presumably have to be analytic, and it is surely not an analytic truth, not even according to Strawson, that beliefs held in accordance with inductive standards are thereby likely to be true.[15] Thus on this construal, either one of the premises is not analytic after all, or else the argument tacitly equivocates. If, on the other hand, "believing reasonably" does not mean, or at least entail, that the belief is epistemically justified in the indicated sense, then Strawson's argument and the attempted justification of induction that it embodies will, like Reichenbach's, offer no real reply to the skeptic and will thus have no clear relevance to the original problem.

It is easier to see that Strawson's argument does not work than to arrive at a definitive diagnosis of exactly how it fails. Perhaps the most plausible suggestion is that the argument equivocates on the phrase "believing in accordance with strong evidence." For the second premise to be analytic, this phrase must mean something like "believing when the evidence is strong according to generally accepted standards"[16]; whereas, for the first premise to be analytic (assuming that "believing reasonably" is construed to mean having beliefs that are epistemically justified), the phrase must mean something like "believing in accordance with evidence that actually establishes a strong likelihood that the belief is true." And whether or not evidence that is strong according to generally accepted standards really does establish a strong likelihood of truth is, of course, precisely what the problem of induction is all about. The only way to avoid such equivocation, while retaining the relevance of the conclusion, is to construe one of the premises in a way that, besides not being plausibly analytic, amounts to begging the question: either premise (1) must be construed as saying that beliefs for which there is strong evidence according to generally accepted standards are thereby highly likely to be true; or else premise (2) must be

---

15 Strawson insists that the claim that induction will continue to succeed is contingent and may even turn out to be false (op. cit., p. 261).

16 Thus it is likely that the underlying mistake is a too casual appeal to ordinary usage of the sort that was rampant in ordinary-language philosophy. For of course the fact that inductive evidence is generally described as strong in ordinary usage does not by itself show that such a claim is part of the meaning or definition of "strong evidence," as would be required to support any serious claim of analyticity with respect to the second premise.

construed as saying that being supported by strong inductive evidence makes a belief highly likely to be true.

The central problem with Strawson's argument may perhaps be made clearer by considering an analogous case. Imagine a religiously oriented community in which judgments on a wide variety of factual issues are made by appeal to a body of sacred literature that is generally accepted as authoritative. If a skeptic were to question whether believing in accordance with evidence of this sort yields beliefs that are epistemically justified, that is, likely to be true, we could imagine a member of the community replying as follows:

Of course believing in accordance with scripture results in justified beliefs! Beliefs arrived at in this way are what we mean by "justified beliefs" in this community. It is an analytic truth that beliefs supported by strong evidence are justified; and it is also an analytic truth that being highly in accord with scripture constitutes strong evidence.

But such a reply to the skeptic is irrelevant to the skeptic's challenge if "justified" does not mean epistemically justified; and either question-begging or guilty of equivocation otherwise. Here too, the basic issue is whether what the community in question accepts as strong evidence really is strong evidence in the epistemically interesting sense. And on this question, the argument just offered, like Strawson's argument concerning induction, sheds no light at all. Nor can any argument that appeals only to generally accepted standards (or to the reflection of such standards in ordinary usage) do any better.

It need not be denied that Strawson's argument, like Reichenbach's, does establish that accepting inductively supported conclusions is reasonable or justified in *some* sense of those multifarious terms. Being in accord with generally or conventionally accepted standards may be conceded to constitute one species of justification – though one that seems even less interesting from an epistemological standpoint than Reichenbach's pragmatic sense. But justification in this sense has no immediate bearing on likelihood of truth and hence is quite compatible with a thoroughgoing skepticism of the sort discussed earlier. As Salmon nicely puts it, such justification seems to amount to no more than this: "If you use inductive procedures you can call yourself 'reasonable' – *and isn't that nice!*"[17] I conclude that this second analytic solution is no more successful than the first in meeting the basic skeptical challenge to induction.

17 Salmon (1972), p. 506.

§7.5. THE INDUCTIVE JUSTIFICATION OF INDUCTION

The argument of the previous three sections may be summarized in the following way. The core of the problem of induction is the problem of finding an adequate reply to the skeptic who questions whether inductive evidence ever provides a good reason for thinking that an inductive conclusion is likely to be true or even that it is to any degree more likely to be true than it would be in the absence of such evidence. It is our inability to answer such a skeptic, or even apparently to say what an answer might look like, that constitutes the scandal of which Broad spoke. To show that inductive conclusions are justified or reasonable in other senses that have no bearing on likelihood of truth, senses like those involved in the pragmatic and ordinary-language justifications, is to leave this central problem untouched. Thus the second part of the received view, which attempts in effect to go between the horns of Hume's dilemma by finding a way of justifying induction that does not involve the claim that inductively supported conclusions are thereby likely to be true, is fundamentally misguided from the outset. And hence, if the first part of the received view is correct, if Hume's dilemma really does establish conclusively that no possible argument or reason can show that inductively supported conclusions are likely to be true, the extreme skeptical conclusion discussed earlier is unavoidable, intellectually scandalous though it seems.

There are only two apparent ways out of this intellectual "coal pit," corresponding to grasping one or the other of the horns of Hume's dilemma: either we must agree with empiricists like Mill that induction can be justified empirically; or else we must adopt a rationalist view, according to which induction can after all be justified on a purely *a priori* basis. For Hume seems correct in his conviction that these are the only possible ways in which inductive conclusions could be established as likely to be true; and we can now see that nothing less than this will truly meet the problem and eliminate the scandal.[18] I will consider the first of these

18 I will not consider in this chapter the possibility of some sort of Kantian or neo-Kantian approach to the problem. Like the analytic approaches already discussed, a Kantian view "solves" the problem in only a Pickwickian sense: it concedes that the skeptic is right, not only about induction but about knowledge of the real world generally, and then proceeds to offer us a pale substitute for the knowledge thus abandoned. (See the general discussion of Kant's anti-rationalism in §1.4, above.)

It has also sometimes been suggested that a coherence theory of justification might provide a solution to the problem of induction. But although I have elsewhere defended such a theory (see *SEK*, Part Two), I do not think that it can help here. The basic point is that a conception of coherence that is rich enough to provide an adequate basis for such a

alternatives in the remainder of the present section and devote the balance of the chapter to the second.

As we have seen, the basic objection to an empirical justification of induction is that it is inevitably circular and question-begging: obviously no set of particular experiential claims can by themselves constitute such a justification, and any attempt to generalize beyond such particular claims will employ the very mode of reasoning whose acceptability is at issue.[19] The few attempts since Mill to defend the idea of an empirical justification of induction against this objection represent variations on a common theme.[20] Their basic gambit amounts to a distinction between different levels of inductive argument: a first level in which induction is applied to things or events in the world, a second level in which induction is applied to arguments at the first level, a third level in which induction is applied to arguments at the second level, and so on. The suggestion is then that each of these levels constitutes a distinct, logically autonomous mode of argument involving its own distinct argumentative principle, and hence that the principle underlying arguments on one level can be justified without circularity by appeal to an argument of the next higher level: first-level inductive arguments by appeal to a second-level inductive argument that generalizes from the observed success of such first-level arguments; second-level inductive arguments (including the one just mentioned) by an analogous third-level inductive argument; etc.

Though this attempt is ingenious, very few have found it convincing. Here I will content myself with two main objections, both pretty obvious. First: The view just sketched clearly involves a kind of regress of justification: first-level induction is justified by appeal to second-level induction, second-level induction by appeal to third-level induction, etc., with the whole chain of justifications being dependent on that offered at each succeeding higher level. But it is obvious that this potentially infinite chain of justifications cannot, even in principle, be completed in practice. For

theory of justification will have to presuppose the cogency either of inductive reasoning or of some other sort of reasoning (such as theoretical reasoning) that raises the same sort of justificatory problem.

19 Strictly speaking, this is a bit too simple. If theoretical or abductive reasoning is recognized (as it should be) as a mode of reasoning that is distinct from instantial or enumerative induction, one could in principle attempt to justify induction empirically by using such theoretical reasoning. But such reasoning seems essentially to reply on induction for its data. And, second, this solution would only slightly postpone the problem, since theoretical reasoning is itself just as much in need of justification, and it is plausible that a justification of empirical theoretical reasoning would be at least approximately parallel to that for induction and would raise most of the same problems and issues.

20 See, e.g., Black (1954); and Will (1947).

201

the argument at each level depends on the evidence provided by the existence and observed success of arguments at the next lower level, so that completing the entire series would require that an infinite number of inductive arguments be actually given and then experientially assessed, a requirement that is obviously impossible to satisfy. Thus even if the general strategy of the hierarchical justification of induction were acceptable, it would inevitably fail in application at some level due to simple lack of evidence. And if this is so, then the whole series of justifications up to that point collapses as well, since each is dependent on those further up in the hierarchy.

Second: An even more fundamental objection is that while the distinction between different levels of induction is unobjectionable in itself, its epistemological significance is extremely problematic. The basic question raised by the problem of induction is whether inductive evidence *ever* constitutes a good reason for thinking that the corresponding inductive conclusion is true, and it still seems plainly question-begging to answer this question at one level by appeal to the same sort of argument at another level. If, as the skeptical objection suggests, no inductive argument ever establishes that its conclusion is likely to be true, then the whole hierarchy of inductive arguments is just as problematic from an epistemological standpoint as a single one would be; and this problem obviously cannot be met by appealing to those very inductive arguments.

There is one other observation that seems to me worth making in relation to inductive justifications of induction. It is easy to slip into a state of mind, especially if one considers the matter very intuitively, in which such a justification seems or "feels" cogent, even though it in fact is not. This is not at all surprising, and does nothing to suggest that an inductive justification of induction might after all succeed somehow. If inductive reasoning is, for good reasons or bad, in fact seemingly cogent from an intuitive standpoint (as it surely is), then the sort of inductive argument that underlies the inductive justification, namely an argument from the observed success of this form of argument in yielding mostly true conclusions in the past to the conclusion that it will continue to yield such conclusions in the future, will be seemingly cogent as well. But the issue with regard to the inductive justification is not of course whether this latter sort of argument seems intuitively cogent or even whether it really is cogent, but rather whether it *would* be cogent if the appeal to such an argument were itself the *only* justification for inductive reasoning. And to this question, for the reasons already considered, the answer must be negative. My suspicion, however, is that those who have found the inductive justification appealing have been confused at this precise point and have been, in effect, appealing to an intuitive cogency in inductive arguments that is either spurious or else due to a justification of some other kind (such as the *a priori* justification yet to be considered), and, in either case, is not legitimately available to them.

§7.6. IS IT POSSIBLE TO JUSTIFY INDUCTION *A PRIORI*?

It thus seems apparent that the second horn of Hume's dilemma cannot be successfully grasped, and the indicated conclusion is that only an *a priori* justification of induction can avoid the extreme skeptical conclusion. Moreover, though this conclusion runs strongly counter to a very high proportion of recent thinking on induction, there is a perspective on the problem from which it can be made to seem plausible, even obvious. The problem of induction arises in the first place after all from viewing induction as a mode of *reasoning* or *argument* that claims to be rationally cogent, that is, one in which the (probable) truth of the conclusion is at least claimed to *follow* in a rationally intelligible way from the truth of the premises. But what does it mean for a conclusion to follow rationally, whether certainly or probably, from a set of premises? I submit that it can mean only that one who understands the premises is thereby in a position to see or grasp or apprehend, either directly or via some series of individually cogent steps, that if those premises are true, then the conclusion either must be true (if the argument is conclusive) or is probably true (if the argument is less than conclusive), where this seeing or grasping or apprehending can only be *a priori* in character. The connection between premises and conclusion must be, one might say, *intellectually visible*. No empirical appeal of any sort can replace the need for such an *a priori* insight, since any such appeal would amount only to adding one or more further premises to the argument, from which the conclusion would still have to be seen to follow. Nor does it make any essential difference if logical rules or principles are added; these would themselves have to be justified on an *a priori* basis, and in any case the person employing the argument would still have to be able to see or grasp or apprehend that the conclusion followed from the total set of premises and logical rules. Thus, as we saw in §1.1, a rationally justified transition from the premises to the conclusion of *any* argument, whether it be classified as deductive or as inductive or as falling under some further rubric, can ultimately only be made on an *a priori* basis; and the result arrived at here is merely the application of this general result to the specific case of induction. The only way to avoid it, as far as I can see, is to refuse to treat inductive "inferences" as instances of reasoning or argument in the first place; this is essentially the course adopted by Reichenbach, but putting its rationale in this way makes the skeptical outcome even more obvious.

Even one who finds the foregoing argument convincing, however, is still likely to feel that its only possible outcome is inductive skepticism, that seeking an *a priori* justification of induction is knocking futilely on doors that have long been firmly and irrevocably closed and boarded up. In this section, I will consider briefly the main reasons for this prevalent attitude and try to show that they have far less force than they are usually credited with. Then, in the following section, I will attempt to sketch, in a necessarily schematic and tentative way, what an actual *a priori* justification of induction might look like.

Why then is it so widely and adamantly believed that an *a priori* justification of induction is impossible in principle – so much so that the possibility of an *a priori* justification is often not even included in the familiar rogues' gallery of possible solutions to the problem of induction?[21] Part of the explanation for the prevalence of this view is the acceptance of one or the other of the general empiricist views concerning *a priori* justification already considered and rejected in Chapters 2 and 3. But there are also some considerations pertaining more specifically to induction that have seemed to many to bar any possibility of an *a priori* justification, and it will be useful to respond to a few of these before actually undertaking this allegedly impossible task.

First. Contrary to the view of Strawson and many others, an *a priori* justification of induction need not constitute a futile attempt to "turn induction into deduction," that is, to show that the conclusion of an inductive argument follows with deductive conclusiveness from its premises. Since inductive conclusions obviously still turn out on occasion to be false, such a deductive construal of an inductive argument would have to be invalid. But, as we shall see, there are other forms that an *a priori* justification may take.

Second. An *a priori* justification of induction need not involve the claim, which so many have rightly found implausible, that the principle of induction (as roughly formulated in §7.1) or some similar principle concerning the uniformity of nature is a self-evident, *a priori* truth. Such a claim seems obviously untenable. It would mean, as has again been widely pointed out,

---

21 See, e.g., Skyrms (1975), chapter 11; and Richard Swinburne, "Introduction," in Swinburne (1974), pp. 1–17.

that a chaotic universe could somehow be ruled out as even an *a priori* possibility; whereas it seems clear on an intuitive basis that this is not so, that such a universe is *a priori* quite possible.[22]

Third. Perhaps the most common way of putting the alleged impossibility of an *a priori* justification for induction, often employed by moderate empiricists, is to appeal to the idea that the conclusion of any piece of *a priori* justifiable reasoning must be *"contained"* (or perhaps "implicit") in the premises; whereas the conclusion of an inductive argument, since it pertains to future or unobserved events, is obviously not "contained" in the inductive premise, which pertains only to past, observed events. But while this metaphor of containment may seem at first glance to have genuine content or explanatory value, it is, I believe, impossible to spell out what it might mean in a way that genuinely sheds light on the issue. My suggestion is that the only intelligible sense in which the conclusion of an *a priori* justifiable argument must be "contained" in the premises is that it must genuinely *follow* from them. There seems to be no more interesting sense in which, for example, "today is Monday or today is Tuesday" is contained in "today is Monday"; or in which "Socrates is mortal" is contained in "all men are mortal and Socrates is a man." (Here again, as with the obfuscating conceptions of analyticity discussed in Chapter 2, it appears that the moderate empiricist who adopts the containment view has taken the necessity and *a priori* justifiability of the propositions or inferences in question so much for granted that he has lost sight of the real epistemological issue and has thus ended up in effect explaining the knowledge in question by appeal to itself.)

Thus in particular, if the conclusion of a standard inductive argument genuinely follows (with probability) from its premises, then the probable truth of the conclusion is in fact "contained" in those premises in the only relevant way. This may or may not turn out to be so, but it is a mistake to think that there is some independently assessable criterion of "containment" that can provide an independent basis for deciding whether it is so.[23]

Fourth: A bit more should also be said about the conception of analyticity that is more or less implicit in Hume's original argument, that according to which an analytic truth is one whose denial is a contradiction.

---

22 More sophisticated versions of the Principle of Induction may escape this objection. Indeed, if an *a priori* justification can be given, then there must be some corresponding principle that is justified *a priori*. But it need not bear any close resemblance to the versions of the Principle of Induction that exist in the literature.
23 For further discussion of this point, see Ewing (1939–40).

The main difficulty with this general conception of analyticity was discussed in §§2.2 and 2.3. If by a contradiction is meant an *explicit* contradiction, a proposition of the form "P and not-P," then the conception in question is a reductive conception of analyticity, and cannot account for all *a priori* knowledge because it cannot account for the *a priori* knowledge that propositions of that form are false, nor for the *a priori* knowledge involved in the logical transformations needed to arrive at a proposition of that form. Whereas if, as seems to be the case with Hume, the idea of a contradiction is broadened to that of a necessary falsehood (or perhaps an intuitively obvious necessary falsehood), there is no way to exclude in advance the possibility that an *a priori* justification of induction might turn out to be analytic under this construal, that is, the possibility that the denial that an inductive conclusion follows with probability or likelihood from the corresponding inductive premise might indeed be a necessary falsehood. It is obviously possible, as Hume remarks, that the course of nature might change. Whether, however, it is possible that such a change is not even unlikely in the face of strong inductive evidence is much less obvious and cannot be simply assumed without begging the question. Thus this horn of Hume's dilemma turns out to be vastly less threatening than is usually believed: it either poses a requirement for *a priori* knowledge that cannot be met in general if there is to be any *a priori* knowledge at all or else one that an *a priori* justification of induction may perfectly well satisfy.

§7.7. TOWARD AN *A PRIORI* JUSTIFICATION OF INDUCTION

But how might an *a priori* justification of induction actually go? It will be useful to begin by recapitulating briefly just what such a justification of induction needs to accomplish. What is needed, according to our earlier formulation, is an *a priori* reason for thinking that the conclusion of a standard inductive argument is likely to be true if the premise is true, that is, that if m/n of observed cases of A have been cases of B, given suitable variation of the collateral circumstances and the absence of any further relevant information, then it is likely or probable that, within some reasonable measure of approximation, m/n of all cases of A are cases of B.

In fact, however, the earlier account needs to be modified in one crucial respect. For it cannot be established, and indeed is simply not the case, that such a conclusion is likely to be true in all cases where the evidence satisfies the specification just given. To see this, imagine a case where the relation between A and B is entirely unlawful or random. Depending on what other factors are relevant to each of them, the observed proportion of *A*s that are *B*s might vary indefinitely over time, drifting from one value to another and assuming no stable proportion. In such a case, while at any particular moment there would still be a proportion of observed *A*s that have been *B*s, there would be no reason at all to think that this proportion reflects any objective regularity that can be justifiably extended to unobserved cases or future cases or hypothetical cases. Thus what needs to be added to our earlier specification of standard inductive evidence is the further requirement that the observed proportion of *A*s that are *B*s, rather than varying irregularly over the range of possible values, converges over time to the fraction m/n and thereafter remains at least approximately constant as significant numbers of new observations come in. Subsequent references to standard inductive evidence or to a standard inductive premise will be understood to include the stipulation that this constancy condition is satisfied. (In the case where *all* observed *A*s are *B*s, this condition is of course automatically satisfied – which may be why its importance has usually been overlooked.)

What sort of an *a priori* reason might be offered, then, for thinking that a standard inductive conclusion is likely to be true when such a standard inductive premise is true? The intuitive idea behind the reason to be suggested here is that an objective regularity of a sort that would make the conclusion of a standard inductive argument true provides the best *explanation* for the truth of the premise of such an argument. This idea is not especially novel by itself: something like it has been suggested by a number of other recent discussions of induction, though usually without making clear what the epistemological status of the underlying premises is supposed to be and in particular without construing the resulting justification as *a priori*. I will first offer a sketch of the main line of argument and then consider briefly some further problems and refinements. The justification in question involves two main components, which will be considered in turn.

First. Consider again the situation described by standard inductive evidence, under our revised account: the proportion of observed *A*'s that are *B*'s has converged on some relatively constant value m/n and continues to closely approximate that value as significant numbers of new observations are added. From an intuitive standpoint, the overwhelmingly obvious question to ask is: what is the *explanation* for this situation? *Why* does the observed proportion continue to approximate m/n rather than fluctuating widely as new observations are made? This is not a situation that would obtain for just any choice of *A* and *B*, and some reason seems to be needed for its occurring in the case in question. Of course, it is logically possible that the results in question represent the operation of nothing more than mere random coincidence or chance, but it seems evident, and, as far as I can see, evident on a purely *a priori* basis, that it is highly unlikely that only coincidence is at work, an unlikelihood that increases rapidly as the number of observations is made larger. My suggestion is thus that the following thesis is justified *a priori:*

(I-1) In a situation in which a standard inductive premise obtains, it is highly likely that there is some explanation (other than mere coincidence or chance) for the convergence and constancy of the observed proportion (and the more likely, the larger the number of cases in question).

Indeed, once general prejudices about *a priori* knowledge have been defused, the *a priori* status of (I-1) seems sufficiently obvious to require little discussion.

There is, however, one possible objection to the claim that thesis (I-1) is justified *a priori* that should be considered. Thesis (I-1) does not claim that there must be a non-chance explanation of the evidence in question, but only that it is likely that there is one. But can the thesis that something is *likely* (or *unlikely*), not just definitely true or definitely false, be justified *a priori?* Many philosophers seem to have assumed, often without focusing on the point very explicitly, that *a priori* knowledge could not take this form. I am unable, however, to find any very definite or compelling reason for such a view, and indeed thesis (I-1) provides a plausible counterexample. Perhaps the rationale for the view is simply the idea that anything known *a priori* must be necessary, true in all possible worlds, since *a priori* evidence, being independent of any empirical input from the actual world, could not distinguish one possible world from another. But while I am inclined to think that something like this conviction is correct (see §1.3), I do not see why the meta-thesis that a certain thesis is likely or unlikely could not itself be the necessary truth in question.

Thus the relevant claim would be that it is true in all possible worlds that there is likely to be a non-chance explanation for the truth of a standard inductive premise. This would not mean, of course, that there could not be cases in a particular possible world in which such a non-chance explanation was in fact not to be found. It does not even mean that in a particular possible world, which might of course be the actual world, such cases in which there is no non-chance explanation for the truth of a standard inductive premise could not be substantially more numerous than those for which an explanation exists. But it would mean that such possible worlds involve the repeated recurrence of an unlikely situation – and hence that they are quite rare and unlikely within the total class of possible worlds. And this in turn would make the claim that the actual world is not such a world itself highly likely to be true, which is essentially what thesis (I-1) says.[24]

Second. The other component of the proposed justification is more complicated and also somewhat more problematic. Supposing that (I-1) is accepted, we need to ask what non-chance explanations might be given for the evidence in question. One obvious explanation would be that the observed proportion converges on m/n and thereafter remains relatively constant because (i) it is an objective, lawful fact about the world, deriving presumably from underlying causal processes or mechanisms of some sort, that approximately m/n of all As are Bs, and (ii) the observed cases represent an unbiased sample of As and thus accurately reflect this objective regularity. I will call this sort of explanation the *straight inductive explanation*. If the straight inductive explanation is the correct one in a particular case, then clearly the corresponding standard inductive conclusion is true.

But there are obviously many other possible explanations that might be given for the occurrence of the evidence in question, explanations which, unlike the straight inductive explanation, would not entail the truth of the standard inductive conclusion. The most obvious alternatives, on which I will for the most part focus in the present chapter, are what I will call *normal non-inductive explanations:* explanations that, like the straight inductive explanation, are compatible with the general world view of common-sense-cum-science, but that postulate further conditions that combine to produce a situation in which m/n of observed As are Bs even though it is false that even approximately m/n of all As are Bs. What is needed to justify the claim that the standard inductive conclusion is likely to be true is a reason for thinking that these alternative explanations are, taken as a group, substantially less likely to be true, on a purely *a priori* basis, than is the straight inductive explanation.

What might a normal non-inductive explanation of standard inductive evidence look like? In the first place, such an explanation will still have to

24 This way of putting the matter assumes in effect that it is possible to make sense of the relative size of classes of possible worlds, even though both those classes and the total set of possible worlds are presumably infinite. But I have no space to go into the issues surrounding this assumption and must be content here with saying that its intuitive credentials in other cases (e.g., the claim that there are twice as many positive integers as even integers) seem to me strong enough to make it reasonable to construe the difficulties as problems to be solved and not as insuperable objections.

say that the relation between the presence of property or characteristic A and the presence of property or characteristic B is in some way objectively regular or lawful, since, as we have already seen, a purely random or chance association could not account for the evidence in question. Moreover, this lawfulness cannot involve merely A and B alone: if there is a lawful regularity that depends on no further factor according to which some definite proportion of As are Bs in reality, then it could only be by chance or coincidence that this proportion fails to be reflected in our evidence, and thus there would be no non-chance explanation for the constancy of the observed proportion. Thus any normal non-inductive explanation must apparently say that the relation between characteristic A and characteristic B, though genuinely lawful, depends on the presence or absence of some further property or characteristic or set of such properties or characteristics, in such a way as to falsify the standard inductive conclusion.

The simplest general case, to which it will largely suffice to confine our attention, would be one in which there is a single further property or characteristic C whose presence or absence affects the proportion of As that are Bs, so that the proportion has one value, m_c/n_c, when C is present, and a different value, $m_{\bar{c}}/n_{\bar{c}}$, when C is absent. If this is so, then there are two possibilities regarding the objective proportion of As that are Bs in reality: If the relation between A and C is itself lawful, for example, if it is a law that 30 percent of As are also Cs and 70 percent are not Cs, then the objective proportion in reality overall of As that are Bs will depend on the objective proportion of cases of A that are cases of C and will be the appropriately weighted average of m_c/n_c and $m_{\bar{c}}/n_{\bar{c}}$ (in the example just given, $(.7)(m_c/n_c) + (.3)(m_{\bar{c}}/n_{\bar{c}})$. Alternatively, if the occurrence of C in relation to A is not itself lawful, then there will be no objective proportion of As which are Bs.

In relation to this general sort of case, there are then two main possibilities as to how the existence of standard inductive evidence might be explained in a way that is compatible with the falsity of the standard inductive conclusion: First, it might be the case that although there is an objective proportion of cases of A that are also cases of C, thus leading to an objective proportion of As that are Bs, observations of A are skewed in one direction or the other, for example, by involving a higher proportion of C-cases as compared with non-C-cases, thus leading to an observed proportion of As that are Bs that differs from the true one. Second, it might be the case that even though the occurrence of C in relation to A is not objectively lawful, so that there is no objectively correct proportion of As that are *B*s, observations of *A* nonetheless include an approximately uniform proportion of *C*-cases, thus resulting in an approximately constant observed proportion of *A*'s that are *B*'s. (One extreme instance of either of these two possibilities would be the case in which all of the observations involve either the presence of *C* or the absence of *C*, so that the observed proportion m/n is simply identical to either m_c/n_c or to $m_{\bar{c}}/n_{\bar{c}}$.[25])

It is obvious that either of these two possibilities *might* be realized through sheer coincidence or chance. But it is equally obvious that this is highly unlikely to happen, that is, it is highly unlikely either that the proportion of *C*-cases in the observations would by sheer chance differ in a significant and approximately uniform way from the proportion of such cases in reality as a whole or that there would by sheer chance be an approximately constant proportion of *C*-cases in the observations even though there is no regularity at all in reality as a whole – and that this unlikelihood increases as the number of cases becomes larger and the background circumstances become more varied.[26]

But if these kinds of correlations between observed *A*s and the presence of *C* do not occur by chance (and do not reflect the objective relation between *A* and *C*, if there is one), then the only remaining possibility is apparently that they reflect a lawful connection between the presence of *C* and the fact of observation itself, that is, that the *observation* of a case of *A* itself tends to lead to the presence or absence of *C*.[27] Thus we seem to be justified in concluding that as long as there is no lawful connection between the occurrence of *C* and the fact of observation itself, a normal non-

---

25 One way in which this might be so is if *C* holds in the spatio-temporal area to which our observations are in fact restricted, even though it does not hold elsewhere. This specific possibility will be discussed below (in the third comment at the end of this section).

26 A possibility worth mentioning is that if *C* is itself an observable characteristic and is taken note of, then a careful scrutiny of the relevant data would reveal its relevance to the occurrence of *B* and would thus lead to the replacement of the original inductive argument by two more specific arguments, whose conclusions, if the same problem is not repeated at this new level, would presumably be correct. But of course *C* may not be an observable property or characteristic. And even if it is observable, it may not be regarded as relevant and hence may fail to be taken note of in the formulation of the evidence. (It obviously cannot be a requirement for the acceptability of a standard inductive argument that the standard inductive evidence in question reflect *all* observable characteristics, whether seemingly relevant or not, on pain of making it impossible to ever formulate an inductive argument.)

27 In theory at least, it would also be possible that the presence of *C* in a case of *A* makes that case more likely to be observed or that some third factor both leads to the presence of *C* and makes the case more likely to be observed. But I can think of no very plausible instances of these two possibilities.

inductive explanation of the sort we have been discussing is extremely unlikely, on purely *a priori* grounds, to be true. And this in turn constitutes an *a priori* justification for the following thesis:

(I-2) So long as the possibility that observation itself affects the proportion of *A*s that are *B*s is excluded, the best explanation, that is, the most likely to be true, for the truth of a standard inductive premise is the straight inductive explanation, namely that the observed proportion m/n accurately reflects (within a reasonable degree of approximation) a corresponding objective regularity in the world (and this likelihood increases as the number of observations and the variety of the collateral circumstances of observation increases).

My claim, which will take some further discussion to nail down, is that theses (I-1) and (I-2) together constitute an *a priori* justification of induction. In brief, if it is highly likely *a priori* that there is some explanation for the occurrence of standard inductive evidence, and if the explanation that is *a priori* most likely to be true, assuming that the fact of observation does not itself affect the evidence, is the straight inductive explanation, then it is likely *a priori*, relative to this same assumption, that if a standard inductive premise is true, the corresponding standard inductive conclusion is true also.[28]

I do not mean to suggest here that the possibility that the occurrence of observation might influence the presence of a relevant characteristic *C* can be lightly dismissed. On the contrary, there are many cases in which this possibility is either obviously realized or at least has to be taken quite seriously. One simple schematic example would be a case in which the propensity of a case of *A* to also be a case of *B* is a function of temperature, and in which the requisite sort of observation involves handling the objects in question enough to produce a significant rise in temperature. A somewhat more specific example would be the possibility, which has often been suggested to explain null or near-null results, that parapsychological phenomena might be affected by the stress or anxiety produced in the subject by being closely observed by skeptical investigators. A more general range of examples is presented by various quantum phenomena, such as the famous case of Schrödinger's cat or the EPR thought experiment, in which there is a superposition of different outcomes that is resolved into a definite outcome only by the occurrence of observation − a situation which, given that quantum phenomena are allegedly the underlying reality

28 Obviously this is still somewhat fast and loose. In particular, if the likelihoods in question are low enough and if they obey the standard multiplicative principle for joint probabilities, it will not follow that the overall result is likely. But it seems reasonable to assume that the likelihoods in question are high enough to avoid this problem.

out of which everything else is constituted, might conceivably be quite pervasive. And there is also, of course, the idealist argument that we have no justification for believing that *any* of the things we observe continue to occur when they are not being observed or experienced.[29]

Thus the issue of whether observation itself may influence the evidence is anything but trivial and indeed may be impossible to resolve in a general, non-question-begging way. My suggestion, however, is that this issue does not *need* to be resolved in order to give a justification of induction, since the absence of such influence is *assumed* in giving a standard inductive argument and is no part of the standard inductive conclusion. It is quite obvious and utterly non-controversial that where there is observational influence of the sort in question or where such influence is even an open possibility, the truth of a standard inductive premise provides no serious reason for thinking that the corresponding standard inductive conclusion is true. Clearly it is not reasonable to generalize from observed cases to unobserved cases if observation itself makes a difference to the phenomenon in question. The classical problem of induction is whether and why such generalization from the observed to the unobserved is epistemically justified, that is, likely to lead to the truth, *even when such influence by observation is assumed or stipulated not to be present*. And to this issue, the foregoing argument provides, I believe, the outline of a satisfactory answer.

I will conclude this section with some relatively brief comments and qualifications designed to shed further light on the proposed justification and to suggest some further problems.

First. It is useful to reflect briefly on the relation between the justification just outlined and the insistence by Reichenbach and many others that we cannot know *a priori* that the world is orderly rather than chaotic. Contrary to what might be supposed at first glance, there is no incompatibility at all between the two positions. Reichenbach insists, correctly, that the thesis that the world is completely chaotic is neither impossible nor even unlikely from a strictly *a priori* standpoint, and I have said nothing to dispute this claim. Where Reichenbach and the others erred was in thinking that the truth of this claim precluded any possibility of there being an *a priori* reason why the conclusion of a standard inductive argument is likely to be true *if* the empirical standard inductive premise is true. For the existence of such a reason does not require that an orderly world be *a priori* likely in the abstract, apart from any empirical evidence, only that the particular sort of order asserted by an inductive conclusion be *a priori* likely

29 See W. T. Stace, "The Refutation of Realism," in Feigl and Sellars (1949).

relative to the existence of standard inductive evidence, which is what the argument offered purports to show. The claim, in other words, is that a chaotic world, though perfectly possible prior to the consideration of empirical evidence, is rendered extremely unlikely (in the respect in question) by the occurrence of standard inductive evidence and that it is an *a priori* fact that this is so. (I suspect that confusion over this point, perhaps engendered by formulations of the problem of induction that give prominence to the Principle of Induction or to the claim that nature is uniform, constitutes the main reason, apart from general worries about the synthetic *a priori*, why so many philosophers have taken it to be overwhelmingly obvious that no *a priori* justification of induction is possible.)

Second. It may be thought that the foregoing justification is still defeated by a feature of Hume's original argument, namely the idea that the course of nature might change. All that has been shown at best, the objection would go, is that if standard inductive evidence obtains, then it is likely *a priori* that an objective regularity of the indicated sort existed in the part of the past in which the observations in question occurred. But the truth of the standard inductive conclusion requires that the regularity in question exist as well in the unobserved past and continue to exist in the future, which does not follow from its existence in the observed past.

A fully adequate consideration of this objection would require delving extensively into metaphysical issues that go far beyond the reasonable bounds of the present book. Here I can only provide a brief indication of how the answer would go and of the metaphysical outlook involved. The central point is that the objective regularity that is invoked by the straight inductive explanation must be conceived as something significantly stronger than a mere Humean constant conjunction, and in particular as involving by its very nature a substantial propensity to persist into the future. This propensity need not, I think, be so strong as to rule out any possibility that "the course of nature might change," but it must be sufficient to make such a change seriously unlikely. The justification for conceiving the regularity in this way is that anything less than this will not really explain why the inductive evidence occurred in the first place: the assertion of a Humean constant conjunction amounts to just a restatement and generalization of the standard inductive evidence, but has no real capacity to explain the occurrence of that evidence.[30] Thus, not surprisingly, a solution to the problem of induction depends on the tenability of a non-Humean, metaphysically robust conception of objective reg-

30 I am indebted to the referee for the correction of a serious mistake in this formulation.

214

ularity (or objective necessary connection). Of course, the proper explication of such a conception is notoriously problematic, but the difficulties involved do not seem to me to be insurmountable. Here I can only insist that such a conception is intuitively quite plausible and also seems to provide the only alternative to skepticism.

Third. A rather different sort of problem is posed by the possibility that my observations of A might be skewed in relation to some relevant factor C, not directly as a result of the fact of observation itself, but rather because C holds in the limited area in which all the observations are in fact made, but not elsewhere. It is obviously a quite stubborn empirical fact that all of our observations are made on or near the surface of the earth, or, allowing for the movement of the earth, in the general region of the solar system, or at least in our little corner of the galaxy, and it is possible that C obtains there but not in the rest of the universe, in which case our standard inductive conclusion on the basis of those observations would presumably be false in relation to the universe as a whole, that is, false simpliciter.

It seems impossible to deny that the foregoing sort of situation is at least a possibility. Nor does this possibility seem to be irrelevant to the general issue of the justification of induction in the way that the possibility that observation itself influences the evidence was argued above to be. The best that can be done, I think, is to point out that unless the spatio-temporal region in which the relevant C holds is quite large, it will still be an unlikely coincidence that our observations continue in the long run to be confined to that region. And if it is quite large, then the inductive conclusion in question is in effect true within this large region in which we live, move, and have our cognitive being. It seems plausible to suppose that for many or perhaps most issues to which induction is applied, a spatio-temporal relativization of this kind would detract little if at all from the practical or even the theoretical value of the conclusion.

Fourth. The argument offered above for thesis (I-2) might seem to be incomplete in one way that has not yet been considered. Besides the normal non-inductive explanations considered there, there is a second class of apparent alternatives to the straight inductive explanation, and it might be thought that a complete argument would have to find reasons for excluding these as well. What I have in mind here is what might be called *skeptical noninductive explanations*: explanations that postulate some sort of entity or mechanism, such as a Cartesian demon, which does not fall within the common-sense-cum-scientific world view and which allegedly produces or shapes the observational evidence so that it does not accurately reflect the proportion of As that are Bs, if any, that actually exists in the world. But such possibilities have in fact been already excluded by implication in the earlier discussion. A skeptical hypothesis of the sort in question is just a special case of the general possibility, already discussed above, that the fact of observation might itself influence the evidence, with the action of the demon being the relevant factor C. Thus, for the reasons already offered there, such skeptical explanations are not alternatives to the straight inductive explanation of standard inductive evidence in the way that normal non-inductive hypotheses are and thus need not be considered further here.

With this, I must conclude the present chapter. Though there is clearly much more to be done in this area, I believe that the present discussion is enough to show that an *a priori* justification of induction, in addition to being the only approach that can hope to genuinely solve the problem of induction and avoid the "coal pit" of extreme inductive skepticism, is far more defensible than it has usually been taken to be.

Appendix: Non-Euclidean geometry and relativity

§ A.1. INTRODUCTION

In this appendix, I will try to say something about the implications of non-Euclidean geometry and especially its role in the theory of General Relativity for a rationalist view of *a priori* knowledge. There can be little doubt that from a historical standpoint, the development of non-Euclidean geometries was a major factor in producing the widespread conviction that a rationalist position is untenable. Euclidean geometry was after all the most striking example of seemingly substantive *a priori* knowledge of independent reality, invoked by Kant as one of the crucial examples of the synthetic *a priori*. But, according to the simplest version of the standard story, within a few years after Kant, the development of non-Euclidean geometry by Lobashevsky and others showed that Euclidean geometry was not necessarily true of physical space, making it an empirical issue which geometry correctly describes the physical world. And eventually, or so the story goes, this empirical question was resolved by General Relativity in favor of a version of Riemannian or elliptical geometry and against Euclid. The suggested further argument, often left fairly implicit, is that if the rationalist view fails in this paradigmatic case, there can be no good reason for thinking that it will in the end be any more acceptable elsewhere.

My view is that this picture is oversimplified and misleading in important ways, which I will try to explain in what follows. But there are two important caveats that must be borne in mind throughout. The first is that there is no space here for anything like a comprehensive discussion of these matters, even if that were within my powers. And the second is that a really complete and authoritative discussion is clearly not within my powers in any case: I am not a mathematician or a physicist, nor even a philosopher of mathematics or physics. But I do not think that general epistemology can afford to leave these important issues entirely to specialists (whose grasp

217

of the general epistemological issues is in any case not always beyond question).

One important point is easily made: even if the standard story were complete and accurate in every respect, it is not at all obvious that it would pose a serious objection to the sort of rationalist position that has been developed in the present book, namely a moderate rationalism that recognizes and indeed insists on the fallibility of rational insight. Even prior to the advent of non-Euclidean geometries, geometers and philosophers were worried about the status of the Euclidean parallels postulate: it seemed "less certain" than the others, and it was in fact in the course of attempts to derive it from the other postulates that non-Euclidean geometries were discovered. One further consideration here is that geometry is on any view a very special case. There is no reason to think that the same sort of situation, with different deductive systems covering the same general subject-matter, exists in other areas of alleged *a priori* knowledge: there are no alternative arithmetics, no alternative versions of calculus, etc.; and though some philosophers like to talk about alternative logics, it is far from clear that these are in the end more than purely formal constructions.[1] Thus there is, I submit, no reason why a rationalist could not simply concede that the *a priori* convictions underlying Euclidean geometry were mistaken in just the way the standard story claims, while still insisting that this provides no serious reason for skepticism about *a priori* justification in general. But while I believe that such a guarded response is dialectically adequate as a defense of the rationalist position, I also think that there are other and more interesting responses available, which I will briefly explore here.

§ A.2. THE MATHEMATICAL AND SCIENTIFIC BACKGROUND

We may begin with a somewhat fuller, though still very compressed description of the development of non-Euclidean geometry, followed by a

---

1 An adequate defense of this remark would require a still wider investigation of issues centering around, though not confined to, the philosophy of quantum mechanics, an investigation that is even more obviously impossible here. For present purposes I can only record my conviction that the proposals for quantum logics that have been offered are of no real help in resolving or even understanding the seeming paradoxes that arise there. In a nutshell, what is required to make sense of quantum mechanics, if indeed this is possible, is not a new and better logic, but rather a new and better metaphysics.

similarly brief look at the theory of general relativity.[2] Euclid's presentation of his system of geometry relies on five postulates, the fifth of which has become known as the Parallel Postulate:

If a straight line falling on two straight lines makes the interior angles on the same side together less than two right angles, the two straight lines, if produced indefinitely, meet on that side on which the angles are together less than two right angles.[3]

This postulate is substantially longer and more complicated than the other four. Euclid seems to have regarded it as less intuitively obvious or self-evident than the others and therefore makes as little use of it as possible. In the context of the other postulates it is equivalent to the following more familiar postulate (Playfair's Postulate):

Through a given point not on a given line there exists exactly one parallel (i.e., line that does not intersect the given line) to the given line.

Note carefully that "parallel" here means precisely that the two lines will never intersect no matter how far they are extended, *not* that they are equidistant; and that a straight line is to be taken, at least initially, as simply one whose length between any two points on it is the shortest distance between those points.

Though Playfair's version is somewhat easier to understand than Euclid's original, it too was regarded as less than fully self-evident, and many attempts were made through the years to derive the Parallel Postulate from the other Euclidean postulates. Eventually, in the nineteenth century, it was discovered that if the Parallel Postulate is replaced by one of the conflicting postulates (i) that many parallels exist or (ii) that no parallels exist, alternative systems still intuitively recognizable as geometries result. These systems (Lobashevskian or hyperbolic geometry, resulting from the many parallels postulate; Riemannian or elliptic geometry, resulting from the no parallels postulate[4]) can be modeled within Euclidean geometry

2 I rely on many different sources here, but most of all on Lawrence Sklar's wonderful book *Space, Time, and Spacetime* (Sklar 1976). Parenthetical references in this Appendix are to the pages of this book. Sklar's own view of these issues will be briefly considered below.
3 Quoted in Sklar (1976), pp. 14–15.
4 Hyperbolic geometry retains the other Euclidean axioms and tacit assumptions unaltered, but elliptic geometry requires changes in some of them as well: in fact the existence of parallels (though not of a unique parallel) can be proved from the other Euclidean axioms and assumptions; in addition, the fact that elliptic straight lines are circular or closed (great circles on the surface of a sphere are the most straightforward example) forces alterations in Euclid's implicit assumptions about the idea of betweenness (as made explicit, e.g., by Hilbert). These niceties can, however, be ignored for our limited purposes here.

and hence are formally consistent on the assumption that Euclidean geometry itself is consistent.

This result has by itself been widely regarded, both then and later, as a refutation of the claim that Euclidean geometry provides *a priori* insight into the nature of physical space. It is easy, however, to see that such a conclusion does not follow without an appeal to something like the moderate empiricist view of *a priori* justification, a view that was shown in Chapter 2, to be quite untenable. That non-Euclidean geometries are formally consistent shows indeed that Euclidean geometry is not logically necessary or analytic, that is, not such that its denial results (via merely logical transformations) in a *formal* contradiction. But from Kant's standpoint or that of the traditional rationalist, this is in no way surprising. Their claim, after all, is that geometry represents *synthetic a priori* knowledge, a claim that is *supported* in part, not refuted, by the discovery that competing geometries are formally consistent.

Thus the mere fact that non-Euclidean geometries are formally consistent, and more generally that the mathematics of curved and multidimensional spaces is perfectly acceptable as mathematics, does *not,* in and of itself, show that such theories represent *a priori* possible accounts of the structure of actual physical space. A useful issue for comparison here is that of the number of dimensions of space. There is no doubt that the mathematics of n-dimensional spaces is perfectly clear-cut and unproblematic, no matter how large n is taken to be or even indeed whether it remains finite. But it simply does not follow from the mathematics alone that, for example, fifteen-dimensional physical space is a genuine metaphysical possibility.[5] Analogously, the fact that non-Euclidean spaces are mathematically possible and coherent has in itself no tendency to show that the rationalists were wrong to think that we can know *a priori* that the space of the world is Euclidean.[6]

To give even the appearance of a problem for the rationalist, it is therefore necessary to bring in the physical theory somewhat inappropriately referred to as the General Theory of Relativity. General Relativity is fundamentally an attempt to give an account of gravitation that is consis-

---

5 For an argument, to my mind convincing, that space (as opposed to space-time) could not have more than three dimensions, see Swinburne (1981), chapter 7.

6 One possible source of confusion here is that mathematicians use the term 'space' to refer to any abstract set of relations that has a structure analogous to ordinary space, i.e., roughly one that can be described in terms of locations represented by n-tuples of numbers. In this abstract sense, there is no doubt that non-Euclidean "spaces" are perfectly coherent and possible, as are n-dimensional spaces for even infinite values of n and indeed structures that are even more intuitively bizarre.

tent with Einstein's earlier (and much more strongly confirmed) theory of Special Relativity: one that avoids treating gravitational attraction across space as instantaneous. Einstein accomplishes this goal in part by identifying the structure of the gravitational field with the structure of space itself. Intuitively, the result is a view in which space itself is curved and in which the curvature of space varies with concentration of matter in a particular location, with the curvature being described by a complicated version of elliptical geometry. It is this result that, according to the simple version of the story outlined above, establishes that Euclidean geometry, far from being the *a priori* knowable truth about the physical world that rationalists have claimed, is not true at all.

But, as I have already suggested, this view of the situation is at the very least much too simple. In fact, the classic empirical tests of general relativity do not directly support the identification of the gravitational field with the structure of space. Rather they show such things as that light rays are deflected by the presence of a large gravitational mass. This is why an alternative theory with flat Euclidean space (or rather flat Minkowski space–time) can accommodate the same observations. Such a theory .would postulate what Reichenbach referred to as "universal forces," forces that depend on the concentration of matter and that have the power to deflect light rays, distort measuring rods, affect the movement of clocks, and deflect moving particles. According to such an alternative theory, what Einstein discovered was not that Euclid was wrong about the structure of space, but rather that the effects of gravitation are far more complicated and pervasive than Newtonian physicists had realized.[7]

§ A.3. SOME ALTERNATIVES

What then is the correct thing to say about the geometry of physical space in light of non-Euclidean geometry and General Relativity? We may approach this issue by considering the set of alternative positions distinguished by Sklar[8]:

(i) Poincaré's conventionalism: the choice between (a) General Relativity (with a non-Euclidean account of the geometry of space as a component) and (b) the view that combines a Euclidean account of space with a physics of universal

---

7 See Sklar (1976), pp. 98–101, for further discussion.
8 Ibid., pp. 88–146. I have somewhat simplified Sklar's picture by abstracting from his concern with the tenability of the observational/theoretical distinction.

forces is a matter of convention, with the choice to be decided on the basis of considerations like simplicity. Neither choice is correct in any deep metaphysical or epistemological sense.

(ii) Reichenbach's positivistic empiricism: the fact that both of these alternatives (and indeed others besides) are both logically consistent and compatible with all the evidence shows that there is no metaphysically or epistemologically significant choice to be made; while there may be methodological reasons for preferring one combined view to the other, at bottom they are simply two ways of saying the same thing, not two theories but just two ways of formulating a single theory.

(iii) "Apriorism": the view that Sklar refers to by this label holds that methodological criteria such as "simplicity, systematic power, elegance, etc." (121) provide a rational basis for deciding between empirically indistinguishable theories, where this presumably means one that is relevant to likelihood of truth, rather than to merely methodological or practical virtues (though Sklar is substantially less clear on this point than one would like).

(iv) Skepticism: though the opposed views in question do make genuinely distinct claims about the world, there is no rational basis that is relevant to truth for choosing among them. We are thus forever condemned to ignorance concerning the actual geometry of physical space.

A full consideration of these alternatives would greatly exceed the allowable bounds of the present discussion, but the points that matter for present purposes can be made quite briefly. (Sklar himself does not opt conclusively for any of these views.)

First, it is extremely hard to make clear sense of the conventionalist view. If conventionalism is to be distinct from the empiricist view, it must hold that the combined views in question do indeed make distinct claims about the world. But if this is so, why should it be thought acceptable to adopt one of these distinct views on a merely conventional basis, assuming that such adoption is understood to involve a claim of truth and not merely of practical acceptability? Lacking any good answer to this question, the conventionalist position collapses into skepticism – or else becomes indistinguishable from the empiricist view, if the claim that the two combined views are genuinely distinct is withdrawn.

Second, the empiricist alternative also seems untenable, though in a quite different way. From an intuitive standpoint, it seems obvious that there is a genuine difference between an infinite Euclidean space and a finite (though unbounded) Riemannian one, even if our empirical evidence is unable to distinguish between them. The verificationism that underlies this alternative in effect evades skepticism only by the transparent maneuver of insisting that any question that we are unable to answer must not be meaningful. Such a view has been thoroughly discredited in relation to other epistemological issues, and I can see no reason for taking it any more seriously in this area.

Third, "apriorism" as construed by Sklar represents only a modest improvement over the two positions just discussed. This view concedes, correctly I believe, that the choice between the opposed combined views is genuine and does not try to say that it can somehow be made on a merely conventional basis. But the claim that following methodological criteria like simplicity is conducive to finding the truth of the matter is almost entirely unsupported in Sklar's account and may well be insupportable. More importantly, as Sklar's label recognizes, any argument that could be made with respect to the truth conduciveness of these criteria could only be an *a priori* argument – and, we may add, not one that could be regarded as analytic in any plausible sense.

Thus Sklar's other three views all threaten to collapse into skepticism. Moreover, the most plausible of these purportedly non-skeptical views could be made adequate only by appeal to *a priori* insight of just the sort defended by the rationalist. The specific insights required for this purpose may not in the end be available, in which case the skeptic would prevail. But the fact that there is no apparent non-skeptical alternative to rationalism as an account of how we might have knowledge of the structure of space still seems to constitute a second reason, over and above that offered at the end of the first section above, for thinking that no serious basis for an anti-rationalist argument is to be found in this area.

§ A.4. GEOMETRY AND RATIONAL INSIGHT

There is, however, one further point to be made, in some respects the most fundamental of all. One important question that has not been considered so far is whether there is after all any apparent rational insight or set of insights that supports the claim that Euclidean geometry correctly describes the structure of physical space. This question receives very little attention in the existing literature, where it tends to be assumed, without much discussion, that the seeming obviousness of the Euclidean perspective is merely a kind of psychological illusion.

Such a dismissive view may well be correct, but it does not seem to me obviously so. Nonetheless I will make no real effort to resolve this issue here, except to remark that it seems to me to turn in the end on whether or not we have an intuitive grasp of the notion of straightness that is independent of the identification of straight lines with such physical phenomena as

223

the path of a light ray, one that would make it intelligible to say that all such physical phenomena might follow curved paths. If we have such an intuitive conception of straightness, then the usual discussions that turn on a dichotomy between a "pure geometry" that is merely an uninterpreted formal system and an "applied geometry" or "physical geometry" that depends on the identification of straight lines with physical phenomena omit a crucial alternative: a geometry that is neither merely formal nor in this sense physical, but rather reflects our intuitive notion of straightness and its implications. That there is such an alternative, which is obviously the one to which a traditional rationalism in this area would want to appeal, is far from clear; but to simply assume in setting up the issue that the dichotomy between pure and applied geometry is exhaustive, as so many discussions do, obviously begs the entire question.

My point for the moment, with which I will conclude this Appendix, is the more modest one that *if* there is after all an *a priori* insight or apparent insight that such a non-physical and also not merely formal geometry provides a correct account of the necessary features of space (and if this insight survives further reflective scrutiny), we have found *no reason at all* why it should not be accorded fully as much weight as any other such insight. Far from refuting such an insight, as we now see, the existence of consistent non-Euclidean geometries and the empirical case for General Relativity do not count against it in any way, since both of these results are fully compatible with a theory that incorporates the Euclidean view.

To be sure, if there were an *a priori* case to be made along the lines of Sklar's "apriorism" for the truth-conduciveness of some methodological criterion (or criteria) such as simplicity, and if the General Relativistic view that incorporates non-Euclidean geometry were preferable on the basis of this criterion (as it seems likely that it would be), then the apparent rational insight in favor of Euclid might after all be corrected and hence overridden, with experience playing a role in this result. But this would only be an example of the fallibility and corrigibility of apparent rational insight, as discussed above (see §§4.5–4.6), and thus once again would pose no special problem for the moderate rationalist.

References

Addis, Laird. 1989. *Natural Signs* (Philadelphia: Temple University Press).

Almog, Joseph, Perry, John, and Wettstein, Howard (eds.). 1989. *Themes from Kaplan* (New York: Oxford University Press).

Alston, William. 1991. *Perceiving God* (Ithaca, N.Y.: Cornell University Press).

Alston, William. 1993. *The Reliability of Sense Perception* (Ithaca, N.Y.: Cornell University Press).

Anscombe, G. E. M., and Geach, Peter. 1961. *Three Philosophers* (Oxford: Oxford University Press).

Ayer, A. J. 1946. *Language, Truth and Logic* (New York: Dover).

Bealer, George. 1982. *Quality and Concept* (Oxford: Oxford University Press).

Bealer, George. 1986. "The Logical Status of Mind," *Midwest Studies in Philosophy,* 10: 231–74.

Benacerraf, Paul, and Putnam, Hilary (eds.). 1983. *Philosophy of Mathematics: Selected Readings,* 2nd ed. (Cambridge University Press).

Bender, John W. (ed.). 1989. *The Current State of the Coherence Theory* (Dordrecht, Holland: Kluwer).

Black, Max. 1954. "Inductive Support of Inductive Rules," in his *Problems of Analysis* (Ithaca, N.Y.: Cornell University Press), pp. 191–208.

Block, Ned. 1986. "Advertisement for a Semantics for Psychology," *Midwest Studies in Philosophy,* 10: 615–78.

Boghossian, Paul. 1989. "Content and Self-Knowledge," *Philosophical Topics,* 17: 5–26.

BonJour, Laurence. 1985. *The Structure of Empirical Knowledge* (Cambridge, Mass.: Harvard University Press).

BonJour, Laurence. 1986. "A Reconsideration of the Problem of Induction," *Philosophical Topics,* 14: 93–124.

BonJour, Laurence. 1987. "Nozick, Externalism, and Skepticism," in S. Luper-Foy (ed.), *The Possibility of Knowledge: Nozick and His Critics* (Totowa, N.J.: Rowman & Littlefield), pp. 297–313.

BonJour, Laurence. 1989. "Replies and Clarifications," in J. W. Bender (ed.), *The Current State of the Coherence Theory: Essays on the Epistemic Theories of Keith Lehrer and Laurence BonJour* (Dordrecht, Holland: Kluwer), pp. 276–92.

BonJour, Laurence. 1991. "Is Thought a Symbolic Process?" *Synthese,* 89: 331–52.

Broad, C. D. 1952. *Ethics and the History of Philosophy* (New York: Humanities Press).

Burge, Tyler. 1993. "Content Preservation," *Philosophical Review,* 102: 457–88.

225

Butchvarov, Panayot. 1970. *The Concept of Knowledge* (Evanston, Ill.: Northwestern University Press).

Chisholm, Roderick. 1977. *Theory of Knowledge,* 2nd ed. (Englewood Cliffs, N.J.: Prentice-Hall).

Chisholm, Roderick. 1981. *The First Person* (Minneapolis: University of Minnesota Press).

Chisholm, Roderick. 1989. *Theory of Knowledge,* 3rd ed. (Englewood Cliffs, N.J.: Prentice-Hall).

Dummett, Michael. 1978. *Truth and Other Enigmas* (Cambridge, Mass.: Harvard University Press).

Dummett, Michael. 1981. *Frege: Philosophy of Language,* 2nd ed. (Cambridge, Mass.: Harvard University Press).

Dummett, Michael. 1991. *The Logical Basis of Metaphysics* (Cambridge, Mass.: Harvard University Press).

Edwards, Paul. 1949. "Russell's Doubts about Induction," *Mind,* 58: 141–63.

Ewing, A. C. 1939–40. "The Linguistic Theory of *A priori* Propositions" *Proceedings of the Aristotelian Society,* 40: 221–30.

Feigl, Herbert, and Sellars, Wilfrid (eds.). 1949. *Readings in Philosophical Analysis* (New York: Appleton-Century-Crofts).

Fodor, Jerry. 1981. *Representations* (Cambridge, Mass.: MIT Press).

Fodor, Jerry. 1987. *Psychosemantics* (Cambridge: Mass.: MIT Press).

Gibson, Roger F., Jr. 1982. *The Philosophy of W. V. Quine* (Gainesville: University Presses of Florida).

Goldman, Alvin. 1985. *Epistemology and Cognition* (Cambridge, Mass.: Harvard University Press).

Goodman, Nelson. 1955. *Fact, Fiction, and Forecast* (Cambridge, Mass.: Harvard University Press).

Guttenplan, Samuel (ed.). 1975. *Mind and Language* (Oxford: Oxford University Press).

Hahn, L. E., and Schilpp, P. A. (eds.). 1986. *The Philosophy of W. V. Quine* (La Salle, Ill.: Open Court).

Hardin, C. L. 1988. *Color for Philosophers* (Indianapolis: Hackett).

Harman, Gilbert. 1967–68a. "Quine on Meaning and Existence I," *Review of Metaphysics* 21: 124–51.

Harman, Gilbert. 1967–68b. "Quine on Meaning and Existence II," *Review of Metaphysics* 21: 331–52.

Hume, David. 1739–40. *A Treatise of Human Nature,* ed. L. A. Selby-Bigge (Oxford: Oxford University Press, 1888).

Hume, David. 1748. *An Inquiry Concerning Human Understanding,* ed. Charles W. Hendel (Indianapolis: Bobbs-Merrill, 1955).

Kant, Immanuel. 1787. *Critique of Pure Reason,* translated by Norman Kemp Smith (London: Macmillan, 1929).

Kenny, Anthony (ed.). 1969. *Aquinas: A Collection of Critical Essays* (Garden City, N.Y.: Anchor).

Kim, Jaegwon. 1988. "What is 'Naturalized Epistemology'?" in James E. Tomberlin (ed.), *Philosophical Perspectives, 2: Epistemology* (Atascadero, Calif.: Ridgeview, 1988), pp. 381–405.

Kitcher, Philip. 1983. *The Nature of Mathematical Knowledge* (Oxford: Oxford University Press).

Kripke, Saul. 1972. "Naming and Necessity," in Davidson, Donald, and Harman, Gilbert (eds.), *Semantics of Natural Language* (Dordrecht, Holland: Reidel), pp. 253–355.

LePore, Ernest, and Loewer, Barry. 1986. "Solipsistic Semantics," *Midwest Studies in Philosophy*, 10: 595–614.

Lewis, C. I. 1929. *Mind and the World Order* (New York: Dover).

Lewis, C. I. 1946. *An Analysis of Knowledge and Valuation* (LaSalle, Ill.: Open Court).

Lewis, David. 1979. "Attitudes De Dicto and De Se," *Philosophical Review*, 88: 513–43.

Locke, John. 1689. *An Essay Concerning Human Understanding*, ed. P. H. Nidditch (Oxford: Oxford University Press, 1975).

Lucas, J. R. 1973. *A Treatise on Space and Time* (London: Methuen).

Luper-Foy, Stephen (ed.). 1987. *The Possibility of Knowledge: Nozick and His Critics* (Totowa, N.J.: Rowman & Littlefield).

Nozick, Robert. 1981. *Philosophical Explanations* (Cambridge, Mass.: Harvard University Press).

Orenstein, Alex. 1977. *Willard Van Orman Quine* (Boston: Twayne).

Pap, Arthur. 1958. *Semantics and Necessary Truth* (New Haven: Yale University Press).

Perry, John. 1979. "The Problem of the Essential Indexical," *Nous*, 13: 3–21.

Plantinga, Alvin. 1993a. *Warrant: The Current Debate* (New York: Oxford University Press).

Plantinga, Alvin. 1993b. *Warrant and Proper Function* (New York: Oxford University Press).

Putnam, Hilary. 1975. *Mind, Language and Reality* (Cambridge University Press).

Popper. Karl. 1972. *Objective Knowledge* (London: Oxford University Press).

Quine, W. V. O. 1960. *Word and Object* (Cambridge, Mass.: M.I.T. Press).

Quine, W. V. O. 1961. *From a Logical Point of View*, 2nd ed. (Cambridge, Mass.: Harvard University Press).

Quine, W. V. O. 1966. *The Ways of Paradox* (New York: Random House).

Quine, W. V. O. 1969. *Ontological Relativity and Other Essays* (New York: Columbia University Press).

Quine, W. V. O. 1970a. *Philosophy of Logic* (Englewood Cliffs, N.J.: Prentice-Hall).

Quine, W. V. O. 1970b. "On the Reasons for Indeterminacy of Translation," *Journal of Philosophy*, 67: 178–83.

Quine, W. V. O. 1981. *Theories and Things* (Cambridge, Mass.: Harvard University Press).

Reichenbach, Hans. 1938. *Experience and Prediction* (Chicago: University of Chicago Press).

Reichenbach, Hans. 1949. *Theory of Probability* (Berkeley: University of California Press).

Salmon, Wesley C. 1963. "Inductive Inference," in B. Baumrin (ed.), *Philosophy of Science: The Delaware Seminar, vol. 11* (New York: Inter-science Publishers).

Salmon, Wesley C. 1967. *The Foundations of Scientific Inference* (Pittsburgh: University of Pittsburgh Press).

Salmon, Wesley C. 1972. "Should We Attempt to Justify Induction?" reprinted in
    H. Feigl, W. Sellars, and K. Lehrer (eds.), *New Readings in Philosophical Analysis*
    (New York: Appleton-Century-Crofts), pp. 500–10.
Sellars, Wilfrid. 1953. "Inference and Meaning," *Mind*, 62: 313–38.
Sklar, Lawrence. 1974. *Space, Time, and Spacetime* (Berkeley, Calif.: University of
    California Press).
Skyrms, Bryan. 1966. *Choice and Chance.* (Encino, Calif.: Dickenson).
Sleigh, R. C. (ed.). 1972. *Necessary Truth* (Englewood Cliffs, N.J.: Prentice-Hall).
Strawson, P. F. 1952. *Introduction to Logical Theory* (London: Methuen).
Swinburne, Richard. 1981. *Space and Time*, 2nd ed. (London: Macmillan).
Swinburne, Richard (ed.). 1974. *The Problem of Induction* (London: Oxford Uni-
    versity Press).
Unger, Peter. 1968. "An Analysis of Factual Knowledge," *Journal of Philosophy*, 65:
    157–70.
Will, F. L. 1947. "Will the Future Be Like the Past?" *Mind*, 56: 332–47.

Index

abstract entities, *see* Platonism
Addis, Laird, 185n
analyticity· (*see also* empiricism, moderate),
    Chapter 2 *passim*
  analytic versus synthetic, 32–3
  as "empty of factual content," 44–5
  epistemological significance of, 31, 37–
    8, 46, 47–9
  Fregean conception of, 32–4, 36, 51n,
    73
  and implicit definition, 49–51, 103
  Kantian conception of, 34, 36, 49
  and linguistic convention, 51–8, 95n
  obfuscating conceptions of, 36–46
  Quine's "circle of terms" argument
    against, 67–73
  reductive conceptions of, 32–6
  relation to *a priori–a posteriori* distinc-
    tion, 59–60
  as "truth by virtue of meaning," 36–
    42, 47–9, 101–2
Anderson, Tony, 142n
a priori propositions, 14
Aquinas, St. Thomas, 183–4
Aristotle, 17, 112, 158–9n, 183
Ayer, A. J., 83, 196

Baker, Ann, 168n
Bealer, George, 184, 185
Benacerraf, Paul, 156–61
Berkeley, George, 17
Blanshard, Brand, 112
Block, Ned, 174n, 176
Boghossian, Paul, 179n
Broad, C. D., 188, 195, 200
Burge, Tyler, 125–7, 170, 173
Butchvarov, Panayot, 50–1, 53–4, 56,
    108–9n

causation, 160–1
Chisholm, Roderick, 37, 124–5, 181–2

coherence theory of meaning, 174n
Comte, Auguste, 17
concept empiricism, 9–10, 160
conceptual role semantics, 169–70, 174–9
conceptualism, 158–9n
contradiction
  explicit versus non-explicit, 34, 45–6,
    205–6
  principle of, 21, 39–40, 93–5

Davidson, Donald, 85n
Descartes, René, 17, 84
direct reference, theory of, 169, 170–3
Dummett, Michael, 93, 150

Edwards, Paul, 196
Einstein, Albert, 220–1
empiricism, 17, 62, 98
empiricism, moderate (*see also* analyticity),
    18–19, Chapter 2 *passim*, 98, 150,
    220
  diversity of specific versions, 28–9, 58
  epistemological status of, 59–61
  hypothetical version of, 65–6, 67n
  two main theses, 18–19, 29, 36
empiricism, radical, 19, Chapter 3 *passim*,
    98, 187
  dialectical immunity of, 63
  epistemological status of, 63
  as a form of skepticism, 62–3
Ewing, A. C., 57
experience, 4, 7–8, 76
  direct, *see* observation
externalism (*see also* reliabilism), 96
  and *a priori* justification, 127–9

Frege, Gottlob, 32, 38, 160n
  Fregean conception of analyticity, *see*
    analyticity, Fregean conception of
Fodor, Jerry, 165–6, 168n, 172, 175, 176

229

Reichenbach, Hans, 192–6, 198, 199, 213–14, 221–2
Relativity, General Theory of, 111, Appendix *passim*
reliabilism, 1n, 7n, 96
Riemann, G. F. B., 217

Salmon, Wesley, 30–1, 44–5, 192, 194, 195n, 196, 199
    conception of rationalism, 45
    on truths of logic, 43–4
secondary qualities, 160n
set theory, 3n, 111–12
skepticism, 3–4, 62–3, 86–7, 91, 93–6, 98, 191, 195–6, 199, 200, 215–16
Sklar, Lawrence, 219n, 221–3, 224
Spinoza, Baruch, 17, 112
Strawson, P. F., 67–8, 70, 71, 72, 73–4, 196–9, 204

synthetic, *see* analyticity
synthetic *a priori*, 21–5, 30–1, 45, 220
Swinburne, Richard, 220n

thought, nature of, 162, 164–5
    intrinsic content view, 166, 180–5
        relation to rationalism, 180, 184–5
    symbolic conception, 162–70, 178–80
        account of intentionality, 165, 166
        defining thesis, 165
        incompatibility with rationalism, 162–4
        problem of access to content, 166–9, 179–80, 185

Unger, Peter, 157n

Weller, Cass, 167n
Wittgenstein, Ludwig, 169n

Printed in the United States
29473LVS00001B/13

9 780521 592369